Chuckin' Charlie Conerly
and the New York Football Giants

ALSO BY LEW FREEDMAN
AND FROM McFARLAND

*Caught by Don Hutson! A Biography of Pro Football's
First Modern Receiver* (2022)

*Johnny Mize: A Biography
of Baseball's "Big Cat"* (2022)

*Lightning Strikes Twice: Johnny Vander Meer
and the Cincinnati Reds* (2021)

*Buffalo Bill Cody: The Man Who
Shaped the Wild West Legend* (2020)

Cy Young: The Baseball Life and Career (2020)

Ernie Banks: The Life and Career of "Mr. Cub" (2019)

*Baseball's Funnymen: Twenty-Four Jokers,
Screwballs, Pranksters and Storytellers* (2017)

*Connie Mack's First Dynasty:
The Philadelphia Athletics, 1910–1914* (2017)

The Boyer Brothers of Baseball (2015)

*George Altman: My Baseball Journey from the Negro Leagues to the
Majors and Beyond* (George Altman with Lew Freedman, 2013)

Joe Louis: The Life of a Heavyweight (2013)

DiMaggio's Yankees: A History of the 1936–1944 Dynasty (2011)

*The Day All the Stars Came Out: Major League Baseball's
First All-Star Game, 1933* (2010)

*Early Wynn, the Go-Go White Sox
and the 1959 World Series* (2009)

*Hard-Luck Harvey Haddix
and the Greatest Game Ever Lost* (2009)

Chuckin' Charlie Conerly and the New York Football Giants

LEW FREEDMAN

McFarland & Company, Inc., Publishers
Jefferson, North Carolina

ISBN (print) 978-1-4766-8804-6
ISBN (ebook) 978-1-4766-4962-7

LIBRARY OF CONGRESS AND BRITISH LIBRARY
CATALOGUING DATA ARE AVAILABLE

Library of Congress Control Number 2023024569

© 2023 Lew Freedman. All rights reserved

No part of this book may be reproduced or transmitted in any form or by any means, electronic or mechanical, including photocopying or recording, or by any information storage and retrieval system, without permission in writing from the publisher.

Front cover: Quarterback Charlie Conerly (United States Marine Corps)

Printed in the United States of America

*McFarland & Company, Inc., Publishers
Box 611, Jefferson, North Carolina 28640
www.mcfarlandpub.com*

Acknowledgments

A special thanks for help with this project goes to Lulu Maness and Perian Conerly for sharing their thoughts about Charlie Conerly and to the University of Mississippi athletic department, particularly special assistant Langston Rogers, for their assistance.

Also, the author would like to thank Jon Kendle at the Professional Football Hall of Fame in Canton, Ohio, for research assistance.

Table of Contents

Acknowledgments   v
Preface   1
Introduction   3
CHAPTER 1. The Best Day of All   7
CHAPTER 2. Mississippi Roots   13
CHAPTER 3. Ole Miss   20
CHAPTER 4. War and Ole Miss II   29
CHAPTER 5. Meeting the Mrs.   38
CHAPTER 6. From Ole Miss to the Big Apple   46
CHAPTER 7. Rookie Year   54
CHAPTER 8. New York, New York   61
CHAPTER 9. Loving the Spotlight   68
CHAPTER 10. Giants Become Winners   75
CHAPTER 11. Keeping It Going   83
CHAPTER 12. The Old Man   90
CHAPTER 13. 1953: The Worst Year   99
CHAPTER 14. New Look Giants   107
CHAPTER 15. The New Regime   113
CHAPTER 16. Charlie and Perian   122
CHAPTER 17. Not Quite There   128
CHAPTER 18. Their Turn   138

Table of Contents

CHAPTER 19. World Champs	148
CHAPTER 20. Trying to Do It Again	154
CHAPTER 21. Redemption Tour	161
CHAPTER 22. Greatest Game	170
CHAPTER 23. 1959: Giants–Colts Again	179
CHAPTER 24. The 1960s	188
Epilogue: Retirement	194
Chapter Notes	205
Bibliography	213
Index	215

Preface

It is often said that New York professional athletes benefit in fans' minds and at awards time because they play football, baseball, basketball or hockey under the brightest lights in the media capital of the world.

Somehow, for all his years of playing quarterback, the most glamorous of positions on the gridiron, Charlie Conerly eluded that. From 1948 to 1961, Conerly was center stage for the New York Giants football team and did all right for himself, winning the Rookie of the Year award and a championship ring, being selected to compete in the Pro Bowl, and having his uniform number retired.

Yet he still fell through the cracks when it came to publicity, and that was much of his own doing. Conerly was a native of Mississippi, and he was a homeboy, returning to his roots in the off-season. He was neither a quip-a-minute guy nor a story-telling marvel. He was more of a "yup" and "nope" guy in interviews with sportswriters. He wasn't rude. He just wasn't loquacious. He avoided the limelight, never sought it, was the ultimate let-my-actions-speak-for-my-performance player.

He and his attractive wife, Perian, who was a more outgoing personality and the first female pro football sportswriter, were gadabouts on the town, soaking in all of the excitement of New York when they were free, in clubs and bars and at Broadway shows. That was all about having a good time and taking advantage of the Big Apple offerings before anyone thought to call New York the Big Apple. No one ever called Charlie Conerly "Broadway Charlie," though.

Conerly arrived in New York from Mississippi when the Giants were at a down level. He took his lumps as the team was rebuilt and reborn and became one of the finest. It was a tricky existence, outlasting critics who heaped blame on him for the team's early failings.

Conerly was just about the last man standing from the weak production years (along with Emlen Tunnell) by the time they were surrounded by a galaxy of stars such as Frank Gifford, Andy Robustelli, and Sam Huff, who were elected to the Pro Football Hall of Fame.

That is the one hole in Conerly's resume. He is not a member of the Pro Football Hall of Fame. It is a bit shocking, especially given the spotlight that shone on him in New York, the way he led the others of such great talent who were voted in.

Seven times (seven times!) Conerly was a finalist for induction to the Hall, yet he is still on the outside and would still need to pay admission to visit the exhibits, many featuring his old friends.

Introduction

Some called him "Chuckin' Charlie" because he always had a strong right arm and could throw the heck out of a football. Charles Albert Conerly, Jr., was the center of attention on the gridiron at the University of Mississippi, where he represented his home state with distinction, and in New York City, where he represented the New York Giants behind center during some of that football franchise's most glorious years.

Conerly was the type of leader other men rallied around. He was appreciated for his physical and mental toughness without being a vocal chatterbox, taking charge of the troops with words. He managed to guide both his alma mater and his professional club to football championships.

There was something innately manly and powerful exuded by Conerly, though he was no braggart, and his craggy face, solid build and manner created followers. Those traits may well be what appealed to the makers of Marlboro cigarettes later in his life, when the tobacco manufacturer hired Conerly to play the character of the iconic "Marlboro Man" in advertising.

During a period in American society when Westerns permeated the television airwaves in greater numbers of half-hour black-and-white shows than at any other time in history, Conerly was selected as one of the symbols of the cowboy and the West even though he was no wrangler. He just looked the part. Conerly was born in 1921—at least the record indicates that now, although there was some question about that when he played pro ball—and he passed away in 1996.

Conerly was born in Clarksdale, Mississippi, and the Ole Miss Rebels gave Conerly a scholarship, but World War II interfered with his college playing days, and he saw combat for the United States in the South Pacific in the mid–1940s. He returned to Oxford, led the Rebels to a Southeastern Conference championship under legendary coach John Vaught, and was named an All-American.

Conerly moved on to the National Football League in 1948 and remained with the Giants through the 1961 season. From the Mississippi Delta to the heart of Broadway, Conerly lived through interesting times. He was a pivotal figure as signal-caller for four Giants teams that reached the league title game. The brightest shining moment for Conerly and the Giants in partnership occurred in 1956, when they won the title, crushing the Chicago Bears.

It was a grand time to be a Giant. The big city was embracing the team with more fervor than ever, Conerly was one of the faces of the franchise, and Perian was a public figure as the female sportswriter who pioneered writing on pro football.

Conerly was surrounded by talent on the Giants roster, and many of his friends and teammates were later voted into the Pro Football Hall of Fame in Canton, Ohio. Although Conerly was chosen for College Football Hall of Fame induction in 1966, selection into the Pro Hall has eluded him despite efforts spearheaded by the University of Mississippi and other football fans.

This is partially attributable to the era when Conerly played, a period when running backs were more integral to offensive success than in the 2020s, when quarterbacks routinely throw more than 40 times per game, are kings of the short-yardage style of attack, and pile up more impressive statistics.

Most of the famous Giants of the 1950s, like Conerly, have also passed away, but to them he was much like a general on the field, the one they looked to for guidance in the huddle, and if they had the votes they would salute him into the hallways at Canton.

Receiver Kyle Rote, one of Conerly's prominent teammates, once said, "Charlie commands respect with quiet confidence. He leads and we follow. We have faith in him."[1]

The Giants rallied around Conerly between 1948 and 1961. More than 60 years after his retirement, Conerly's name still dots the football team's record book.

Generations of star quarterbacks have followed Conerly, making their own legends at Ole Miss and in New York. But the name Manning glitters as if in blinking lights in Mississippi. Archie Manning, father of Hall of Famer Peyton Manning and champion Eli Manning, was born in 1949, a year after Conerly broke into the NFL, in Drew, Mississippi, and played for the Rebels in college, starting in 1968. Then, he, too, advanced to the pros.

When he was a youth, though, before he became a beloved Mississippi figure, Archie Manning followed football intently, along with his father, Buddy. It was Buddy who first rooted for Conerly, native of Mississippi soil and alum of Ole Miss.

Introduction

"He was my first football hero," Archie Manning said of Conerly, and the Mississippi connection was reason enough to applaud one of his own predecessors. "I knew he was from Ole Miss and Clarksdale, and that was enough for me."[2]

Charlie Conerly made more friends and fans on a much larger stage. He may have had Mississippi dirt between his toes, but he had New York at his feet.

The hard country Charlie Conerly came from is one of the steamiest sections of the United States. It is a region where sweat born of high temperatures that register triple digits on the thermometer and the same in humidity conspire to keep a man soaking wet in the summer.

That was true in working the fields, or working out, an athlete trying to make something of himself, trying to become the best he could be. But it was the kind of environment that was pretty much a backdrop for a whole 'nother way of life than New York City, the heart of Yankee land up north.

Conerly was Mississippi proud yet bridged the differences, connecting the disparate places by exhibiting his impressive skills in managing football games.

Chapter 1

The Best Day of All

Charlie Conerly didn't even start the game on the best day of his professional football life. A day filled with football drama began as a day filled with rotten weather at Yankee Stadium, but it concluded with grand celebration for Conerly, the Giants, and New York.

On December 30, 1956, the Giants met the Chicago Bears to settle that season's National Football League championship. It was 18 degrees with rain, snow and sleet mixed in the air, ordinarily a day most people would prefer to sit at home in the dry. Although there were about 11,000 tickets left over, some 56,836 paid for the privilege of sitting outdoors in the chill.

The match-up for the crown offered suspense. The Giants, at 8–3–1, won the Eastern Conference, and the Bears, at 9–2–1, won the Western Conference, sending both squads to the title game in this pre–Super Bowl era. The added twist was that the same teams met on the field five weeks earlier and tied, 17–17, which suggested a close game.

Conerly was chosen to appear on the cover of *Sports Illustrated* for the December 3, 1956, issue after the tie game and before it was apparent that the teams would meet to decide the league crown. The magazine touted the tie as a battle between two of the NFL's best teams.

On this occasion, Don Heinrich spent most of the time at quarterback for the Giants. Heinrich was given a list of scripted plays, and Conerly stood on the sidelines listening to the team's third-string quarterback, Bobby Clatterbuck, relay information from the press box. Conerly took over later as the Giants led, 17–3, and worked to fend off a Bears comeback. That worked inasmuch as New York was able to preserve a tie, but they could not grab the win.

This approach allegedly gave Conerly the ability to spot tendencies in the Bears' play, though much later he said he never believed in the system.

"You don't see much of a game when you're in," Conerly said in the magazine. "You're looking for the guy you're going to pass to, or the guy you're making a handoff to, and you don't see much else. I guess I wouldn't even recognize half the guys I play against in a game if I saw them on the street afterward."[1]

Still, Conerly had learned enough versus the Bears so recently he could apply some knowledge in the title game. There was one danger in believing too much in information picked up in the tie game and applying it to the title game—the weather shift. In 1934, the Giants and Bears faced off for the NFL championship on a similarly icy field at the Polo Grounds, and New York outsmarted the Bears by discarding its usual footwear in favor of sneakers to grip the ground. The game was termed the "Sneakers Game." In unlikely circumstances, history repeated itself 22 years later, only the Giants knew their history, and the Bears flunked their history exam. This became known as "Sneakers Game II."

Assessing the weather, New York coach Jim Lee Howell indulged in a short experiment prior to kickoff. He ordered two players to test different types of shoes on the seemingly treacherous turf. Defensive back Ed Hughes trotted onto the field wearing cleats. Halfback Gene Filipski ran out wearing sneakers. Hughes took a few steps, slipped, and fell. Filipski's footing was not affected. Howell called for everyone on the team to wear sneakers.

Perhaps most impressively, the Giants had a stash

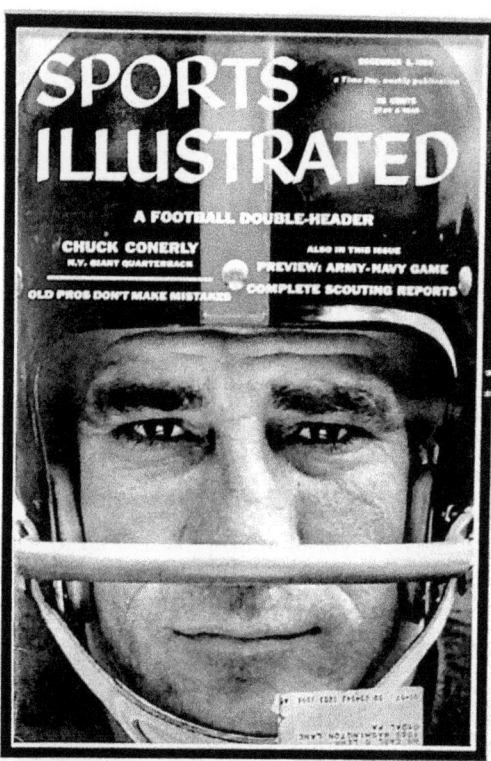

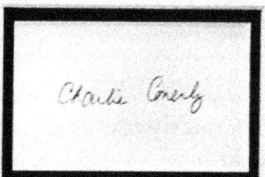

Charlie Conerly was on the cover of *Sports Illustrated* in 1956 while playing for the New York Giants (photograph by the author).

Chapter 1. The Best Day of All

of sneakers handy to don. Defensive lineman Andy Robustelli, one of the several future Hall of Famers in New York's lineup, owned a sporting goods store in nearby Greenwich, Connecticut, and he had ordered a supply of rubber-soled shoes. Robustelli had the inventory handy for use.

The Giants and Bears were two of the league's traditional powers and regular participants in the NFL title game since the league was founded in 1920 and the Giants joined in 1925. However, both squads had been in a championship lull. New York had not won a crown in 18 years. The Bears had not won in 10 years.

Kickoff took place at 2:05 p.m., and the National Football League worked in conjunction with NBC-TV to pull together a post-game film of the action. It was almost all play-by-play with very limited featuring of individuals. The camera did pause on Conerly as the announcers, Earl Gillespie and Chris Schenkel, termed him "the Grey Eagle." As the players jogged onto the field, they crossed a fresh coating of an inch or so of white.[2]

Don Heinrich, who twice led the nation in passing at the University of Washington, had been a Giant since 1954. Although Heinrich never threw more than 88 passes in a season in a career that lasted through 1962, Dixie Howell sometimes juggled his quarterback rotation. Heinrich started the title game, completing three of six passing attempts for 21 yards, then gave way to Conerly, the rightful starter.

Outplaying Chicago quarterback George Blanda, taking advantage of the Giants' wise selection of footwear, and guiding a superior offense, Conerly masterfully directed New York to score after score. As the Giants rolled to a 47–7 thrashing of the Bears, Conerly completed seven of 10 passes for 195 yards and two touchdowns.

In some ways, this was the most bizarre season of Conerly's pro career. Teams played a 12-game regular season at the time, and whatever Howell was thinking, he started Heinrich in every one of them while using Conerly for more time in each contest. So the quarterback who didn't start games came in and led his team to victories by completing 90 of 174 passes for 10 touchdowns. Remarkably enough, this "bench" player was chosen for the Pro Bowl at the end of the season, his second all-star selection.

The championship game had its own all-star cast of announcers, teaming Chris Schenkel, Jack Brickhouse, and soon-to-be-enshrined in the shortly-to-be-built Pro Football Hall of Fame Red Grange. Despite the recent tie between the teams, oddsmakers made Chicago a three-point favorite. They were wrong.

New York played close to a perfect game, appropriate enough since earlier that autumn, on October 8, also in Yankee Stadium, Yankees hurler Don Larsen shut out the Brooklyn Dodgers 2–0 in Game 5 of the World Series. It remains the only perfect game pitched in the history of the Series.

The Giants crushed the Bears, the only exception to their perfection being a nine-yard touchdown run by Chicago fullback Rick Casares and the subsequent extra-point kick by Blanda. If the field itself was as dicey for travel as much as the asphalt outside the stadium was for fans, the comfort zone for anyone supporting the Bears was that much more distressing.

Ed McCaskey, team founder George Halas' son-in-law and eventually president of the Bears, was in attendance. "It was the coldest I'd been in my life," McCaskey said.

> We attended "My Fair Lady" the night before the game and when we left the theatre an ice storm set in. It was a miserable night and the next day the field was a mess. We were sitting with George Halas [Paddy Driscoll was the coach at the time] in the upper deck and the cold and the wind were unbelievable. After the Giants scored the first touchdown, Halas left the stands and went down to the sidelines. He couldn't save us and we got beat soundly.[3]

The Giants went ahead, 13–0, after one quarter and led 20–0 in the second period when Casares scored the Bears' touchdown. The lead expanded to 34–7 at halftime, and although the Giants missed an extra point on their next TD, they added two more before the final gun.

The last two New York touchdowns came from the arm of Conerly. He hit Kyle Rote on a nine-yard score in the third period and found Frank Gifford open for a 14-yard score in the fourth. The game film had a good view of Conerly throwing to Rote at the goal posts, right between them, and the narrative suggested this was "just how touchdowns are made."[4]

Although he missed the extra point after the Rote touchdown, kicker Ben Agajanian made five extra points and kicked field goals of 17 and 43 yards early in the game when the score was still close. Agajanian was a rare figure in pro football lore. He was born in 1919 in Santa Ana, California, and played ball for the University of New Mexico.

In 1941, Agajanian was working an off-season job running a freight elevator at a soft-drink company. He had an accident when the elevator forced his kicking foot against concrete and crushed it. That resulted in the amputation of his toes. Until then he had been a defensive lineman and wide receiver. But despite the incident, Agajanian made it in pro football as a kicker using a square-toed shoe, gaining the nickname "The Toeless Wonder." He had a long career spanning the 1940s, 1950s and into the 1960s in the All-America Football Conference, the National Football League, and the American Football League.

"Lot of guys said I was cheating because I had the hard, square toe," Agajanian once said. "I said, 'Well, you can do it, too. If it helps you, why not?'"[5]

No doubt few would be willing to sacrifice toes to give it a try. Agajanian, who lived to be 98, had two terms with the Giants, the prime one being the stretch where he helped the team win this title. He also was with the Green Bay Packers in 1961 when they won the championship.

Agajanian did his share to beat the Bears in the 1956 championship game, but so did many others in the New York lineup, including Gifford, who termed the victory the most memorable game of his career. He played in five NFL championship games, but this was the time his team won.

When the game concluded, New York fans behaved the same way followers on college campuses did after big wins. They rushed onto the field and tore down the goal posts.

This was also Conerly's only pro championship. Years later, Conerly's wife, Perian, said the quarterback gave the triumph the same designation as Gifford. "Charlie counts this victory, along with the resulting designation as World Champions of 1956, as his greatest pro thrill," she said.[6]

Conerly was never outspoken as a collegiate player or a pro football player, never a go-to quote man in the locker room. Sportswriters who covered his teams regularly grew to realize that, although they did often try to interview him. He was just not very forthcoming with his emotions, and he was not one to reveal his innermost thoughts. He was not contentious, just reticent.

However, it would have been fortunate and wise to listen to words coming out of Conerly's mouth after the satisfying title victory over the Bears. It wasn't clear how many people heard, but his wife was a sportswriter, too, after all, and no doubt she had the advantage over the rest of the scribes in obtaining quotes.

"That evening he muttered over and over to anyone who would listen," she reported, "'Do you realize we're champions of the whole wide world? That covers a mighty lot of territory.'"[7] For sure, the world was a geographical entity, though the specific accuracy of the statement would refer to the more limited football-playing world.

Teammates responded in the same spirit, in part teasing Conerly about his declaration, though not disagreeing about becoming world champs. "Hey, Charlie, don't forget Afghanistan!" one shouted in reply. "Or Outer Mongolia. Or New Guinea."[8] No sports federations representing any of those nations would protest.

That year the NFL, gaining in popularity, was able to secure a rights deal for radio and television broadcasting that helped lift the proceeds from the title game to $517,000. Although that is infinitesimal compared to present-day payoffs, that meant each of the players competing for the Giants earned a check for $3,779.

Conerly shared the wealth with his wife by buying her a mink stole.

Chapter 2

Mississippi Roots

Clarksdale was always home for Charlie Conerly. The county seat of Coahoma County, the community borders the Sunflower River and carries the nickname "the Golden Buckle on the Cotton Belt." He was born there on September 19, 1921, and regularly returned during his professional football playing days' off-seasons.

Conerly grew up in Clarksdale, Perian hailed from there, he ran businesses in the city, and he was a local legend for his exploits on the gridiron.

Cotton counted. So did football. Though above all, throughout a long and checkered history of race relations, music may have mattered the most. Clarksdale is situated in the heart of the Mississippi Delta, the home of the Blues, and rests on the western edge of the county adjacent to the Mississippi River. The place was established in 1848 to harbor a timber business owned by a John Clark. The brother of the woman he married was a cotton grower.

Native Americans, Choctaws and Chickasaws, had long populated the area, but the ever-westward expansion of the United States pushed them aside, as happened to many tribes first in the East, then on the Plains, in the Rocky Mountains, and finally in the West.

In 1860, on the cusp of the Civil War, the city, which had blossomed with cotton plantations, had a population of about 6,600 souls—about 25 percent of them White and 75 percent of them Black slaves. Clarksdale was a tinderbox of race relations for a long time. Tension between races defined Clarksdale before and during the Civil War, during Reconstruction, and for many decades after, the community also over time morphing from a hotbed of denied rights into a Civil Rights battleground. This was the general environment, the backdrop for the creation of a form of music exported around the world. Conerly was no musician, but he did enjoy listening to it, especially in adulthood when he and his wife visited the hottest clubs in the Harlem section of New York.

It may not always have been the same kind of music growing from the ground in Clarksdale. Author James C. Cobb once explored the history and status of the Delta, and the title of his 1992 work was *The Most Southern Place on Earth*. In general, the Delta was not a wealthy place, and even after the Civil War ended with the South's defeat at the hands of the Union in 1865, it was very much a land of sharecroppers and tenant farmers. Legalities changed with the freeing of slaves, but attitudes did not. In 1935, sociologist Rupert Vance described the Delta as "cotton obsessed. Negro obsessed." He was quoted by Cobb as saying that and noting that the region had actively preserved the vestiges of the Antebellum history.

Mississippi, the Delta, and Clarksdale are credited as the birthplace of the Blues form of music. There is a Mississippi Blues Trail series of markers for historic sites, and Clarksdale has its share. Bessie Smith died at the Riverside Hotel there, and while there is little supporting evidence that Charlie Conerly played such tunes or sang such songs, it would have been difficult for him to avoid hearing them.

Conerly is one of the best-known native sons of Clarksdale, but his competition on the fame meter of those with origins in the Delta is heavily populated with individuals from the musical world, including such artists as Robert Johnson, Sam Cooke, Muddy Waters, John Lee Hooker, and Ike Turner. Bluesman McKinley Morganfield (Waters) worked the cotton fields before leaving for Chicago. Playwright Tennessee Williams, who authored such magnificent stage shows as *A Streetcar Named Desire*, was not born in Clarksdale but moved there as a youngster. His written words were spoken, not sung.

Other football players besides Charlie Conerly came from Clarksdale and had college and professional success, but none of them rivaled his. Most of the others of note passing through Clarksdale registered their success due to their way with words. Apparently, those who lived and died with slavery, who resided where the results of the Civil War were slow to take hold, where the oppressive heat, averaging 90 degrees in July and August, and where it once reached 109 degrees, had plenty to talk, sing and write about.

Robert Johnson was born in Hazlehurst, Mississippi, in 1911, and as a Black man he had difficulty breaking into a top level of show business. He wrote songs, played guitar, and sang, but he performed on street corners and in clubs in one-night deals. He recorded heavily in 1937 and 1938 and then died at 27 in 1938, essentially an undiscovered talent. His music had a small group of supporters, and it was not until the 1960s, when he became better known and more popular, that some small details of his life became clearer.

Chapter 2. Mississippi Roots

It is not known how Johnson died in Greenwood, Mississippi, or where his grave is. Any clue to the mysteries of his existence, more than a century after his birth, are found in his music.

One of Johnson's songs was titled "Walking Blues." Some of the lyrics go

> "Well, some people tell me that the worried blues ain't bad,
> Worst old feelin' I most ever had,
> Some people tell me that these old worried old blues ain't bad,
> It's the worst old feelin' I most ever had."

Lyrics of his "Crossroad Blues" include

> "Yeoo, standin' at the crossroad, tried to flag a ride,
> Ooo eee, I tried to flag a ride,
> Didn't nobody seem to know me, babe,
> Everybody pass me by."

Johnson may well have sought a ride to Chicago, where so many Black Mississippians exiled themselves from their original homes as part of the Great Migration, as the shift of population from the Deep South to the big-city North was termed. They fled for opportunity and to avoid discrimination.

Johnson may have spoken with a powerful voice and a powerful pen, but nobody outside of his immediate vicinity heard his plaintiveness and way with music until long after his passing.

Conerly was the son of Charles and Winford Conerly. His birth certificate name was Charles Albert Conerly, Jr. One oddity about the football Charlie's fame was that his name was often misspelled "Charley," and he never corrected anyone or cared which way it was written. That was so even to the extent that autographs he signed conformed to that spelling. Most of Conerly's football cards produced later in his career read "Charley," as did many photograph captions and newspaper articles.

"He just did whatever was on the card or the photo," said Lulu Maness, Conerly's goddaughter from Clarksdale.[1]

Conerly's birth certificate did not read "Chuckin' Charlie," either, as some wags might have speculated following his fame as a football quarterback. Indeed, although the "Chuckin'" appellation seemed appropriate for a football player who frequently threw the ball, there is some dispute about what Conerly's nickname really was. There are many references in print to "Chuckin,'" yet his wife said that may have been corrupted from "Chunkin.'" And "Chunkin'" is a local term. Since Conerly pretty much always looked slender, that moniker did not seem to mean much when applied to him.

Charlie was the only boy among three children, with sisters named Ruth and Ray, who outlived him. Always a great athlete, he aspired to become a professional football player at a time when the game was far from America's number one sport in popularity. In the late 1930s, pro football was still in its leather helmet days.

The top sport in the country during Conerly's coming-of-age years was baseball, with boxing and horse racing next on the list behind the national pastime. Even college football had more support than pro football, still finding its way from its founding in 1920, the National Football League being just one year older than Conerly.

One day, when Conerly was a youngster, his mother asked what he wanted to be when he grew up. Anticipating the routine answer many little boys offered at the time, she continued, "A policeman? A fireman?" His answer was illuminating. "No, ma'am," Charlie Jr. said, "a professional football player with the New York Giants."[2]

The specificity of his reply was more than slightly surprising. His mom thought she knew her sports, and her answer was "You mean a baseball player." Winford Conerly thought her son was referring to the New York Giants baseball team of Mel Ott playing in the Polo Grounds. "No, ma'am," Charlie repeated. "Football, but I might play baseball, too." Mother Conerly occasionally recounted the story, but said she never probed young Charlie's thinking. "He never would tell me where he got the idea, but from then on, the Giants were his team," she said.[3] That is, the football Giants, winners of NFL titles in 1927, 1934 and 1938, within his lifetime to date. Given his refusal to reveal the sources of his fandom, it's not evident whether Conerly knew and rooted for such luminaries of the past champion teams as Red Badgro, Ken Strong, Mel Hein, Pete Henry, Cal Hubbard, Joe Guyon, or Steve Owen, who would one day become his coach. Whether or not Conerly ever met most of them, his name would ultimately be connected to theirs in Giants lore.

Further cementing Conerly's mental affinity for New York as a teenager while growing up in Mississippi, in an action and attitude rare for his time, he had enough curiosity about the big city that loomed in so many ways over American life that he developed a burning yen to visit. Clarksdale, which only has about 15,000 people now, was a blip on the map compared to New York City, which had nearly seven and a half million people in 1940.

"I always liked New York," Conerly said. "When I was a teenager, me and this friend of mine hitch-hiked up there to go to the World's Fair, and I remember going to the Polo Grounds when we got there to see a Giants baseball game. It was really something, I thought."[4]

Conerly may have aspired to play pro football in the largest city in America, but that would be a long way off, and there would be only so much he could do to effect that result. As he said to his mother, he might play baseball as well as football, and, as it turned out, he was quite adept at that game.

Many of the finest high school athletes, even in this modern age of specialization, possess the versatility to devote themselves to more than one game when they are still young. Even if their hearts belong to one sport, and even though many more young athletes focus on only one game, many still do participate in several sports while in school.

The famous three-sport athlete image stems from high school days when the seasons were shorter. When it came to the top male athletes (and in Conerly's day and for many days later, girls had no teams to play for), it was often routine, especially in small towns, for a star to compete in football, basketball and baseball. Basketball, in the pre–NBA days, hadn't quite taken hold as one of the regular big-time sports for those guys. Conerly focused on football in the fall and baseball in the spring at Clarksdale's Bobo Senior High School.

Conerly didn't know how Bobo High got its name, but it was fairly new when he enrolled. The school was completed in 1930 and was named after an early Clarksdale family, though many years later its name was changed from Bobo to Clarksdale High. The Bobo family, which owned an adjacent plantation, donated the land for the school's construction. However, it became an abandoned, decaying building, its Gothic revival architecture fraying after it shut down in 1999. Window frames were empty, and boarding blocked some. The school does have a Mississippi Landmark designation.

Still marking the property is a graveyard called Bobo Cemetery. The once lively school building abuts the Sunflower River. The headstones in the graveyard themselves date back far earlier than the building, to the earliest years of the 19th century, indicating the cemetery was used as a place of rest long before rambunctious local students took their lessons inside.

One member of the Bobo family of Clarksdale served as head football coach at Mississippi State Teachers College, the forerunner of the University of Southern Mississippi. William Herschel Bobo coached the team for four years in the 1920s, when Conerly was in elementary school. He spent much longer coaching high school baseball before passing away at 79 in 1975.

In its earliest years—and that included Conerly's attendance years—Bobo Senior High was segregated, as was the rest of Clarksdale. It opened its doors to Black students beginning in 1970. Conerly never had a Black teammate in high school.

The 1941 Ole Miss freshman football backfield: (from left) Doug Kenna, R.C. Britt, Charlie Conerly, John "Bud" Bowen, and Ray Woodward (courtesy University of Mississippi Athletics Department)

Another nickname Conerly picked up as he was growing up, although it was much less frequently referred to in his pro football days, was "Roach." One day, a group of friends just began spewing nicknames at one another.

There are two possible origins of this less-flattering and less-known nickname. It was suggested that Roach Conerly sprang into existence because of the awkward way Conerly ran the bases for his high school baseball team. It probably was not a supreme compliment. Indeed, he never was a true runner with the ball in football, either by instinct or with much speed.

Maness, who said it was accurate to say that Conerly was not a picturesque sprinter in any sport, said other lore points to a different answer to the Roach mystery.

"No, he was not a pretty runner," Maness said. Others said Conerly picked up the nickname through another sport altogether when he was a youngster. "That was because he caught roaches for fish bait during the Depression."[5]

Perian Conerly once admitted that sometimes back in Mississippi during off-seasons, she called Conerly "Roach."

Conerly was a local football star in Clarksdale and a coveted player

Chapter 2. Mississippi Roots

for Mississippi. After he graduated and his old school was getting ready to play a new season without him, his departure was still lamented. The *Delta Times-Democrat* headline on the high school's pre-season preview in 1941 read "Eleven Lettermen Are Back This Fall with Clarksdale" with this subhead: "Loss of Charlie Conerly Is Big Blow to the Wildcats." The preview went on to state, "Charlie Conerly, one of the greatest triple threat (running, passing and punting) men ever produced in the Delta area, leaves Clarksdale High to pick up his new duties with the Old Miss football squad. Loss of Conerly in the backfield is a severe blow."[6]

Although it is not clear how focused he was on New York at that time, it turned out to be a long intermission between Bobo High and the New York Giants for Conerly. In 1941, he enrolled at the University of Mississippi in Oxford. While Ole Miss has had a devoted fan following over its 125-year football history, its reach has often exceeded its grasp, the spectators' hopes extended beyond the achievements of the team. There are plenty of lean seasons on Ole Miss's record.

Well known, but not yet famous, certainly not beyond the boundaries of Mississippi, Conerly hit the road for Oxford, just 64 miles east of Clarksdale, responding affirmatively to a scholarship offer and naturally not knowing what lay ahead for him, never mind even in the very near future. Not long after Conerly began college and as his freshman football season concluded, in December of 1941, the Japanese bombed Pearl Harbor in Hawaii, drawing the United States into World War II.

Charlie Conerly, like most Americans who had any awareness, could not be ignorant of the burgeoning international tensions that had already embroiled Great Britain in war with an aggressive Germany. Most Americans feared the worst but hoped for the best, that President Franklin D. Roosevelt could keep the United States out of the conflagration.

In the end, no political action by the U.S. government could do that, and within a few months of Conerly's freshman fall at Ole Miss and not long after the completion of his first season of college football, the landscape had dramatically changed. Soon enough, America was at war.

Chapter 3

Ole Miss

The University of Mississippi pretty much dominates the community of Oxford, although technically it is an independent place called University which is surrounded by Oxford. Just plain University, its own self-contained entity. It's not clear how many people ever refer to Ole Miss as being situated in University, but looking back over the years, it is easy to find football stories that use "University" on the dateline. The average non-resident might not know where he is when he crosses a street.

Compliments pour forth about Oxford, Mississippi, these days. One can't cast his eyes more than a few paragraphs into a story about the place without coming across the word "charm" and, specifically, "Southern charm." In some ways, Oxford's architecture and lifestyle epitomize the nicest atmospheric things about Southern charm. The Grove alone, standing as the grandest tradition in college football, wins the community an untold number of bonus points.

However, Oxford wasn't born yesterday, nor in the 1990s. It has a wild, up-and-down, often testy history, receding by the minute, but not without some scars. The city of 25,000, nearly burned down by occupying Union troops, once nearly imploded by race riots, has become one of the most desirable towns to reside in across this region. It is a college town oozing with that charm, home to the University of Mississippi and its 19,000 students, and it is the heartbeat of culture, music and literary wisdom for the state.

Oxford, where Charlie Conerly chose to attend college and play football after graduating from high school in Clarksdale, has been many things, served as a symbol for many, during its longevity stretching back to its founding in 1837, when the city was named after the Oxford in England. Foremost among those historical moments that helped define Oxford in the eyes of many far away was its landlord-ship of Ole Miss since it was chartered in 1844.

Appropriately enough for a place with a complicated history, not

Chapter 3. Ole Miss

only was Oxford home to one of the country's ultimate men of letters, William Faulkner, but his old manse is a museum called Rowan Oaks. A visitor can view the old-fangled typewriter the Nobel Prize–winning author used to write such novels as *The Sound and the Fury*, *Light in August*, and *As I Lay Dying*, among others, even if younger tourists may not even recognize what a typewriter is.

A centerpiece and jewel of the community is the Downtown Square, and one of that area's special locales is the Square Bookshop. If the singers of the Delta sang the Blues, the authors of the area wrote the Blues in distinctive styles, with critical eyes, yet with passionate devotion. A browser is more likely to discover autographed copies of sterling works by Willie Morris, prominent journalist Curtis Wilkie, and more current, ever-popular John Grisham than within any other four walls. Eudora Welty, Richard Wright, and Tennessee Williams let their thoughts pour out in crisp sentences, sometimes in disturbing stories.

A College Football Hall of Fame souvenir cup featuring a young Charlie Conerly during his Ole Miss football days (photograph by the author).

When it comes to objective viewing of the old trees and stately homes, Oxford earns raves as one of the best small towns in America, a place with a lively music scene, quality restaurants, and night-life offerings and where the people are friendly.

They didn't used to be, however. At various times in Oxford's history, they were virulently unfriendly to Blacks, whole-heartedly devoted to slavery, despised Yankees, and held a grudge following the Civil War. During the Civil Rights movement in the 1960s, a White man from the North visiting was seen as the enemy and regularly treated as such. Oxford of the 2020s is a very different place than it once was. Some refer to Oxford as "The Little Easy," a play on New Orleans' nickname "The Big Easy."

As someone who attended a White-only high school in Clarksdale, Conerly did not share space with Black players on his football and baseball teams' rosters. Neither did he have a Black teammate on the football team or the baseball team at the University of Mississippi, an institution as segregated from the start as the rest of the state.

The school's first football team was organized in 1893, but officially the team did not begin play until 1902, and through 2021 it had competed in 116 seasons. The fans may have been behind the squad, but Ole Miss was an independent team through 1921. The school then joined the Southern League and played in that conference through 1932 before becoming a stalwart member of the Southeastern Conference in 1933, where it retains affiliation.

The fact is that on very few occasions before linking up with the SEC was Mississippi very good in football. In 1910, the team finished 7–1 under coach N.P. Stauffer. That represented the most victories in a season through Southern Conference days, and it was flanked by many losing seasons and roughly .500 seasons. The good old days were not so good for the gridsters at Ole Miss.

Yet the Rebels broke out in 1935 under coach Ed Walker, going 9–3 and gaining an invitation to the Orange Bowl. They lost that post-season contest, but it was a memorable season in Oxford. The game was played on January 1, 1936, and Mississippi fell to Catholic University of America, 20–19. Through the 2021 season, Mississippi has been invited to 39 bowl games, an indicator of fairly sustained success in recent decades, though there have been periods of ups and downs.

This happened shortly before the Mississippi athletic teams changed their nickname. In the 1920s, the teams were referred to as the somewhat unwieldy "Mississippi Flood." Then the Great Mississippi Flood took place in 1927, causing great damage, and the name was deemed unpopular, if not politically incorrect.

The teams representing the school switched to the Rebels, which many still consider politically incorrect, and is taken as a symbol by those in the North, in particular, that those at this school, in this state, and in the South are still fighting the Civil War. Until the late 1990s, around 1997, Confederate flags, emblematic of the Southern split with the Union in the 1860s, still waved at football games.

Through 2015, the similarly identified song "Dixie" was played at Ole Miss football games and had been played by the school band regularly since 1948. But it was removed from the play book for 2016 home games. Opponents characterized that as ditching Southern tradition. The university announced in an August 2016 press release that the move was made in the interest of "inclusivity."

Chapter 3. Ole Miss

An opinion writer for Fox News ridiculed the decision, saying, "It's only a matter of time before Ole Miss replaces fried catfish and sweet tea with fermented soy sandwiches and beverages made from lawn clippings—all for the sake of inclusivity."[1] The same writer quoted the other side, a student seemingly identifying with Black students. He said, "It's an important step forward for our university as we attempt to reconcile and understand our relationship with our Old South. Ending the use of 'Dixie' promotes inclusivity and makes room for traditions that all UM students can connect with."[2] The Old South mentioned, of course, refers to racism—and worse—in harking back to the slave era.

Much as it was in high school in Clarksdale, Charlie Conerly never had a Black teammate on the football team at Ole Miss. The school was still completely segregated, and when the University of Mississippi did integrate, it came forcibly and was a nationally-followed drama that involved President John F. Kennedy's White House, the courts, university officials, Mississippi state authorities, and the military. Ole Miss integration was among the most memorable and Earth-shaking challenges of the Civil Rights movement period, closely watched by citizens around the country—and most likely around the world, although technology and television itself were far more limited in 1961 when the process began.

James Meredith was the bold individual who wished to enroll at Oxford. He was born in 1933 in Kosciusko, Mississippi. Meredith attended segregated schools through 11th grade, then finished high school in St. Petersburg, Florida. He returned to Mississippi, spending two years at Jackson State, an historically Black university. Then he joined the Air Force.

Meredith was much older than the traditional undergraduate college student when he heard and was inspired by JFK's inauguration speech. Subsequently, he applied for admission to Ole Miss to complete his undergraduate studies. School officials worked to delay his admission. But eventually, employing the argument that Mississippi was a state-funded institution and it was his right to enroll, Meredith won the backing of the United States Supreme Court to sign up for classes.

Meredith had been correct to put his faith in the Kennedy Administration. At that time, Robert F. Kennedy, the president's brother, was the attorney general of the United States, and as head of the Department of Justice, he intervened on Meredith's side. The case had spilled over to 1962, yet when Meredith showed up for his classes, the segregationist governor, Ross Barnett, and lieutenant governor, Paul Johnson, Jr., stood in the doorway to prevent Meredith's entrance into the proper building.

As they took this action, a howling mob surrounded the grounds, yelling at Meredith. Three different times, the U.S. Circuit Court of Appeals for the Fifth Circuit declared both Barnett and Johnson in contempt of court, applying $10,000 daily fines.

To ensure that Meredith could enter the school, John F. Kennedy, in consultation with his brother Robert, sent U.S. marshals, border patrol agents, and federalized Bureau of Prison guards to help maintain order. It was not enough. After Meredith was escorted into the school on September 30, 1962, a riot broke out. Violence exploded and expanded, and the federal government kept adding forces to the uniformed men trying to quell the disturbance. Individuals from the National Guard and other agencies became involved. All told, 30,000 peacekeepers were needed as Whites threw rocks, burned cars, and threatened individuals.

This confrontation took place in front of the academic building known as the Lyceum. The structure was named after Aristotle's Greek Lyceum, and during the Civil War, it was used as a hospital for Confederate casualties. Of some irony is that the federal soldiers and law enforcement figures who came to Oxford to enter Meredith in school used the Lyceum as their headquarters. Ultimately, because of the circumstances, the riot, and Meredith's desegregation success, the Lyceum was placed on the National Register of Historic Places and is included as a National Historic Landmark.

For quite some time, Robert Kennedy was a despised figure in Mississippi, yet somewhat ironically, several years later, when Charlie Conerly was inducted into the College Football Hall of Fame, RFK, who had become a United States senator representing New York, and his wife, Ethel, were guests and posed for a picture with Charlie and Perian Conerly. The couples were all smiles.

While many did not recognize the significance of Meredith's determination originally, the more time passed, the more appreciated his actions have become as he approaches his 90th birthday. Meredith became a long-term civil rights activist, and the university commemorated the 40th anniversary of his becoming the school's first Black student in 2002 and celebrated the 50th anniversary in 2012.

Meredith spent just two semesters at Ole Miss, and throughout much of that time, White students harassed him, literally turning their backs on him in the school cafeteria and bouncing basketballs on the floor above the ceiling of his room to make it difficult for him to sleep.

In 2006, a new generation of school leadership, representing a different era, had a statue of James Meredith erected on the campus, acknowledging the role he played in the Civil Rights movement.

The admittance of Meredith as the first Black student at Mississippi occurred right about the time Conerly retired from pro football

Chapter 3. Ole Miss

and returned to live permanently in Mississippi. He left Clarksdale for Oxford in the autumn of 1941, very much with football on his mind and believing he could continue to excel at the game.

Conerly was not exposed to much sophisticated offense in high school or when he was a freshman at Mississippi. The passing game was in its infancy compared to later decades. The ground game was still king, and few teams embraced a wide-open throwing offense. If Conerly sought a role model for what could be by 1941, he could study the Green Bay Packers and their outstanding pioneer end, Don Hutson, who virtually invented new pass routes weekly, or he could keep an eye on Washington Redskins star passer Sammy Baugh.

Soon enough, the Chicago Bears adopted the T-formation and spread the deadliness of the offense. But in high school and at Ole Miss, Conerly was slotted in at tailback, with only some of the responsibilities of the modern-day quarterback. Conerly was a signal caller, but the signals he called represented plays that were much more conservative than the routine calls of the game in the 2020s.

On future rosters and on the Giants' football cards issued later when he was playing in New York, Conerly was listed as standing 6-foot-1 and weighing 185 pounds. At the time, that was a firm enough figure, though these days a scout might well suggest that he was too small to be a pro QB or even an NCAA Division I quarterback. These days, teams like their quarterbacks to be taller, so they can more readily throw over the heads of the gargantuan defensive linemen they face, and they prefer those leaders to be heftier, certainly more than 200 pounds and sometimes more of a 220-pound-or-so pillar, making them harder to knock down when hit in the pocket.

As Conerly worked his way through high school to college ball, it was a very different football world in the late 1930s and early 1940s from the modern style of play. Indeed, there are photographs from early in Conerly's career when his head was adorned by a leather helmet with no face mask.

The NFL decreed in 1943 that all players must wear helmets. Dick Plasman, a wide receiver for the Chicago Bears, had an eight-year pro career without wearing a helmet. The rule change kicked in while Plasman was in the service during World War II. He returned to play two more years, 1946 and 1947 for the Chicago Cardinals, but the league grandfathered him in to go without a helmet, making him the last NFL player to play bareheaded.

Before coach Clark Shaughnessy masterminded Stanford University's employment of the T-formation and spread it to the pros through the Chicago Bears in the 1940s, many teams relied on the single wing.

The single wing, created by legendary coach Glenn "Pop" Warner, featured the ball hike flipped to a player rather than snapped between the center's legs directly into the quarterback's hands. The formation relied on an unbalanced offensive line, and the man most often handling the ball was the tailback, with the quarterback used as a blocking back the way future fullbacks evolved.

When he was younger, Conerly was a tailback in the single wing. Later he picked up what he referred to as the A formation, the brainchild of Giants coach Steve Owen. New York was the best practitioner of the A formation for some time. For many years, Conerly was not the traditional quarterback the way the job is defined these days. This meant his passing statistics at all levels were not as large as one might expect.

The tailback physically took a bigger pounding from defenses than the quarterback in the T-formation, and when, after all of his years of being slotted in one role, Conerly graduated to full-fledged throwing quarterback, he was grateful.

"And that's what saved my life," Conerly said, citing his frame as being roughly 180 pounds at the time. "It was just too tough playing out of the A with all of the blocking and running that went with it."[3]

That was an introspective mouthful for Conerly, who as a high schooler, college player, and a professional player in New York said little. He rarely gave away his thoughts and was known as someone who carried a big gun (his right arm) and shot first, but spoke in detail later—practically never.

That was a reputation established early, and it stuck. Conerly spoke with a Southern drawl, but he mostly talked in clipped sentences to sportswriters who asked questions. He was one of the original one-word-answer guys. No one suggested he wasn't smart, but everyone suggested that he chose not to say much, selecting one word when more was sought and choosing two words instead of a longer sentence. Conerly stood out at Ole Miss and later in New York, but he was a low-profile guy in a high-profile sport.

Sam Huff, the linebacker who was one of Conerly's more glamorous teammates, said that was just his way. "He was a silent leader," Huff said. "Charlie never talked to anybody. He came in, sat in front of his locker and read the paper. Some people thought he was grumpy. He just didn't talk."[4]

In 1941, when college football seasons were shorter, Ole Miss played nine games and finished 6–2–1, a good start to Conerly's college career. The Rebels were coached by veteran leader Harry Mehre, who was making the last stop in a 17-season career that concluded in 1945 with a record of 98–60–7. Before coming to Oxford in 1938, he was the long-time coach at Georgia.

By 1942, the program was, like the nation as a whole, a bit shakier. World War II had impacted the country and swept up millions of young male citizens, athletes included. Instead of sitting in classrooms or running up and down playing fields, they began flying in bombers, sailing on gigantic ships, and dodging enemy fire in fields and jungles.

After the bombing of Pearl Harbor, the United States began engaging in war on two fronts, in the South Pacific focused against Japan and in Europe, and in Europe fighting Germany and the spread of Naziism. It was initially unclear whether organized professional sports would even continue.

Major League Baseball was the flagship team sport of the time, and Commissioner Kenesaw Mountain Landis took the initiative, writing a letter to President Franklin D. Roosevelt seeking guidance on whether or not to play. FDR's response, which became known as "the green light letter," gave the go-ahead. Roosevelt's position was that baseball would serve as good entertainment for the civilian population working hard in factories for the war effort, but he emphasized that no players would be given special consideration for exemption from service in the Army, Navy, Marines, and the forerunner of what became the Air Force.

A healthy athlete who was drafted and passed the physical served. Some athletes rushed to enlist; some waited to be drafted. In baseball, among the most prominent future Hall of Famers whose careers were interrupted or delayed were Bob Feller, Ted Williams, Warren Spahn, Joe DiMaggio, Yogi Berra and Stan Musial. Just two major leaguers, Harry O'Neill and Elmer Gedeon, perished in World War II.

Other sports took their cue from baseball, though the National Hockey League consisted of just six teams at the time and the National Basketball Association had not yet come into existence.

The National Football League did play on, though with some difficulty. There was a shortage of personnel, stretching rosters very thin, and for one season, 1943, the Pittsburgh Steelers and Philadelphia Eagles merged, playing under the banner of the Steagles. It was an uncomfortable alliance. In 1944, the Steelers and Chicago Cardinals shared one team, operating under the unwieldy name Card-Pitt.

Some 21 men connected to the NFL died during World War II, 19 of them either active or former players, one a former coach, and one an executive. Marine Jack Lummus had been an end with the New York Giants. He died while fighting in the South Pacific and was recognized with the Congressional Medal of Honor.

Given the worldwide fighting and uncertainty affecting daily activities, life and death were on people's minds more than the result of any individual sporting contest. If you were a college coach, it was unlikely you cast a wide net in recruiting. The pool of players kept shrinking as young men pulled on uniforms of a different kind. And that was after a crop of players left for war instead of staying through graduation.

Harry Mehre, who was born in 1901 in Huntington, Indiana, and played football and basketball for Notre Dame in the early 1920s, was a good get for Ole Miss when he came from Georgia. Although it was not especially prestigious at the time, before he coached the Bulldogs, Mehre coached the NFL's Minneapolis Marines to a 4–5–2 record.

Mehre's first four Mississippi squads had been quite good, with none losing more than two games. The situation changed in 1942, Conerly's second season. The Rebels had previously finished 9–2, 7–2, 9–2, and 6–2–1 under Mehre. This time they went 2–7. Anyone who observes old photographs of Conerly from his first college football days will recognize him in his No. 42 uniform jersey. He wore that number throughout his college and professional days.

Initially, the new season shaped up like the recent ones. Mississippi trounced Western Kentucky, 39–6, on September 26. The 1–0 record looked and felt good. But it turned out there was only one additional W on the horizon. On October 31, Mississippi hammered Memphis State, 48–0, in Memphis.

That was pretty much a home game for both teams. In those days, the University of Mississippi played several home games in nearby Memphis, 86 miles away, so Oxford was practically a suburb of the Tennessee city. The Rebels played four games in Memphis during the 1942 season. The other three visits produced losses.

Mississippi fell to Georgetown 14–6, Georgia 48–13, Louisiana State 21–7, Arkansas 7–6, Vanderbilt 19–0, Tennessee 14–0, and in-state rival Mississippi State 34–13. The Rebels did not earn much in the way of bragging rights in their neighborhood. Mississippi was outscored 163 to 132 that year.

When Ole Miss' 1942 season concluded November 28 with that Mississippi State defeat, Charlie Conerly may well have been looking forward to an improved Rebels junior football season, but American life in the early 1940s was volatile and unpredictable. Conerly did not resume his third year of schooling and football for several years.

Soon enough, the tailback for Ole Miss was lining up as tailback for the United States Marines.

There were two evenly divided parts to Charlie Conerly's student-athlete days at the University of Mississippi, two-year segments split by a different sort of time spent in the trenches, time spent at war.

Chapter 4

War and Ole Miss II

As taciturn as Charlie Conerly naturally was, it should be of little surprise that he spoke little about his time in the Marines, which he entered as a private rather than returning for his junior year of college at Ole Miss in the fall of 1943.

That was not uncommon among the American men who served their country during World War II. Many brothers and fathers who saw terrible things happen, who participated in bloody battles, wanted to forget more than remember, to start fresh rather than relive those experiences.

Lulu Maness, now in her early 70s, is the goddaughter of Charlie Conerly and Perian (whose name was pronounced Perry-Ann). Maness, whose maiden name was Malvezzi, came from a family in Clarksdale that was always close to the Conerlys. She describes her father Tony as Charlie's best friend since the age of five and says her grandfather, Angelo Malvezzi, taught Charlie how to drive. Much later, Lulu and her sisters (there were five Malvezzi siblings in all, including one boy) were like the Conerlys' own children since they had none, and they were caretakers for Perian during the last years of her life.

Conerly went into the Marines as a private and emerged from the service as a sergeant. Much of his service took place in combat on Guam, in the Mariana Islands. This was the site of one of the more famous battles in the South Pacific in 1944. Guam was a United States possession, acquired after the Spanish-American War of 1898. Japan moved in to occupy the island just three days after the assault on Pearl Harbor, on December 10, 1941.

This was the early period of the war, when an ill-prepared United States, short on men in arms and equipment due to previous isolationist political factions nipping at President Franklin D. Roosevelt's policies, received bad news after bad news. At Pearl Harbor, the Hawaiian base's losses included 2,403 dead and 160 aircraft, most on the ground during the two-hour surprise attack that began at 8 a.m.

Pearl Harbor was the spark bringing the United States into World War II, but the sneak attack set the early tenor of the war. More defeats occurred as America sought to gear up in a hurry to combat the Japanese in the Pacific and the aggressive Germans in Europe. The earliest positive impact was the seemingly near-suicidal mission led by Jimmy Doolittle on April 18, 1942. Doolittle, who was awarded the Congressional Medal of Honor for his leadership, spearheaded a group of 16 pilots in B-25s over Japanese territory to inflict bomb damage on the government and people who believed themselves invincible. In a heroic undertaking that required the men to parachute on chance afterward into China as their planes ran out of fuel, the bold action lifted American morale.

The U.S. began a re-invasion of Guam on July 21, 1944, determined to take back the land. There were 59,400 Allied troops in the attack. Under the command of Marine major general Allen H. Turnage and under cover of naval offshore bombardment, the American and other troops charged ashore. It took until August 10 to re-establish supremacy. There were 1,783 Allied men killed and 6,010 wounded. The Japanese suffered 18,300 deaths with 1,250 men captured.

By the time the fighting on Guam occurred, the United States had begun turning the tide of the war and was putting heavy pressure on Japan in the lead-up to the atomic bomb being dropped on Hiroshima and Nagasaki in August of 1945, ending the war in the Pacific. Whatever Charlie Conerly's experience was during combat on Guam, he basically kept quiet about it. He did not tell war stories, to newspapermen who later interviewed him about resuming his football exploits or to his family or friends.

"He never talked about it," Lulu Maness said.[1]

Only one story from Conerly's Marine combat life seemed to follow him home to Mississippi—and not one lavishly illustrated by his words. It was more of a show-and-tell event. When he returned to Clarksdale and was visiting with his mother Winford, he gave her a damaged rifle clip. It was a leftover piece from his weapon, one that had been shot out of his hands by a Japanese sniper aiming from a tree.

Conerly was not wounded in the incident, even if his gun was. He brought the small remaining piece from the rifle home without saying much about its origins. Conerly knew he was fortunate. The close call was neither something he bragged about surviving nor told to strangers. Later, Winford gave the rifle clip to Conerly's wife, Perian.

Goddaughter Lulu Maness said Perian kept the item for years but eventually lost it along with other possessions in a flood.[2] This was a catastrophe much later than the Great Flood of the 1920s.

Chapter 4. War and Ole Miss II

There was one much more amusing anecdote related to Conerly's war service. Conerly had played two years of football at Ole Miss, in 1941 and 1942, before joining the Marines. If he had remained in school, he would have played the 1943 and 1944 seasons, completing four years of eligibility.

Instead, Conerly was in the Marines and spending those years in the South Pacific, not the South. Still, based on the evidence of his talent shown for the Rebels during his first two college seasons, the Washington Redskins chose him in the NFL draft. Winford notified Charlie by letter that the pros had picked him. Of course, he was otherwise occupied in a U.S. Marines uniform, hardly able to pull on a Redskins uniform. Conerly teasingly wrote back to his mother, "Tell them I'll be glad to come."[3]

Actually, it is too simple to state outright that Conerly never spoke about his war experience to any-

Charlie Conerly, as a member of the Ole Miss football team in 1947, after returning from World War II service (courtesy University of Mississippi Athletics Department).

one at all. Once, when talking to his friend and wide receiver Kyle Rote of the Giants, Conerly said, "If a war breaks out in the future, do all you can to stay out of it. I was scared to death all the time I was in the Marines in the Pacific."[4] It was a candid comment from a man who at almost all times refused to voice deeper thoughts.

The professional athletes who returned to the normalcy of American life once they were discharged from the branches of the service had decisions to make. All were rusty and in need of training camp regimens and practice. Many returned to their former teams. Some, in the best of health, not nursing resulting disabilities or harm from wounds, seemed to seamlessly fit back in, especially the big stars. Some players lost critical prime years of their career but overcame that obstacle to become great stars, Yogi Berra and Warren Spahn among them in baseball. Some players, in baseball and football both, never played the game at a high level again.

Although he had been selected to play for the Redskins, Conerly had two years of college eligibility left at the University of Mississippi. He chose that comparative stay-at-home route, re-enrolling as a student in the fall of 1946, with the 1947 season stretched before him too. He could have gone either way. Langston Rogers, the former long-time sports information director at Ole Miss, and more recently a special assistant to the athletic director, said, "Charlie had thought about leaving."[5]

Anyone who lost three years of his life to military service in wartime conditions was probably anxious to get on with the calling of his professional life. But Conerly chose the comfort of hometown Mississippi, of Oxford, Clarksdale, and the familiar as a way to ease back into everyday living, and at the same time he could still hone his football skills.

During his first two seasons at Ole Miss, Conerly had shown promise, but he was not necessarily the go-to guy at the center of the offense. When he returned, he was that guy, the epicenter of the action for the Rebels. He was the man who made the offense go, running and passing, and he was a key figure for his punting too.

As had the entire world, Mississippi football had undergone changes in the early 1940s, not least the suspension of the team for the 1943 season. Unlike Major League Baseball, acting on its green-light letter from President Roosevelt, and the National Football League, colleges gauged the appropriateness of playing football during wartime, and a limited number pulled the plug temporarily as so many young American men signed up for military service. Mississippi took the year off, as did fellow Southeastern Conference teams Mississippi State, Alabama, Auburn, Florida, Kentucky, Tennessee, and Vanderbilt. Teams in other leagues were also sidelined. The United States Naval Academy in Annapolis, Maryland, and the United States Military Academy in West Point, New York, did field teams.

Mississippi coach Harry Mehre was at the helm for 1944 when the Rebels played ball again. They finished 2–6 that year. Mehre's final season at Old Miss and as a head college football coach was in 1945, when the Rebels finished 4–5.

Chapter 4. War and Ole Miss II

When Charlie Conerly rejoined the Rebels for the 1946 season, there was a new head coach in Red Drew. Drew was head coach at Birmingham-Southern in 1924, finishing 4–4–1, and he was not a coach again until taking over at Mississippi in 1946. Drew and Conerly went just 2–7 that year.

Born in 1894 in Dyer Brook, Maine, as Harold Drew, "Red" played football at Bates College in Maine and Springfield College in Massachusetts. By the 1930s, he was an assistant football coach at Alabama and the track and field coach in Tuscaloosa. He spent three years in the Navy at the start of World War II, and his stay in Oxford was brief, just one season, before he returned to Alabama as head football coach and took the Crimson Tide to three major bowl games. In all, Drew's head football coaching record was 96–68–14.

There were a limited number of highlights for Drew and Conerly on the field in 1946. The Rebels defeated Florida, 13–6, and Arkansas, 9–7. That was the eye-opener. Arkansas was favored by three touchdowns entering the game, played in Memphis, so the Ole Miss victory was an upset of tremendous proportions.

A headline in the *Clarion-Ledger*, based in Jackson and Mississippi's most important newspaper at the time, read, "Ole Miss Comes of Age in Porker Win; Rebs Now Men." Part of the game story read, "Of course, Charlie Conerly's punting and passing had a lot to do with Old Miss superiority over Arkansas."[6]

That season, Conerly became a more active passer than had been called for during his first stint at Mississippi. He completed 65 passes in 124 attempts, a hint of what might follow his senior season.

Although the Rebels played many home games in Memphis, they had their own Oxford home field, too, called Hemingway Stadium. The building opened in 1915 and was named after Judge William Hemingway, who was a professor of law and chair of the school's athletic committee. Hemingway was the first big backer of football and sports at the campus. From the time it opened, through 1949, or just after Charlie Conerly's playing days, Hemingway Stadium's attendance capacity was 24,000. Given the success and popularity of Mississippi football since then, a number of expansions have followed. The current listed capacity is 64,038, though the all-time attendance record is 66,176 for a game versus Alabama in 2016.

The other major difference in the stadium from Conerly's playing days is that since 1982, the stadium has been known as Vaught-Hemingway Stadium. That name change honors Johnny Vaught, the long-time prominent coach of the Rebels who was an assistant in 1946 and took over the program in 1947, just in time to tutor Conerly for his last college season.

Vaught was born in 1909 in Olney, Texas, and was 96 when he passed away in Oxford. He did more than any other coach to build Mississippi into a football power after playing guard for Texas Christian in the early 1930s and working as an assistant coach at North Carolina. No one realized when Vaught came to Mississippi that he was there to stay. Vaught got to see the foibles of Old Miss up close in 1946, but he provided the cure in 1947, presiding over the biggest college thrills Conerly experienced.

It was a whole different ballgame in 1947. The Rebels put together a 9–2 record and were basically two well-placed touchdowns shy of finishing unbeaten. They won close games, and they beat up on some teams, thrashing them thoroughly. It was the first time in years there had been such excitement for Ole Miss.

The season played out with good vibes from the start. On opening day, September 20, the Rebels topped Kentucky, 14–7. A week later at Florida, Mississippi prevailed, 14–6. Ole Miss moved to 3–0 by hammering South Carolina, 33–0, early in October. On October 11, Mississippi was ranked 18th in the country, but opponent Vanderbilt was ranked 10th and was the home team. The Commodores hung on for a 10–6 victory.

Before the Vanderbilt game, Vaught played it sly. He acted out the role of the self-deprecating coach downplaying his own team's ability, telling sportswriters that Mississippi had no chance to win against such an outstanding club. "We just aren't good enough," Vaught said, "big enough, experienced enough, or even enough. Look what they did to Harry Gilmer [the Alabama quarterback in a 14–7 loss], rushed him off his feet, that's what. Now how can we be expected to keep them from doing the same thing to Charlie Conerly. And Charlie Conerly's just about our entire offense."[7]

By all measures, Conerly was terrific that season, but he was not a one-man offense. A prolific thrower, he was complemented by a dangerous pass receiver in Ray Poole, the combination helping Ole Miss average nearly 25 points a game.

Whether Vaught was playing games with expectations or not, the Rebels were good enough to threaten, if not take down the 10th-ranked team in the land. One story about the result made Conerly and Poole out to be one of the most formidable duos outside of Batman and Robin. "Charlie Conerly and Barney Poole could be one of the best scoring combos in the South," the report read. "Conerly is one of the South's best triple threat backs. Poole's ham-like hands can snare aerials from any angle and he is a wizard in ripping away from pass defenders."[8]

Mississippi split its next two games, handling Tulane, 27–14, on the

Chapter 4. War and Ole Miss II

road and falling to Arkansas, 19–14, the second close loss and the last one of the season. After edging 17th-ranked Louisiana State, 20–18, and thumping Tennessee, 43–13, Ole Miss was back in the rankings. The 15th-ranked Rebels crushed Chattanooga, 52–0, and rival Mississippi State, 33–14. That moved Mississippi to its highest ranking—13th—of the season.

The Conerly-to-Poole tandem dazzled. As an illustration of how removed the passing game was in 1947 from what it is in the 2020s, the duo set national records that are routinely surpassed by multiple teams in the same conference. For their time, however, their numbers were extraordinary. During the 1947 season, Conerly set national records. His 133 (in 233 attempts) completions were a new mark, and his completion percentage of 57.1 was a new record. He threw for 18 touchdowns and 1,366 yards. The old record of 114 completions was set by Wilson "Bud" Schenk of Washington University in St. Louis, and the previous percentage mark was set by Texas Christian's Davey O'Brien at 55.7 percent. That season, Conerly also ran for nine touchdowns, and his punting average was 40.2 yards per boot.

It was later on that Perian Conerly, who had just gotten to know her future husband, joked about having that season's statistics imprinted on her brain. "I could rattle off his 1947 statistics as fast as a blasé fifth-grader can say the pledge of allegiance to the flag," she said. And, she noted, on the other side of the ball, Charlie, quoting a sportswriter, "defended with consummate skill on every occasion."[9] It is often forgotten that even the best offensive players of the era played on the other side of the ball too, doubling up on the defensive side with quarterbacks and running backs contributing in the defensive backfield.

Conerly's passing partner, Barney Poole, also went on to the pros, following his older brothers Jim "Buster" Poole and Ray Poole. In 1947, Ray Poole, who was from Gloster, Mississippi, caught a college record 52 passes. The old record was 50 catches by Harry Stanton of Arizona in 1940.

Mississippi finished its 1947 regular season with an 8–2 record. The surprise prize was the championship of the Southeastern Conference, the school's first. The other reward would have likely been a slot in one of the 13 established bowl games.

However, at that point Mississippi had not been to a bowl game since the 1936 Orange Bowl and had not won nine games in a season since 1940. Insecure about its new status, when Memphis, the Rebels' second home, announced the creation of a new post-season game called the Delta Bowl and offered Mississippi an early invitation, the athletic department grabbed it rather than compete for a spot in a more prominent bowl after the season ended. One thing that made the January 1, 1948, match-up intriguing was that the opponent was to be Texas Christian, Vaught's alma mater. The Horned Frogs did not seem to be the most threatening opponent in the country with a 4–4–2 record.

Ole Miss seemed willing to play any team in any bowl game. The Memphis founders of the Delta Bowl planned to build this first-ever contest into an annual event that would gain prominence on the holiday calendar. Although some years later Memphis adopted the Liberty Bowl as a regular local event, there was only one more Delta Bowl after this one, between William & Mary and Oklahoma A&M (later Oklahoma State), in 1949.

January 1, 1948, turned out to be a chilly, uncomfortable day at Crump Stadium in Memphis, 25 degrees with a 35-mph wind, though attendance was still given as 28,120. For a long stretch, Mississippi played what shaped up as its worst game of the season, and a lot of it could be blamed on Conerly. He threw an interception that was run back 28 yards for a touchdown and had a punt blocked for a safety, all in the second quarter. TCU's lead held up at halftime and into the fourth quarter.

Time was running short when Conerly put Ole Miss on the scoreboard for the first time, trailing 9–6. Subsequently, Conerly completed a 52-yard pass to Johnson that moved the ball to the Texas Christian 13 yard line, and then on the next play, he hit Dixie Howell for the winning score.

That concluded Mississippi's season with a 9–2 record and left TCU 4–5–2. Johnny Vaught, the new coach, was an instant hero, and it was only the start of a memorable career as the leader of Ole Miss football. Vaught's lifetime coaching record, his entire career spent at Mississippi, was 190–61–12. His teams won national championships in 1959, 1960 and 1962, and the Rebels won six SEC titles under his guidance. He was chosen as the league's Coach of the Year six times between 1947 and 1962, and he was inducted into the College Football Hall of Fame in 1979.

Honors piled up for Conerly after that season, and his reputation spread across the country. He was a unanimous first-team Southeastern Conference pick and an All-American.

Professional sports teams, whether major league clubs that expect their new acquisitions to spend several years in the minors working their way up, or NFL teams, which, especially in the late 1940s, did not pay particularly high salaries or count on many players to stick around

Chapter 4. War and Ole Miss II

until their late 30s, certainly not their 40s, generally eyeballed young talent.

Baseball players typically signed pro contracts right out of high school at 18 or 19 years old. Football players who earned a degree were generally 21 or 22 years old. It was not widely known, however, just how old Charlie Conerly was.

He was old enough when he showed up to play at Ole Miss in September of 1941. Then he played two additional years at Ole Miss after his time with the Marines in the mid–1940s. Without the Internet as a source in the late 1940s and early 1950s, it may not have been as handy to discover someone's official date of birth.

Conerly was born on September 19, 1921, which by the start of the fall football season of 1948 made him 27. Few knew it. When Conerly returned to Oxford from the South Pacific, the Ole Miss sports information office added just a single year to his age in his school biography. Conerly never questioned it. The truth only came out, in a most casual manner, some years later when sportswriters covering the Giants asked about his age.

"Upon his return to the Old Miss campus, compilers of the 1946 Rebel team roster took no official note of Charlie's three-year absence," Perian Conerly said. "They merely lifted his vital statistics from the 1942 program and charitably added but one year to his age. Later, the unsuspecting Giant publicity director adopted the conservative Ole Miss version. Now, Charlie has never made a secret of his age. It was just that nobody ever asked him what it really was."

Nobody asked him until some years later in the Giants' locker room after a New York story ran noting just how amazingly well he was doing at 33. A reporter asked when he was going to turn 34, and Conerly said, "Been there. I'll be 36 on September 19."[10]

Perian Conerly said that was big news in all the New York papers for a while—and at that time there were a lot more New York newspapers than there are now.

Chapter 5

Meeting the Mrs.

Perian was five and a half years younger than Charlie Conerly. She was in eighth grade when the football star graduated from high school. Although she was also from Clarksdale, she had never met him.

A college woman, but not a student at the University of Mississippi, in the summer of 1947 she had completed her junior year at Mississippi State College for Women, which was located about 90 miles from Oxford.

However, for the adventure of it, and because she had an older sister who was a member of the faculty at the University of Wyoming, Perian spent a chunk of her summer in Laramie. Although she did make mention of there being a huge disparity in the ratio of men to women there, when she called the area a utopia, it was not clear if she was talking about that circumstance or the mountain scenery.

By August, she was back in Clarksdale, and one day she stopped at the municipal pool, where she had worked three summers as a lifeguard. She was sitting at the side of the pool with the present lifeguard, a high school classmate, chatting about what she had missed locally during her stint in Wyoming. The young man, who had a date that night, tried to talk her into picking up the rest of his shift so he could get ready for his evening out.

While they were shooting the breeze, another old friend, Farley Solomon, walked over to say hello. He had a pal with him, and he introduced Charlie Conerly to Perian. The three of them drifted away to the Coca-Cola stand. No one guessed that this chance meeting would lead to much more.

Thinking back on the occasion, Perian recounted her first impressions, including processing that this guy was the big football star everyone talked about.

"Now, of course I knew who Charlie was," she said later. "Anyone in town able to read a newspaper could hardly escape knowing. Of course I knew him." More like *of him*, not personally because of their

Chapter 5. Meeting the Mrs. 39

The 1947 Ole Miss backfield featured (from left) Charlie Conerly, Buddy Bowen, Eulas Jenkins, and Jerry Tiblier, who led the Rebels to their first Southeastern Conference title and a 13–9 victory over TCU in the first Delta Bowl in Memphis, Tennessee (courtesy University of Mississippi Athletics Department).

age difference. "So it is understandable that our paths had not crossed socially."[1]

Perian was a social person. She was outgoing, chatty, friendly, her demeanor in that sense contrasting with Conerly's. He was close-mouthed and quiet, though that was one thing about him that appealed to her.

"I was immediately taken with his dark, good looks and his engaging shyness," she said. "And he had lean, low-slung lines peculiar to athletes and Cadillacs. I have always been partial to both."[2] It has long been jokingly said (before professional football salaries grew so significantly) that quarterbacks drove Cadillacs. That was a symbol of their being the highest-paid players on their teams.

There was an immediate attraction going both ways, or "reciprocal," as Perian called it. Conerly asked her out on a double date for that very evening, and they began going out regularly right away. Soon enough, they dated exclusively. "We continued to see each other almost every night until the pre-season practice sessions called him to Ole Miss several weeks later." She also spoke of tying up a few loose ends and obligations leading to their exclusivity, implying she had other suitors whom she put on ice in favor of Conerly.[3]

Cadillac preference or not, Perian seemed partial to the "baby blue" Buick Conerly purchased with his war-time salary savings, since he did not spend much money while in the service. She did teasingly say the sight of that car was common on her college campus once the school year began.

Perian was already a football fan, a sports fan in general, and was more rough-and-tumble as a girl than genteel. "I was a tomboy growing up," Perian Conerly said in a 2019 interview. "I enjoyed playing ball with the boys more than with dolls with the girls. I was always a sports fan. My motto was, 'If it wears a number, I will watch it.'"[4]

She previously had been a backer of Mississippi State, not Ole Miss, which was less than 30 miles from the women's college. As she shifted her allegiance to Conerly, she likewise shifted her gridiron support to Mississippi. She once described their dating situation as "keeping company,"[5] an old-time phrase that has gone out of style but sounds a bit sweeter than simply saying "going out together."

Perian became the editor of her school newspaper, *The Spectator*, and later a pro football columnist in New York, the first woman in American newspapers to handle such a role. Even as she was transferring her allegiance from the team she formerly rooted for—the Bulldogs of Mississippi State—to Charlie's Rebels of the University of Mississippi for the 1947 season, she took note of his nickname, "Chucking'" or "Chunkin,'" and she offered the most declarative and clear distinction and application to clear up some confusion.

She claimed that in the South, "the colloquialism" for throwing is "chunking." Therefore, he is "Chunkin' Charlie" in Southern newspapers. "Chuckin' Charlie" is what he was called in Northern newspapers, but she could almost be seen grimacing in adding, "heaven forefend, Chuckin' Chuck" in Northern publications.[6] That was her take on the whole thing, and it did the job of explaining as well as anyone else who may have taken a crack at it.

Perian made it to three of Charlie's home games during that 1947 season. Road trips for single women at colleges for women were regulated and limited as well as dorm hours permitting visits by men. By the end of the season, Charlie and Perian were committed to one another and were serious about their relationship. But in the eyes of the world and college administrations, they were just another couple keeping company. The ripple effect of that came when December 3, 1947, rolled

Chapter 5. Meeting the Mrs.   41

around and Clarksdale, the hometown of both young people, staged a celebration for Charlie which she was not permitted to attend. If they had been engaged, the school authorities would have let her go, but she didn't want to lie.

So "Charlie Conerly Day" in Clarksdale went on without Perian present. Mississippi football fans from everywhere made the pilgrimage to Clarksdale to celebrate Conerly, and the guest of honor was given a new Chevrolet automobile. (Still no Cadillac.) Sort of. The car was given to Winford, Charlie's mother, instead of to him. He couldn't accept it or he would have been declared athletically ineligible. That wouldn't do because he planned to play one more season of baseball for the Rebels. He did so that spring, hitting .467. Presumably, Conerly's mother let him drive the Chevy once in a while.

Only a few weeks after his day, Conerly proposed marriage to Perian. He asked for her hand on Christmas night. While she did wish to marry him and her reaction was a "yes," she had one caveat. She wanted to postpone marriage until after she graduated from college. At that point, she had a year and a half, or three semesters, to go for a degree. Charlie wasn't that excited about waiting, but he agreed. One thing Perian took note of was that she was about to become editor of the newspaper, and from the vantage point of many years later, she wryly recalled thinking, "Never know when newspaper experience will come in handy."[7]

A week after the agreement-in-principle to get married later on, Charlie Conerly pulled out his Ole Miss football uniform one more time for participation in the hard-fought Delta Bowl game against Texas Christian. Come spring, he did represent Mississippi on the diamond.

Going back from the time when the Washington Redskins selected Conerly in the NFL draft in 1945, when he was busy being a Marine, Charlie had become a much more valuable commodity. However, the Redskins still had Sammy Baugh, one of the greatest quarterbacks and football players of all time, running their offense, so they didn't feel they needed Conerly.

Washington owner George Preston Marshall traded Conerly's rights to the New York Giants for fullback Howie Livingston, who had played four seasons with New York. Livingston was the brother of Cliff Livingston, a Giants linebacker star who became a Conerly teammate a little later. Although he did play a few more seasons, Howie Livingston's best years were behind him. It was an all-around steal of a trade for the Giants.

When school ended and Conerly was prepared to make decisions about his future, the Giants were the team to negotiate with in the NFL.

But there was at least one other football option. A bit of public confusion followed, and perhaps because Conerly was also a good baseball player, there was thinking he might try that sport. Also, there was a new football league on the horizon with a prominent baseball executive heavily involved.

The United States prospered after World War II. Peace introduced innovations and expansions in many areas. The automobile and television set both saw tremendous growth as goods for average income families with the improvement in the economy.

In 1946, the All-America Football Conference, an idea initiated by Arch Ward, the *Chicago Tribune* sports editor who created baseball's All-Star Game, began play. There were eight teams in the league determined to compete with the NFL. Many of those initial franchises are little remembered today, but some made a huge impact, most notably the Cleveland Browns, the dominating team in that league, later absorbed into the NFL. This was the origin of the San Francisco 49ers, too.

Another league club was the Brooklyn Dodgers, not to be confused with the longstanding baseball Brooklyn Dodgers, but easily creating some lack of clarity. Compounding the name overlap was that the football Dodgers were fronted by Branch Rickey. Rickey is best remembered as the leader of the Dodgers who brought Jackie Robinson to the majors, breaking the Major League Baseball color line barring Black players. Robinson was already signed and in the fold, and he played a year with Brooklyn's Montreal AAA club in 1946 and made his famous big-league debut in 1947.

In Mississippi, up until then, Rickey was best-known for his association with the St. Louis Cardinals baseball team. Rickey, later inducted into the National Baseball Hall of Fame in Cooperstown, New York, had been the brains behind the successful Cardinals teams of the 1930s, the Gashouse Gang of Dizzy and Paul Dean, Joe Medwick, Pepper Martin, and Frankie Frisch.

Of all the sports teams, the one Conerly should have been most familiar with was the Cardinals. Prior to games being nationally televised and baseball's expansion beyond eight teams in both the American League and National League, the team of the South was the Cardinals. They were the closest franchise to the region, as well as one of the winningest.

Rickey was general manager of the Cardinals when Conerly was finishing up high school—and during his first years of college—before Rickey moved on to the Brooklyn Dodgers baseball team in 1943. Yet he was interested in Conerly for the football Dodgers.

There was talk that Rickey offered Conerly $100,000 to play for him, which would have been an outrageous sum of money at the time. But Conerly, thinking Rickey made such comments as a public relations gambit, said that information floated to the surface and into the public only after he turned Rickey down in favor of the Giants.

It might also well be remembered that Rickey was renowned among his own star players with the St. Louis Cardinals for being more of a skinflint than a spendthrift. At various times, he had salary disputes with Dizzy Dean, Joe Medwick, and Johnny Mize, established All-Stars all, spurning their requests for raises.

It is difficult to imagine that Rickey had such big bucks to throw at Conerly's feet. Conerly said stories appearing in some New York newspapers were all bosh "that they were going to give me a $40,000 bonus or some such. There was all this stuff in the papers about money—big money, $15,000 a year for so many years—but it was all talk."[8]

The Giants had acquired the rights to Conerly before he even finished the season at Ole Miss. "During that year the Redskins, I guess, decided they didn't want me anymore," Conerly said.[9] Wellington Mara, of the Giants' founding family, made a trip to watch Conerly play the final game of his college career.

"So I saw that I was going to New York, which wasn't all that bad," Conerly said of escaping the shadow of Baugh. "And I also felt New York was the place to be if you were going to play professional sports."[10]

Around that time, Conerly said, he did receive a visit from someone representing the Brooklyn Dodgers baseball team. No wonder everyone was confused. Nonetheless, Conerly joined the New York Giants football team, as he had pledged to his mother long before, and stayed with them his entire professional athletic career. Who would have guessed that would come to pass? Not Winford.

Still, although it was a bit tricky to sort out, the football Dodgers did draft him in the other league's selection process, and Rickey did make a pitch, although it did not reach to the sky the way some of the newspaper reports suggested. "They offered me some money," Conerly said, "a little more than the Giants, as I recall. But they were a new team, and I just felt the Giants had been playing football, what, twenty-some-odd years, and that sure seemed like a safer place to go."[11] Safer, as in more secure.

Conerly remembered the newspapers talking about the $40,000 bonus and said real dollars in that amount might have changed his mind about his destination. "I might have taken it. That was a lot of money in those days."[12] And yes, even the $100,000 figure, spread over a long-term contract, was bandied about. The actual deal Conerly signed with New York was a five-year contract for $62,500. At that time, such an amount was very lucrative in pro football.

Perian remembered the Rickey offer as hitting the $100,000 mark, but she also remembered his public remonstrances that appeared in newspapers after he was spurned by Conerly. "Mr. Rickey howled in print that free enterprise was being imperiled when a boy could be persuaded to accept an offer so vastly 'inferior' to another," she said.[13]

For once, the reticent Conerly spoke up, indicating that that Brooklyn offer discussed in the papers was made after the Dodgers knew he was beholden to the Giants. Conerly said he never seriously considered joining Brooklyn and told their scout that from the beginning. "I guess they announced that offer to make themselves look good and make me feel sorry for myself," Conerly said. "I don't."[14]

What did the Giants want from Conerly in exchange? Of course, they wanted him to win. They wanted him to lead the team to championships. Just what position he might be assigned to was a bit of a mystery, mostly because of the morphing nature of offensive formations.

It should be noted that although Conerly is always described as a quarterback and that is how he is remembered for his time with the Giants, in high school, college and his earliest days in New York, he was mostly a tailback in an offensive formation that did permit him to pass but also required him to run. This was before the T-formation completely revolutionized football and more sophisticated offenses later gave quarterbacks—true quarterbacks—more flexibility to throw than ever.

This was the heyday of the College All-Star Game, another creation from Arch Ward's fertile brain that pitted the defending National Football League champion against a selection of college stars who had finished school and were on their way to joining their pro teams for training camp. The All-Star Game was played between 1934 and 1976, mostly at Chicago's Soldier Field, before it was discontinued.

Conerly, far more experienced in football and life than he was as a teenager when he made his fun trip to New York, was anxious to get going with the Giants. The All-Star Game, which generally resulted in the professional defending champs overcoming the fresh-out-of-college guys, was almost always contested in late August. Receipts from the game benefited area charities, and that helped boost the inclination to attend among football fans. The spectacle in the very large stadium almost always attracted major crowds, three times topping 100,000.

Conerly's year, 1948, the NFL opponent was the Chicago Cardinals, led by back Charlie Trippi, and attendance was 101,220. The game was not close. The Cardinals overwhelmed the collegians, 28–0.

This was Conerly's first real, live exposure to pro football, but he later said he and several others on the roster felt there was little chance

Chapter 5. Meeting the Mrs.

they would even get in the game. The head coach was Notre Dame's Frank Leahy, and he stacked the roster with a number of Irish players, Conerly said, leaving many others on the outside. One player on the Cardinals was Zig Czarobski. Conerly said that during the practice lead-up to the games, he and other back-ups spent their free nights at Czarobski's restaurant and bar. It was hardly outrageous for Conerly to drink. Not only was he not subject to any college team rules, but he would also be turning 27 years old in less than a month, even if the football world thought he was more like 24.

"We were really hungry to get to our training camps," Conerly said, "and all of us were glad when the game was finally over."[15] After he and Perian became engaged and he discussed money matters with her, he told her he planned to apply his first-year salary to buying a house for them.

As he guessed ahead of time, Conerly barely played in the All-Star Game, going in to make one punt.

After Conerly began collecting money from the Giants, he made an investment. He bought a chunk of farmland on the outskirts of Clarksdale. "With the bonus the Giants gave me, I made a down payment on 225 acres south of town," Conerly said. "Dad has always wanted to raise cotton and will manage it for me."[16]

When Charlie Conerly joined the Giants in 1948, he learned that his favorite Mississippi number, No. 42, was available. He claimed it for his professional team, too, and wore it throughout his long NFL career, spending every season with New York through 1961.

Chapter 6

From Ole Miss to the Big Apple

Despite being a guy from the Delta, Charlie Conerly had long harbored a fascination with the bigness of New York. Although this may have seemed surprising or odd to his high school buddies and college teammates, in keeping with his quiet nature, he didn't speak of it very often.

The Clarksdale of 1948 was a sleepy, rural town. The New York of 1948 was the center of American cultural life. New Yorkers liked to think they had the biggest and best of everything, the finest places to eat, and the best live entertainment on Broadway, and they were the kings of the sporting world with three Major League Baseball teams, a big-time National Hockey League team, a professional basketball team in the new and fledgling National Basketball Association, top-notch colleges, and yes, a premier, established professional football team as well as another pro football team in the secondary All-America Football Conference.

People came to New York to try to make it big in their field. And they came to New York to see Times Square, all hustle and bustle, and the Empire State Building and the Statue of Liberty, the sights they had always heard about. It would have been easy for Conerly to leave Mississippi in his rearview mirror for good, but while a part of him enjoyed the bright lights, another part of him was a homebody, linked to a simpler way of life. Besides, Perian was still in Mississippi, finishing college, and he was waiting for her so they could marry.

There was so much newness for Conerly to digest, but he was no wide-eyed lad. He was an older rookie who had spent three years in the Marines and seen a part of the world in wartime that he didn't care to vacation in again. He had a college degree and four years of college football experience. He was a man, not a youth, turning 27 years old when the Giants' season was starting, even if everyone outside of his family and friends thought he was 23 or 24, maybe.

Chapter 6. From Ole Miss to the Big Apple

His college team, the University of Mississippi, had made a breakthrough with him and its new coach, Johnny Vaught, the prior season, and it was about to embark on its most glorious run of football since it began playing in 1902. Vaught transformed Rebels football into a national power, leading the squad to Sugar Bowls, Cotton Bowls, and others as the line-up of bowls increased. Ole Miss became a regular fixture in the Associated Press rankings.

Oxford and Hemingway Stadium expanded as a destination lure for fans throughout the region. The Grove became the place to be on Saturdays in the fall. The first references to the 10-acre, oak-rimmed park in the middle of the University of Mississippi campus as "the Grove" seem to date from 1893. Generally, it was a peaceful place and only gradually morphed into the epicenter of pre-game tailgating where thousands upon thousands of fans gather and party leading up to kick-off. Celebrating shifted from more casual activity to more intense over the years.

When newspapers or sports-oriented publications rate the best places for spectators to gather for beers and grilling, they invariably come around to ranking the Grove the finest place for tailgating. And that's with the parking lot of the Florida–Georgia game being termed "the world's largest outdoor cocktail party."

The Sporting News labeled the Grove experience as "the Holy Grail of Tailgating."[1] Lulu Maness, the Conerlys' goddaughter, said it is estimated that 100,000 or more people show up for the tailgating on game day.[2] *Sports Illustrated* once made a similar calculation when ranking Ole Miss as the best place in the sport to tailgate.

One other element sets Mississippi apart which adds to the lore. Future coach Billy Brewer, who took over the reins of the program in 1983, wanted his players to feed on that atmosphere, and he began a ritual of leading the team from the athletic dorm to the stadium through the Grove, a journey that became increasingly frenzied. Fans lined the walk route screaming support and reached out for high-fives and the like. In 1998, an arch describing this march as the "Walk of Champions" was constructed on the east side of the Grove.

The popularity of the ritual keeps growing as the tradition becomes more ingrained. "We had a motor home and parked it off to the side of the Grove," Maness said. "We brought sleeping bags with eight or nine kids. We would watch [people in] the Grove." The area has become so jam-packed, the university has established regulations prohibiting people from staking out advantageous positions until closer to game time, she said. "Now it is so filled up. It's huge. It really has become that. It's not just the students. It's the alumni. The tradition is the big thing."[3]

The atmosphere is incomparable, not just for the massiveness of it, but because many believe it speaks to the best traits of Mississippians and their friendliness. In a statement borrowed from the *New York Times*, a locally provided illustration was contained with the quote:

> Ole Miss's Stadium accommodates 60,580 people and devotees of the Grove argue that the Grove accommodates more. It is every kind of party you can describe, at once: cocktail party, dinner party, tailgate picnic party, fraternity and sorority rush, family reunion, political hand-grab, gala and networking party-hearty—what might have inspired Willie Morris, one of Mississippi's favorite sons—to declare Mississippi not a state, but a club.[4]

There is more, from the *New York Times* via hottoddy.com:

> There are seven home-game weekends at Ole Miss. And people in the Grove know how to have a good time down there—they can stretch the party over three days, from Friday night into Sunday morning. It is pimento cheese sandwiches and silver trays, candelabra and fried chicken tenders, button-down shirts, rep ties and khaki shorts, pearls, expensive sunglasses and flip-flops in your purse for when your high heels become history.[5]

What that summation sounds like is Kentucky Derby Saturday in Louisville seven times a year, without the hats.

These days, the volume of fans who flood the Grove must be regulated. There is not enough space to accommodate the number of cars and recreational vehicles whose owners desire to come, so the university put some rules in place. Tents are permitted but cannot be staked until the night before the game.

Conerly missed the heyday of the tailgating and the gradual institutionalization of the Grove as a stronger tradition, but quarterbacks for whom he paved the way at Ole Miss participated one way or another, through the Walk of Champions or otherwise. One of Conerly's famous QB successors was Eli Manning, son of the heralded Archie.

"We went a lot when I was in middle school and as a kid," Eli Manning said.

> You'd play pickup football in your best clothes and your parents would come looking for you. They'd find you all muddy and sweaty. As a student, after games, I would go back into the Grove. My parents always had a tent and we had the full setup. [We] always had some sort of shrimp dish, being from New Orleans. And some sandwiches.[6]

Outside of extreme inebriation, the tradition of the Grove is far more innocent than much of the other history that played out in Mississippi, though football Saturdays in the Grove were pretty much a White person's holiday. It should be remembered that Charlie Conerly never had a Black teammate in high school or at Mississippi. There were no Black students in Clarksdale's Bobo High when he attended, and his college football days took place pre–James Meredith.

Chapter 6. From Ole Miss to the Big Apple

It should also be noted that finding any printed evidence that Charlie Conerly had a prejudiced bone in his body is impossible. He is never quoted as making any type of disparaging remark about his Black neighbors. There are sportswriters who covered Conerly's playing days over a 20-year span of college football and professional football who never tugged complete sentences out of him despite how hard they tried. And their questions were about the games, not sensitive matters.

This was a guy who in a sense would not even gush about himself, would not make the case for his own All-Star capability, even when asked. "'Yep' and 'nope' seemed to be his favorite responses at post-game press conferences," one author said many years later after dissecting Conerly's verbal record.[7]

Conerly was one of the immediate NFL successors to Sammy Baugh of the Redskins and Sid Luckman of the Chicago Bears as the 1940s turned into the 1950s, but when others compared him to those future Hall of Famers, one did not hear Conerly even saying his name belonged in the same sentence.

"I don't know if I was a good passer or not, but I could see the field," Conerly said. "I thought I was average. I couldn't throw the ball too far, but then, I usually never had anybody who could go deep."[8]

In his self-effacing approach, he did not help his own case for recognition or reputation, something Hall of Fame defensive end and teammate Andy Robustelli said in sticking up for Conerly.

"Charlie was unflappable in good times and bad," Robustelli said. "He was a ruggedly handsome, soft-spoken Southern gentleman."[9]

It is not exactly clear what being a "Southern gentleman" meant to those from the North in the late 1940s and throughout the 1950s, though it is obvious Robustelli meant it as a compliment.

Between the 1920s and the end of World War II, the National Football League was a league only for White players. That began to change after Jackie Robinson integrated Major League Baseball in 1947, and then others such as Roy Campanella, Don Newcombe, Minnie Minoso, Willie Mays, and Hank Aaron followed. Significantly, even though Blacks had been held back despite risking their lives for their country during the war, President Harry Truman integrated the Armed Forces with an executive order on July 26, 1948.

Running back Kenny Washington, who had played college ball with Robinson at UCLA, and end Woody Strode, who later became a Hollywood film actor, joined the Los Angeles Rams in 1946, the NFL's first Blacks to play in the so-called modern era. Public pressure demanded that the Rams sign African Americans if the team, having just moved from Cleveland, wanted to play in the publicly financed Los Angeles Memorial Coliseum.

At roughly the same time, Cleveland Browns founder Paul Brown, looking to build the best team he could, and having been exposed to the talents of some Black stars during the war, brought in Marion Motley and Bill Willis for his new club.

However, by the time Conerly was entrenched in New York, the Giants also had Black stars in their line-up, and for the first time the Mississippi native was counting on African Americans to help aid the cause of winning. By the mid–1950s, major contributions were being made by Black Giants. Tackle Roosevelt Brown, whose job was to protect Conerly from pass rushers with evil intent in their eyes, was one. Rosey Grier, as well known on the defensive line but someone who became better known later for his television acting and his hobby of knitting, regarded as an unusual avocation for a 300-pound football cruncher, was another. Then there was Emlen Tunnell, a defensive back, who like Brown was later inducted into the Pro Football Hall of Fame.

Tunnell, the first African American to play for the Giants, intercepted 79 passes as a safety, the second-most in league history. He was chosen for Pro Bowls and was a Conerly teammate for 11 seasons. Lulu Maness said she was once told a story by an old-time sportswriter who informed her of something Tunnell said about her godfather.

The writer told Maness he was interviewing Tunnell about the slow pace of NFL integration and asked him to name his all–Black team. Tunnell, who died young at 50, responded that he had a problem with that because his personal, permanent, first-team quarterback was Charlie Conerly, a White man from the South.[10]

Maness also said she once met Rosey Brown's wife, who told her stories about how when her husband was a teammate of Conerly, he took him to jazz clubs in Harlem.[11] This was something Conerly and Tunnell did together, too.

That all sounds as if Conerly, a man of the South, a man with Mississippi roots, was someone who was not carrying around the average prejudices of his time and place. That was not true of the university and football program he left behind to join the Giants, not for some time.

The Charlie Conerly–Johnny Vaught tandem had taken the Rebels to their greatest heights in 1947, winning that Southeastern Conference title. Conerly was gone, but Vaught was literally just getting started. He remained head coach through the 1970 season and then made a brief return for two-thirds of a season in 1973. Vaught stayed in Oxford for the rest of his life and was always regarded as a coaching legend and sports department hero.

The times they were a-changin,' though, even in the heart of Dixie. Civil Rights demonstrations broke out throughout the South, and

Chapter 6. From Ole Miss to the Big Apple

the movement gained in intensity everywhere. Federal government responses to those demanding their God-given rights were sympathetic. The U.S. Supreme Court in 1954 struck down separate but equal provisions in schooling in *Brown vs. Board of Education*. In 1964, the Congress passed the Civil Rights Act, and President Lyndon B. Johnson signed it into law.

The Civil Rights movement made lasting heroes of those on the right side of the issue, tearing down Jim Crow laws, implementing voting rights, and assaulting discriminatory practices in place since the Civil War. Dr. Martin Luther King, Jr., became a martyr to the cause. All Rosa Parks wanted to do was sit down near the front of the Montgomery bus after a long day of work, and her refusal to budge from the first four rows led to a boycott and her own involvement in the cause.

These were very troubled times, and Mississippi was often a frontline battlefield.

In 1955, 14-year-old Emmett Till of Chicago was vacationing with relatives in Money, Mississippi, in the Delta, when he was kidnapped, tortured and killed because he had irritated a White woman in her family's grocery store. Later, a jury acquitted the accused, and forevermore this stood as one of the prime examples of injustice in the South. Medgar Evers was a National Association for the Advancement of Colored People representative in Mississippi when he was assassinated by a White man. In 1964, three White Civil Rights workers from the North were murdered by the Ku Klux Klan near Philadelphia, Mississippi.

The worst form of discrimination is murder, and in 2021, the *Washington Post* reported an even-now story suggesting that there have been eight lynchings of Black men and young people over the last 20 years.[12]

If it had been up to some, the integration of the University of Mississippi would never have occurred, as evidenced by the riots that took place when James Meredith enrolled in 1962. At that time, Vaught was as entrenched in his job as the leader of Ole Miss football as one could be. When the disturbances and protests took place, he adopted the stance of standing clear of what was going on and advising the same for his 1962 football players, who were about to embark on a 10–0, best-ever season that included a Sugar Bowl victory.

Decades later, reflecting on the unrest of the time, Vaught said, "It was pretty bad then. If it hadn't been for football, they would have probably closed Ole Miss." He said that at the time he instructed the Rebels to "stay away from it. Don't get into it. Don't associate with it. It doesn't bother us. Whatever is going to happen will happen."[13]

Things were going so well for Vaught and his football team that he didn't want to tamper with the status quo. Mississippi continued to win in later years, well beyond 1962. It was not until 1967 that the first Black football player entered the Southeastern Conference, when Nate Northington, a defensive back from Louisville, suited up for Kentucky.

As doors of opportunity gradually opened for Black students and athletes, the issue was a common topic in SEC towns. Vaught told reporters he wanted to recruit African American football players to Mississippi, but quickly retracted the comment, saying he was "just kidding." He seemed to anticipate Title IX or some similar law altering the landscape when he added, "We have to comply with some sort of act to get federal funds. We fill out a form to show that we have looked at one. By the time we find someone good enough, I'll be gone. Let someone else do that."[14]

It was not until after Vaught's retirement as coach that Mississippi did recruit a Black player. The wooing took place in 1971, and defensive lineman Ben Williams and running back James Reed went to Oxford in 1972. Williams, from Yazoo City, played as a freshman that year, which credited him as the one who broke Ole Miss' football color barrier. Williams was selected All-SEC three times and became an All-American as a senior in 1976, then played professionally for the Buffalo Bills.

His nickname, for his off-field demeanor, was "Gentle Ben," and when he was a senior, fellow students voted him "Colonel Rebel," an ironic honor for a Black man. The Colonel caricature was the official sports mascot until 2003, when it was replaced for being much too reminiscent of Ole Miss instead of, as advertised later in life by Meredith, "New Miss."

The 6-foot-3, 250-pound Williams was a defensive end for Buffalo between 1976 and 1985 and made one Pro Bowl. Jim Carmody, an assistant coach at Mississippi, who knew him well, and then coached Williams with the Bills, raved about his character after he died at 65 in April of 2022. "His teammates loved him," Carmody said. "His coaches loved him. Obviously, he was really popular on campus, as well. The only people who didn't love him were the guys who had to play against him."[15]

Charlie Conerly did not engage in politics, and from 1948 on, his professional life was centered in New York, more than 1,000 miles from Clarksdale and Oxford. But he was always in touch with Mississippi doings through family members, because he and Perian followed his old team and returned to their original home in the off-season.

As Perian thought when she first met Charlie, one had to know who he was if they only read the newspaper. The same was true about the sometimes-cataclysmic happenings in Mississippi that brought their home state to the forefront of the national news. Still, for a stretch of the

Chapter 6. From Ole Miss to the Big Apple

THE FOOTBALL WRITERS ASSOCIATION OF AMERICA

Designates For The 1947

Look All-America Football Team

Charles Conerly

OF *University of Mississippi*

AS *Back*

Charlie Conerly was chosen as an All-American his senior year at Mississippi (courtesy University of Mississippi Athletics Department).

year, they fully embraced being New Yorkers and fully threw themselves into that big city life.

The Conerlys were a young couple in love, regardless of where they were, and they bridged two different worlds fairly effortlessly, if only temporarily, each year.

Chapter 7

Rookie Year

America was on the move again in the late 1940s, the normalcy of everyday society replacing the tension of a nation at war. Soldiers were home, re-entering the work force. Automobiles were changing the mobility of Americans, providing more freedom. Television was invading living rooms.

And the sports world so disrupted, as were all facets of American life, was part of the fun of it all again. It was okay to invest emotion in the fortunes of the home team. It was quite all right for an athlete to go pro rather than enlist to serve his country overseas.

Many players in all sports, of course, had completed service in the Army, Navy, Marines and fledgling Air Force. They had seen combat. They had taken long time-outs from their athletic pursuits. Charlie Conerly was one of them. His college football career at the University of Mississippi had been split in half.

Now he was finished with college play, and the National Football League was interested in his skills. The NFL draft pre-dating the 1948 season took place on December 19, 1947, in Pittsburgh. Some 300 players were selected over 32 rounds, and Conerly's name was not called. This was not a specific omission. This was because Conerly was listed in the group eligible in 1945, when he was representing his country at war, not his football team on the field.

Conerly was off the board because he had been selected in the 13th round of the 1945 draft by the Washington Redskins. He was the 127th player chosen, even though he was hardly in any position to show up for training camp. There were 32 rounds that year as well, with 324 players drafted. This selection made Conerly the property of Washington well before he graduated from college.

Conerly never came close to playing for Washington. Three years after the Redskins drafted him, and the season after his final season of college eligibility, he surfaced with the New York Giants. Conerly signed a five-year deal with the Giants.

Chapter 7. Rookie Year

"The Redskins, I guess, decided they didn't want me anymore, so they traded my rights to the Giants," Conerly said. The Giants shipped Howie Livingston to Washington. Conerly said he remembered New York owner Wellington Mara attending his last college game for Mississippi. "So I saw I was going to New York, which wasn't all that bad. After all, the Redskins had Sammy Baugh at the time [which meant he wouldn't play]. And I also felt New York was the place to be if you were going to play professional sports."[1]

It had been clear for some time that he and Perian were going to get married. She was still wrapping up college and sported an engagement ring, and Conerly used his pro contract bonus to make a down payment on 225 acres of land that he expected his father would manage. On August 1, Conerly left Mississippi to prepare for the College All-Star Game, and by August 20, he was in the Giants' training camp. He and Perian did not see one another from August until December, when the season ended.

The Giants squad Conerly joined was dismal in 1947 with a 2–8–2 record. The player called the tailback that season was Paul Governali, who threw 14 touchdown passes and 16 interceptions and gained 1,461 yards through the air. Governali, who had a short NFL career after his schooling at Columbia, was out of the league after 1948.

The job was rookie Conerly's for the asking that year. This was expected. Conerly had set national collegiate records, and New York was counting on him to take over as its field leader. It was a whole different world offensively for the Giants with Conerly in charge in 1948. Conerly set Giants rookie records when he completed 162 out of 299 pass attempts for 2,175 yards and 22 touchdowns.

New York scored nearly 300 points, but the Giants' defense was weak and surrendered 388 points. So the overall record was only slightly improved at 4–8. Pro football was still in an adjustment phase, and the Giants under head coach Steve Owen were linked to the A formation, not yet moving to a T-formation system. So instead of quarterback, though that was his basic role, Conerly was described as playing tailback.

Conerly said that at his size, 6-foot-1 and around 180 pounds, he took a beating playing the A formation, and he was happy when Owen shifted the offensive game plan to the T-formation.

"And that's what saved my life," Conerly said. "It was just too tough playing out of the A with all of the blocking and the running that went along with it. We did pass a lot, though, after I joined the Giants."[2]

On December 5, in the next-to-last game of the season, the Giants faced off against the Pittsburgh Steelers. While Pittsburgh won, 38–28, before 27,645 fans at Forbes Field, Conerly recorded an extraordinary game, especially for the era. Conerly completed 36 out of 53 pass attempts for 363 yards, including three touchdown passes.

"I threw so often that day," Conerly said, "which was an NFL record at the time, and hell, we still lost the game. So I always felt the record didn't mean much of a damn because we lost the game. You weren't out there to set records. You were out there to win the darn ball game."[3]

Conerly's primary receiver that day was Ray Poole, an old friend and teammate from Mississippi. Poole caught nine passes. Poole was the same age as Conerly, born in 1921 in Gloster, Mississippi. He attended the University of North Carolina but transferred to Ole Miss. Like Conerly, Poole was absent from college for three years during World War II, and he played one year for the Rebels after the war.

Ray Poole, a sturdy 6–2 and 215 pounds, was drafted by the Giants in 1944 while still in the service. Poole had two brothers, Barney and Jim, who were also star athletes. It was Barney Poole, who was 6–2, 231, who caught 52 passes in a season in 1947 for Mississippi with Conerly in command. While he did play some for the Giants, he was more of a defensive end for the New York Yanks. Jim was older, and he too played some end for the New York Giants. Ray Poole later spent 20 years as an assistant football coach for the Rebels under Johnny Vaught.

During Conerly's rookie year with the Giants, Ray Poole was in his second season and caught 35 passes. He and Conerly often compared notes about the bright lights of New York compared to the sleepier environs of Mississippi they had both known growing up, as they shared an apartment during the 1948 season.

Part of a display recognizing Charlie Conerly at the University of Mississippi (photograph by the author).

Chapter 7. Rookie Year

Conerly and Barney Poole worked some football magic together in college at Oxford. When Poole caught 52 passes for the Rebels during the 1947 season, he set an NCAA record. The old mark was 50 catches during the 1941 season by Harry Stanton of Arizona. Conerly was friendly with the whole family.

"We were just a couple of country boys," Conerly said of spending rookie time with Ray Poole in New York. "We would catch a subway to go to practice at the Polo Grounds, which was where we were playing in those days. We always kept saying, 'Hey, this is a little different from where we come from.'"[4]

Few people have ever made direct comparisons between daily life in New York City and Mississippi, but Conerly and Poole had one another to share it with. The Giants were far from a loaded team during Conerly's rookie season, although soon enough they would be. For the time being, they would take lumps from other league teams.

There was some talent on the roster, just not enough. Bill Swiacki out-caught Poole, with a team-high 39 pass receptions. The Giants' ground game was on the weak side with Gene Roberts amassing just 491 yards rushing. Except for Conerly and standout defensive back Emlen Tunnell, a future Hall of Famer, the list of Giants in 1948 did not feature household names, and most players did not endure in New York lore. By the time the team became a regular playoff and championship contender in the 1950s, Conerly and Tunnell were the only two players of note left.

Conerly did appreciate his receivers his rookie year, even beyond Poole. He said nice things about Swiacki, who came out of Columbia, and Gene "Choo Choo" Roberts. Swiacki was also a rookie and a first-team All-American in 1947. Roberts, who attended Chattanooga, led the NCAA in scoring in 1946 with 117 points.

"He wasn't all that speedy, but he sure could get open," Conerly said of Swiacki.[5] Conerly did not know it at the time, but he would be blessed with better receivers later in the 1950s.

Another game that stood out in a major way during Conerly's 1948 rookie season—and was more satisfying than the performance against the Steelers—was a November 21 contest against the Green Bay Packers. New York pummeled Green Bay, 49–3, and Conerly threw three touchdown passes and ran for another TD. He went 20 for 30 passing, for 291 yards. Governali saw some action and added 43 yards to the total.

Conerly had given the Giants' organization good reason to appreciate him in his first year. They had backed him from the start, publicly too, when he had spurned Branch Rickey and his Brooklyn Dodgers football club. Tim Mara, the original owner of the Giants when they began NFL play in 1925, responded to Rickey's comments when Conerly took the team's $62,500 pay offer instead of the rumored $100,000-plus Rickey offer, the one whose accuracy Conerly disputed.

"Maybe the kid figures he'll have better security with the Giants," Mara said when it became known that Rickey was offering well-regarded veteran pitcher Ralph Branca just $14,000. "Maybe he's [Conerly] looked over the All-America Conference and realized we've been here 24 years, whereas Brooklyn's had three, four owners."[6]

Tunnell came cheaper. He was the equivalent of a walk-on for a college team. He showed up at the Giants' offices in New York and boldly asked for a job. He had had limited college exposure at Iowa, but some people knew he was talented. Tim Mara granted him a tryout and then, quickly enough, a contract. Defensive back Tunnell established himself swiftly, and he could also tell very quickly that the main man on offense for the foreseeable future was going to be Conerly.

Tunnell was the type of man everybody liked and who tried to see the best in everyone. Outsiders wondered from the start whether the proud Black man and the prominent White star from the South would get along. Tunnell said he understood where those thoughts originated, but he never worried about such a thing, believing that from the first minute when they were introduced, he and Conerly bonded. Yes, Conerly was from Mississippi, a dangerous place for Black Americans, a place with a reputation for extremist segregation. But Tunnell was someone who never judged a book by its cover, nor a man by his geographical background.

"Everybody has been intrigued by this association," Tunnell said of his connection with Conerly. "Over the years the one question that inevitably has been asked by my friends, Negro and White, went like this: 'How did you and Conerly really get along?'"[7]

Tunnell said the word "really" made the question a loaded one, carrying the assumption that there had to be some friction between the men from different races and backgrounds. Not so, Tunnell said. "The truth of the matter is that I consider Charlie Conerly to be one of the best friends I have in the world, and I have reason to believe that he feels the same way about me. We hit it off right from the start. Charlie was a war veteran like myself."[8]

As an older rookie, one who spent several years in the service and saw much of what war could bring, Tunnell felt Conerly was more mature than a rookie who would be around 22 years old.

> Another thing we had in common is that neither of us carried our race on our sleeve. We judged one another as football players and guys. Conerly demonstrated his class that very first day [of workouts]. "Emlen, this is Gene Roberts. I hope the three of us are going to be together for a long time."[9]

Chapter 7. Rookie Year

Tunnell was born in Bryn Mawr, Pennsylvania. There is some question about whether he was born in 1922, 1924 or 1925, but his date of birth is most commonly given as March 29, 1924. Whatever the accurate year, Tunnell, like Conerly, was an older rookie, having spent time in the service, delaying the start of his pro football career.

Growing up in the Philadelphia area, the Garrett Hill section of Radnor Township, Tunnell began his college education at the University of Toledo, but after spending three years in the U.S. Coast Guard, in 1946 and 1947 he competed for the University of Iowa. At Toledo, Tunnell suffered a broken neck, which could have ended his football days. However, he recovered. Although the injury kept him from being drafted and caused his rejection from some branches of the service, he was able to join the Coast Guard. While in the service, Tunnell earned medals for saving shipmates' lives. At Iowa, Tunnell was more of an offensive threat, carrying the ball and catching it. At no time would anyone have predicted that Tunnell would emerge as one of the greatest professional football defensive backs of all time. He ended up becoming a nine-time NFL All-Star.

Tunnell was a free agent who just showed up in camp. Conerly was a heralded rookie who had just set NCAA passing records. Tunnell said that if Conerly was a different type of person, he might have "lorded it" over him and other rookies as a prima donna. "Conerly was *the* rookie."[10]

A close watcher of the other rookie, with whom he would remain teammates in New York for a decade, through 1958, Tunnell said Conerly's first play from scrimmage in 1948 was notable.

"Charlie demonstrated the quality that won the respect of all the Giants, old ones and young ones," Tunnell said. Conerly tossed a pass to another rookie, Skippy Minisi, who was in the clear but dropped the ball.

> Most rookie quarterbacks would have been shattered. A chewing-out was not unexpected. No criticism. Charlie didn't even mention the pass, didn't say a word about it. That play was gone forever. Now he called the next play. That was the kind of man he was and the kind of man he would remain. That's why we busted a gut for him for so many years.[11]

Conerly and Tunnell emerged from the 1948 crop of rookies as the two most important Giants for the future, and they stayed together, played together, and remained teammates for years.

As a rookie, Conerly shared that apartment with fellow Mississippian Ray Poole, but his status changed the next season. During the off-season, after their long period of dating and a lengthy engagement, Charlie married Perian.

Marriage had been waiting until Perian finished college. She finished in the spring of 1949, and the Conerlys married in June, three weeks later, on what she said was the hottest day of the year. Which in Mississippi is saying something, although she did not specify the level of humidity.

Logically enough, the couple married in Clarksdale, choosing the First Methodist Church for the ceremony. Perian recalled that most of Charlie's groomsmen were former football teammates at the University of Mississippi, and her bridesmaids were high school and college friends, plus a sister.

The day before and the day of the wedding were quite hectic and included some faux pas. One bridesmaid left the sash of her gown at home in Indiana. Perian learned on the day of the ceremony that she had forgotten to issue a proper wedding invitation to Charlie's family. She believed she was dooming herself to a poor start with the in-laws. When dressing, Perian's father discovered he was missing the appropriate black tie to go with his outfit. As the day wore on and the reception commenced, some strangers came and went. Perian figured out later that they were newspaper reporters, chronicling Charlie's nuptials because he was a big cheese. Her mother, she found out, had been hoping for attention on what were then called society pages, or women's pages, and was disappointed when some reports of the scene ended up in sports sections.

A honeymoon followed, but their time together was cut short at the end of the summer when New York Giants training camp, set for Saranac Lake in upstate New York, beckoned. Wives were not welcome at training camp, Perian learned to her irritation, only after the regular season commenced.

As a native of Mississippi, Perian had not had a youthful fascination with New York City the way Charlie had. Her immediate family members had once vacationed there, but they were worried about how the big city would treat their girl in her early days of marriage. To reassure her mother, Perian told her that if she couldn't find anything to do with her time, "I'll just sleep."[12]

Boredom never seemed to afflict the Conerlys during their move to New York for the 1949 season, nor in the ensuing years. They were able to find ways to keep busy and soak up the excitement offered by the big town.

Charlie Conerly became one of the most recognizable of New York athletes, and Perian became a pioneering female pro football writer. New York would prove very good to them both.

Chapter 8

New York, New York

The New York City newlyweds Charlie and Perian Conerly moved to New York for the autumn of 1949. The city was thriving in a post–World War II environment, the center of the universe for trendy Americans seeking excitement. The iconic song "New York, New York" lay in the future, recorded first by Liza Minnelli in 1977 and then by Frank Sinatra in 1979, but its essence was part of daily life more than a quarter of a century earlier.

Indeed, if you could make it in New York, you could make it anywhere. According to the 1950 census, New York was populated by 7,891,957 individuals. It was the largest city in the United States, and it was the hub of the American universe.

New York had the busiest streets and the tallest buildings, was the center of the art and music worlds, and was definitely a city that never slept. By comparison, the 1950 census for the entire state of Mississippi was 2,173,373.

World War II had left many of the world's prominent cities devastated by bombs and combat. An untouched New York City assumed a more significant role on the world stage. When the United Nations opened, it opened in Manhattan. Already a city dotted with gleaming office buildings and towers such as the Empire State Building, the center of Manhattan grew anew with major construction.

In the communications capital of the country, fierce newspaper battles, hustling for every scrap of news of every type, were ongoing between the *New York Times, New York Daily News, New York Post*, 10-year-old *Newsday* on Long Island, and other papers which have since folded.

One of the front lines of the newspaper wars was reportage of professional sports. The National Basketball Association and the New York Knickerbockers were new to the scene in the late 1940s. The National Hockey League, featuring the local New York Rangers, seemed to receive secondary coverage. The biggest news always was produced by Major League Baseball.

There were three big-league teams in New York, led by the American League's perennial champion New York Yankees, the kings of the world. The National League had the Giants and the Brooklyn Dodgers, intense rivals, who as often as not during this era emerged as pennant winners only to lose to the Yankees in the World Series.

Under new manager Casey Stengel, underrated at first, the Yankees of Joe DiMaggio at the end of his career and Mickey Mantle at the beginning of his, plus Yogi Berra, Whitey Ford, Allie Reynolds, Vic Raschi, and Ed Lopat, ruled the sport.

Between 1949 and 1953, the Yankees won all five AL pennants and all five World Series. In three of those years, the Yankees topped Brooklyn for the championship, and once they bested the Giants. This stretch of time, lasting through 1956, spawned the phrase "Subway Series," since the opponents were situated so close to one another that fans could take a subway train between them.

The New York football Giants were founded in 1925, helping give the young National Football League credibility. When the NFL was founded in a car dealership in Canton, Ohio, and throughout much of its first decade of the 1920s, many of the franchises were semi-pro in nature, situated in smaller communities which loved the game but were not viewed as big-time settings.

Many teams from the earliest days of the NFL could not withstand the financial pressures, including such franchises as the Rock Island Independents, Canton Bulldogs, Hammond Pros, Muncie Flyers, Sheboygan Redskins, and Dayton Triangles.

After the first fledgling days of the league, there was a desire and commitment to make sure there was a New York franchise involved. It was about prestige, a symbol of being big league, and a mark of credibility. The same was true for any new competitive conference born to compete with the NFL.

The first American Football League, which popped up in 1926, was created by promoter C.C. ("Cash and Carry") Pyle to showcase the talent of superb running back Red Grange. It did not last long. The All-America Football Conference, established in 1946 and lasting through the 1949 season, had that Branch Rickey Dodgers team in Brooklyn and a New York Yankees football squad. It was common for football teams to steal the nicknames of firmly established baseball clubs, hoping to receive reflected glory and attention. In the NFL, this was also true of the Pittsburgh team. Before becoming known as the Steelers, the squad was called the Pirates, like the National League baseball team. Of course, the same applied to the New York Giants, borrowing from John McGraw's baseball men.

Chapter 8. New York, New York

A mix of Charlie Conerly football cards from the 1950s (author's collection).

Even though the baseball Giants still exist, since the late 1950s they have represented San Francisco. The New York Giants may have been in the shadow of the baseball Giants in the 1920s but long before created their own identity.

By 1949, Charlie Conerly's second season, the football-playing Giants had been around for just shy of 25 years. Fans knew who they were. They just were not very impressed with the on-field product. For good reason. The late 1940s was the most fallow period in the team's operation to date.

Just two years after the inception of the team, in 1927, the Giants won their first NFL crown. The team, which was playing its home games at the Polo Grounds, the same place as the baseball Giants, finished 11–1–1. Defense was the strong point under coach Earl Potteiger, 34, a player-coach. The defense provided a surreal strong point, posting shutouts in all but three games and not allowing more than seven points in a game. The Giants lost, 6–0, to the Cleveland Bulldogs and tied the Bulldogs, 0–0, in the only blemishes on the schedule.

Fullback Jack McBride was as close to a big offensive gun as New York had, scoring 57 points. In the big picture of history, however, there were others on the roster more notable, better remembered for longer, who wrote better careers.

Running back Joe Guyon, 35 at the time, had attended the Carlisle Indian Industrial School, where he was coached by Pop Warner and played with Jim Thorpe. In 1966, Guyon was inducted into the Pro Football Hall of Fame. Time spent with these 1927 Giants represented the last season of his pro playing career.

Tackle Wilbur "Pete" Henry, who stood 5-foot-11 and weighed 245 pounds, was nicknamed "Fats." Henry was a standout who played collegiately at Washington & Jefferson, then starred with the Canton Bulldogs prior to competing for the Giants. He was inducted into both the College Football Hall of Fame and the Pro Football Hall of Fame. He was one of the most enduring names from the 1927 championship Giants, although he only appeared in four games for New York. Immediately before and after, Henry played for the Pottsville Maroons, one of the early NFL teams that did not last.

Another extra-large lineman on the 1927 Giants was Cal Hubbard, whose dimensions were 6-foot-2 and 253 pounds. Hubbard excelled more with the Green Bay Packers later in his playing career, and he was acknowledged as a Pro Football Hall of Famer. After football, Hubbard became a Major League Baseball umpire and subsequently was inducted into the National Baseball Hall of Fame in Cooperstown, New York, as well.

So the Giants wrote some impressive history early in their existence. The 1930s were very good to New York, with the Giants taking first place in the Eastern Division in 1933, 1934, 1935, 1938 and 1939, and just as World War II was about to snare the United States in its grasp, also in 1941.

Of those six championship game appearances, the Giants were triumphant only twice, in 1934 and 1938. But New York was clearly one of the league's powerhouses. Benny Friedman, an early success as a throwing quarterback from 1929 to 1931 with the Giants, was one of several Giants selected for the Hall of Fame from the pre–World War II era. He was joined by ends Red Badgro and Ray Flaherty, running back Tuffy Leemans, halfback-kicker Ken Strong, Jim Thorpe himself (in 1925), owners Tim and Wellington Mara, and Steve Owen.

When Owen was born in 1898 in Oklahoma, it was still a territory. He played for four other teams in the NFL in the early 1920s, then was purchased by the Giants for $500 in 1926. By 1930, Owen was co-head coach, and when Conerly joined the team in 1948, Owen was still the field boss.

As a player, Owen was listed on rosters as 5-foot-11 and 237 pounds. As a coach, Owen was known as an innovator with New York, and even subsequent to his 24 seasons in charge when he worked as an assistant coach for the Philadelphia Eagles and then for a few more years in the Canadian Football League with the Toronto Argonauts, Calgary Stampeders, and Saskatchewan Roughriders. Owen's career NFL coaching record was 153–100–17.

Owen was the head man when New York won its NFL titles in 1934

Chapter 8. New York, New York

and 1938, but besides those early division crowns, Owen twice more led the Giants to the league championship game, losing to the Packers in 1944 and the Chicago Bears in 1946.

A Giants tailspin followed with the slumping 2–8–2 mark of 1947, the 4–8 finish in Conerly's rookie year of 1948, and the hopeful signs of a turnaround with a 6–6 record in 1949.

While Owen was credited with being a sharp offensive thinker because of his reliance on the A formation, it was obvious by then that the T-formation, adopted with great success by the Bears in the 1940s, was the offense of the future. Conerly was used to the A formation but hungered for change so he would not endure as much of a physical onslaught in games.

After Owen's partial role leading the Giants in 1930, the team went in search of a new full-time coach. Yet Tim Mara, or other members of the family ownership group, kept telephoning Owen and picking his brains for ideas on who the right man might be. Owen recommended different people, but after considering the other candidates, Tim Mara turned back to Owen. "I knew very little about football, but I believed that an ability to handle men was essential," Mara said. "He knew how to handle rough customers with tact."[1]

Owen adapted. A four-time league All-Star, he first visited New York as a player for the short-lived Kansas City Cowboys, who long pre-dated the Kansas City Chiefs. He was wearing a cowboy hat before changing into his football helmet.

After lifting the Giants to what ultimately became eight division titles, Owen knew the team was in trouble after the poor 1947 season. It was a swift fall from reaching the 1946 title game. "We need help," Owen declared.[2] It was a plea that registered with fans and ownership. That led to the heavy pursuit of Conerly, fresh off setting NCAA records as a passer. Washington's indifference to retaining Conerly related both to their reliance on the great Sammy Baugh and also on having picked Alabama's Harry Gilmer as his successor.

When Wellington Mara traveled to Mississippi to ink Conerly to the long-term deal he signed, the only competition for his football services was the Brooklyn team in the All-America conference.

The Giants were hoping they were hiring a savior, but there are 22 starters on a football team, 11 on offense, 11 on defense, and while one player can shine, he cannot often lift a whole club on his shoulders and carry it across the goal line.

Rarely can football teams make sudden turnarounds, going from being well under .500 to well above .500 in a single season. The NFL draft can help. Signing free agents is useful. Conerly came via the draft and trade. It did not take long for him to be inserted as the starter running the offense. That also made him a target for defenses, which found easy paths into the Giants' backfield through a porous offensive line.

"In those early years, when we didn't have a very good team, he used to take a terrific physical beating," Tim Mara said. "Getting sacked six or eight times a game was every day of the week for Charlie. We just didn't have very good teams. But he never complained. He wasn't a charismatic character, but he was a very quiet leader."[3]

The 1949 Giants were better than the 1948 Giants, but going 4–8 did not win many plaudits. There was no such thing as winning the quarterback job for Conerly, as there had been in 1948. There were no challengers. He was the man. In a 12-game season, Conerly threw almost all the passes New York attempted that year.

Chuckin' Charlie attempted 305 passes, which was a high number for that era and 12-game schedule. He completed 152 of them, and 17 went for touchdowns. Only 17 other passes were attempted by members of the team all season. Ray Mallouf was 3-for-16 and Gene Roberts, the Giants' leading rusher with 634 ground yards, was 0-for-1. Mallouf was a full-time punter.

Roberts, aka "Choo-Choo," scored 17 touchdowns on his own, nine by rushing, eight by catching passes, for 102 points. Emlen Tunnell, already a star in the defensive backfield, intercepted 10 passes and was the chief punt returner, averaging 12.1 yards per return. Conerly, as was expected in that era, did play defense, too. This was before teams realized how foolish it was to risk valuable arms by playing guys both ways, but it was also what the rules required. Steve Owen was a strong backer of two-platoon football.

Before losing their last two games of the season, the Giants were 6–4 and headed for a winning record. They couldn't pull it off. During the 1949 season, New York lost twice to the Pittsburgh Steelers, twice to the Philadelphia Eagles, and to the New York Bulldogs and the Detroit Lions. Wins came over the Bulldogs, the Washington Redskins twice, the Green Bay Packers, the Chicago Bears, and the Chicago Cardinals.

There was good reason to believe the Giants were on their way back. Going 6–6 did not provoke much excitement, but it was a positive sign for a team that had been in a two-year slump. Steve Owen had rebuilt the Giants before, so there was good reason to think he could resuscitate the club again.

Charlie Conerly and Emlen Tunnell were two major weapons and leaders who could restore the Giants to the top of the Eastern Conference standings. They were keepers from 1948 who as second-year players were now obvious cornerstones on what the future might be built.

Decades later, one sportswriter seeking answers about how the Giants made their rebound from bottom feeders in the standings to one of the consistently best teams in the league, again pinpointed the dual efforts of Conerly and Tunnell for their contributions.

It was noted how few of their teammates stuck around after the losing 1948 campaign and how the addition of more capable players in 1950 set the Giants on the right road, as Owen had hoped. "Those two [Conerly and Tunnell] came from different areas of the country and seemed to have little in common, but they quickly became friends on and off the field," a sportswriter noted in 2017.[4]

They complemented and complimented one another in leadership and in performance.

Chapter 9

Loving the Spotlight

When the married Conerlys together moved to New York from Mississippi for the fall of 1949 because of Charlie's career, it was with a great sense of expectation. Charlie, of course, had been enamored of New York since his teens. The bright lights also appealed to Perian, who was as outgoing as her husband was shy.

Perhaps the oddest aspect of the Conerlys' relationship to outsiders in Clarksdale was that they often seemed to be splitting up and reconciling. It was an inaccurate perception, but Perian described the situation that way. Although it seems to be a most gossipy and simplistic way of looking at matters, she suggested that hometown residents just didn't get it that Charlie was going off to training camp for the Giants for a number of weeks. Somehow, they did not grasp that was how things worked in pro football.

But if that seems peculiar, the perceived properness of society, or rules governing expected behavior in the late 1940s, had already affected the Conerlys at least once in a way they never would today. Famous for his football exploits at the University of Mississippi, after Charlie completed his college playing days, grateful fans feted him. December 3, 1947 was declared "Charlie Conerly Day" in Clarksdale. By then Charlie and Perian were an item, and it seemed automatic that she would be at his side for the special event. But no, she was not permitted to be present.

"I was unable to attend the celebration because it took place on a Wednesday," Perian said. "Mississippi State College for Women girls were allowed to make out-of-town trips only on weekends, except in extraordinary circumstances."[1]

Despite the honor of the attention bestowed on her beau, this was not deemed extraordinary enough. Two other elements of the day were extraordinary. One was that his adoring fans were gifting Conerly a new car, a Chevrolet. The other was that he turned down receipt of it to preserve his spring baseball eligibility.

Chapter 9. Loving the Spotlight

Ole Miss' "Team of the Century" in 1993, which included six College Football Hall of Famers and two members of the Pro Football Hall of Fame. Charlie Conerly is seated front row, second from left, at the black tie gala held to honor the team (courtesy University of Mississippi Athletics Department).

If Charlie Conerly Day had been scheduled a year later, following their marriage, Perian would have been allowed to go. Perian was not especially fond of the forced split between spouses as Giants policy, either. She was prepared to start a riot with the team but decided to wait a while before challenging the status quo.

"A bride of six weeks, I took a rather dim view of the accepted procedure whereby players' wives remain at home until the start of the regular season," she said.[2]

That was very much a serious-business outlook projected by the Giants and other teams, a statement that training camp was all about getting players ready to perform at their top level for when the games counted. The weeks-long camp also put jobs on the line. The coaches were kings during training, and part of their role was to trim the list of hopefuls who showed up and to shape a final roster. Women, wives included, were perceived to be a distraction.

Perian accepted her exile from her husband's life, though she didn't have to like it. "But I decided to wait at least one year before overthrowing the heartless Giant regime and grudgingly fidgeted away my nine-week widowhood in Clarksdale," she said.[3]

When Perian finally departed from Mississippi and replanted herself in New York, she and Charlie landed at the Concourse Plaza Hotel. Unlike many other players connected to the team and unlike many others on the rosters of modern-day National Football League teams, the Conerlys did not investigate buying a home in the vicinity of the employing team.

That was a less-common procedure in the late 1940s for several reasons. The season was shorter than it is now, with only 12 regular-season games on the schedule and playoffs concluding before the end of the calendar year. Salaries were lower, so it seemed less practical to purchase a second home since the rest of the Conerlys' lives were centered in Mississippi. Also, despite Charlie operating on a five-year contract, job security was limited.

When it came to New York, there was a ready alternative. The Concourse Plaza, located in the Bronx, was quite close to the Polo Grounds home field and within walking distance to Yankee Stadium, and it was famous for housing big-name professional athletes connected to the city's Major League Baseball teams and the football Giants.

The 12-story hotel opened in 1922 and for decades served as a regular-season home for such prominent star athletes as Babe Ruth, Mickey Mantle, and Roger Maris of the Yankees, and Frank Gifford and other members of the football Giants. It was the most convenient plush hotel in the neighborhood.

Many of the players who resided at the Concourse were single, but some Giants lived there with their wives. Charlie had lived in an apartment his rookie year with a teammate, but Perian was a New York newcomer, and they needed higher quality digs. The Concourse was handy for practice and games and a respectable location for his wife to stay while he was busy at work.

Eager to experience the sights and sounds of what for her was a new and grand place, while Charlie chucked the ball on the gridiron, Perian explored the surroundings and sought entertainment from the vibrant city that seemed to offer it all to tourists and residents alike. In a sense, in the early days of her marriage in New York, Perian Conerly had two love affairs going at once, one with her new husband and the other with her new city. As long as she was in New York, she wanted to learn what it was all about.

Perian linked up with a willing partner, Joanne Fennema, whose husband Carl was a center on the Giants. Carl Fennema had played his college ball at the University of Washington in Seattle, and his wife was

Chapter 9. Loving the Spotlight 71

from that large Pacific Northwest city. Like Perian, she was anxious to experience New York's charms. Perian described Joanne Fennema as "another newlywed with a penchant for adventure," and Perian said they were a good match for her "See-and-Do Club."[4]

They made an effort to see all of New York's famous sites, but when the weather was rainy and they did not feel like making a long jaunt, they walked across the street from the Concourse and entered the Bronx County Courthouse to sit in on entertaining trials. They considered themselves lucky if they discovered a murder case being presented.

Another satisfying pastime was taking in the best theater offered in America, dropping in on the Broadway shows that were the hottest in the land. "Joanne and I saw literally every play on Broadway," Perian said, "for matinees were priced as low as $1.20. We didn't mind sitting in the balcony since most of the theatres are approximately the size of the Clarksdale High School Auditorium, and even the last row affords a reasonable view of the stage."[5]

The hot ticket at the time was the new musical *South Pacific*, and Perian and Joanne got into the theater on the day-of-show, stand-in-line sale. Over time, as Charlie's football career extended in New York, and the show likewise extended on Broadway, friends from Mississippi coming to visit all wanted to see it, and the Conerlys ended up seeing the stage performance based on James Michener's book *Tales of the South Pacific* five times. This Pulitzer Prize–winning collection of stories issued in 1947 was the book that launched Michener to stardom as an author. Perian said it was a much different view from the second row of the theater when one friend put their tickets on an expense account.

While this would be little surprise to any fan of New York, Perian also said she and Charlie had a ball sampling the wide variety of high-caliber food offered in restaurants. Although professional sports teams have made serious efforts recently to improve the nutritional value of eats served to players in training camp and in locker rooms, it is almost impossible to find sports-page references to athletes talking about how much they love what teams serve.

Upgrades were sought when the Conerlys dined out and discovered favorite places. Perian said eating was something she considered a favorite hobby and declared at the time of her introduction to New York that she was mentally game to try just about every restaurant around. She did take note, however, how impossible such a task would be since the city guidebook she was consulting made mention of 20,000 restaurants. As she put it, "One for every man, woman and child in Clarksdale." (Or was that the whole county?)[6]

The Conerlys enjoyed New York nightlife, but had no intention of sampling alcoholic refreshment at all of the city's 20,000 bars. However, during this era, and for many years afterward, there were famous watering holes that particularly welcomed New York's best-known, biggest-star athletes. The Conerlys became habitues of such establishments, such as Toots Shor's, Mike Manouche's, P.J. Clarke's, Eddie Condon's, Downey's and 21. They were part of the see-and-be-seen crowd.

Those were the places Perian cited as special hangouts, where sports in general were embraced and the athletes could mingle and enjoy themselves. P.J. Clarke's, which opened its doors in 1884 and is also well known for dinner, is still in operation. Toots Shor's Restaurant was perhaps the most legendary among these sites. Bernard "Toots" Shor was the seemingly ultimate host of this saloon in the 1940s and 1950s at 51 West 51st Street.

In New York and Los Angeles, there were places where athletes, actors, actresses, and other famous personages were known to congregate, celebrities who in the vernacular were there "to see and be seen." The signature element at Toots Shor's was a large, circular bar. The second signature element was Toots Shor himself. Shor could be a discreet host, protecting privacy with the proper table in the corner of his establishment while befriending all. He was sensitive to the needs and desires of big names who wanted to be alone, or at least not hassled by the average patron, perhaps Joe DiMaggio, the Yankees' superstar, most particularly.

Shor was a character who had his own way of doing things. More than the proprietors at the other prominent bars on Perian Conerly's list, Toots Shor, the individual, was part of the attraction at his drinking location. Shor extended courtesies, especially if he liked you. He insulted you, sometimes because he liked you, but also because you may have broken one of his unwritten rules. While Shor might well rush a prominent figure such as DiMaggio right to a table, others of note, made to wait in line to enter the always-crowded bar, were not as fortunate.

Shor was a raconteur, a host, and above all a sports fan. When someone first introduced Ernest Hemingway to Shor as a writer, Toots said, "What paper are you with, Ernie?"[7] Ernie, by then, had put such newspapers as the *Kansas City Star* and *Toronto Star* in his rearview mirror and was dominating the best-seller lists the way Shor's friend DiMaggio dominated the baseball diamond.

As one example of how the Shor mentality worked, if a celebrity was in his inner circle, Shor called him a "crum-bum." If one were not held in such high esteem, he might be forced to stand and wait for a table along with tourists and New Yorkers who were just off the street. Once, Louis B. Mayer, the famous Hollywood motion-picture magnate, grew touchy because he was forced to wait 20 minutes for a table and growled something about hoping the food was worth it. Shor retorted that he had waited in line longer to see one of Mayer's lousy movies. In 1969, a decade after Shor, who was often referred to as the saloon keeper to the stars, sold his bar for $1.5 million, well-known journalist Bob Considine wrote a biography of the restauranteur.

In the early 1940s, when Frank Sinatra was just making his mark, Shor invited him to dinner at the bar. Before too long, Sinatra, Bing Crosby, former heavyweight champ Jack Dempsey, and Babe Ruth were sharing a table with Shor. One thing the Conerlys never had to worry about when they dropped in at Toots Shor's was the nature of the company. They were new to it all from Mississippi, and it was enough to put their heads on a swivel.

On Sundays, Charlie wore his no. 42 jersey, and he was just shifting away from his leather helmet to a more protective, hard-shell helmet that in its own way symbolized a shift in the modernization of pro football as the 1950s began.

The New York Giants, whom Perian watched on the field in 1949 when she wasn't hitting the Broadway plays, provided a better show than in 1948. Charlie Conerly had taken control of the offense, and his statistics improved. By going 6–6, the team improved from the lousy performances of the two preceding years.

Besides Conerly, Emlen Tunnell, the anchor of the defense, gave the offense a boost by sometimes carrying the ball. He gained 251 yards on the ground in this limited duty. Although New York did not appreciably improve itself in the draft, the talent on hand jelled better than it had. The only notable rookie was defensive tackle Al DeRogatis, who in later years became better known as a broadcaster.

One of the most intriguing players on the 1949 team was Ben Agajanian, a kicker who played college ball at New Mexico and was minus four toes on his kicking foot. Yet he put together one of the longest NFL careers of anyone on this roster, staying active through 1964. He scored 655 points on field goals and extra points.

Bill Austin, a 6-foot-1, 223-pound lineman, was a rookie who was also a keeper. Coming out of Oregon State, Austin stuck with the Giants from 1949 through 1957 and then embarked on a long coaching career. He was one of those pieces coach Steve Owen was looking for when it came to rebuilding New York after the 1947–1948 debacle.

Owen, who had been with the Giants as a player and coach for nearly three decades at that point, was confident he could restore his team as a top-notch contender as long as he had sufficient time. Owen was sure he knew talent, and he knew he still needed to add more of it for a Giants resurgence.

In Conerly, he believed he had the long-term solution to run his offense. But Owen was an innovator on defense who created the 6–1–4 defense for certain circumstances. This came to be called the "umbrella" defense. This was his brainchild, but as it so happened, at one time during the early days of its existence, Toots Shor's was a gathering place for Owen and a couple of other well-known football coaches, Jock Sutherland and Greasy Neale. The three men exchanged ideas while having some refreshments, and new ideas were born.

It seemed appropriate that a man whose nickname was "Stout Steve" took such pride in defense and the shut-outs his D produced. With his mind oriented in that direction, he needed someone he could truly trust to generate offense. That connection was made with Charlie Conerly. Conerly, the older-than-average-rookie (although few knew how old at the time), was developing the necessary skills to lead a professional team, much as he had been the front man for the Ole Miss football team in college.

Chapter 10

Giants Become Winners

Steve Owen was right. He was able to lead the New York Giants to a swift turnaround, back into the winner's column, back into the championship contender column. After a few sub-par seasons, New York, with Charlie Conerly at quarterback, finished 10–2 in 1950.

That put New York in a first-place tie in the revamped National Football League standings, knotted with the Cleveland Browns in the American Conference. The new-look NFL had absorbed three teams when the All-America Football Conference folded, the Browns, the San Francisco 49ers, and the Baltimore Colts.

The AAFC had mounted the most vigorous challenge to the NFL since it was created in 1920, though a decade later the second American Football League would more dramatically change the landscape of pro football.

The seismic shift was announced on December 9, 1949, at the tail end of the previous season. The transition was something noted by the Conerlys after Charlie's flirtation with Branch Rickey's Brooklyn club, one of the teams left by the wayside as the AAFC disappeared. That left the NFL with 13 teams.

Cleveland's arrival in the new American Conference produced an instant rivalry with the Giants, one of the fiercest and closely watched in the 1950s. Cleveland showed up in the NFL ready-made as a top-performing team. The Giants began trending that way in 1950.

Under legendary coach Paul Brown, the Cleveland squad had dominated the AAFC. The Browns owned that league, winning the title in each of the four years of its existence and compiling a record of 47–4–3. That included a 14–0 mark in 1948.

The Browns of that period were supremely talented. Led by quarterback Otto Graham, the Browns were also at the forefront of breaking the pro football color barrier, welcoming such Black stars as Marion Motley and Bill Willis into their line-up. Later, all three, plus tackle-kicker Lou Groza and receivers Dante Lavelli and Mac Speedie, became inductees

75

into the Pro Football Hall of Fame. Lineman Len Ford, another African American, who played the bulk of his career with Cleveland, though he also competed elsewhere, was another member of that group.

During the four seasons when the AAFC was alive, it was common among NFL figures to disrespect those associated with the upstart league. Disparagement of the overall quality of play was a regular topic on the NFL side. Completely overlooked in such debates was the talent on the Browns' roster, and the imposing Cleveland record was very much an indicator that the Browns were on equal footing with the best the NFL could offer.

There was no doubt the Browns were underrated by NFL stalwarts. The prevailing opinion from those representing the older league was roughly on the order of "We'll show them what real opponents are like." It was felt that the Browns' stunningly phenomenal record had been amassed against a group of AAFC inferiors. From their beginning in the NFL, however, the Browns demonstrated that they were really that good. Schedulers seemed eager to make the point of NFL superiority right away, so they pitted the Browns against the Philadelphia Eagles in Cleveland's first-ever NFL regular-season game.

The Browns were the defending champions of the defunct AAFC, and the Eagles were the defending champions of the NFL. Fans were curious to get a closer look at the Browns, and some of the pre-game billing of the matchup of 0–0 teams called the contest "The World Series of Pro Football." Certainly that was hype, but it described what was on some followers' minds. This was a credibility game as much as anything else. The Browns wanted to show they were for real. The Eagles defended NFL honor.

The Eagles hosted the game on September 16, 1950, and tickets were not a hard sell. More than 71,200 fans turned out. To the shock of most and the dismay of many, the Browns slaughtered the Eagles, 35–10. This was no one-off, either. The Browns emerged as one of the league's elite teams, winning those 10 games to equal the Giants during Cleveland's inaugural NFL year. Cleveland was about as good each year for seven of the next eight seasons.

The early success of the Browns caught many in the NFL establishment off guard in 1950. That could be said to include the Giants, but the Giants' own bounce-back was catching many by surprise, too. It had taken Owen a few years to restock, but the Giants of that season resembled some of his best elevens of the 1940s.

Conerly may have gained more seasoning as the chief operator of the offense, but he was not asked to throw the ball nearly as often as previously. Chuckin' Charlie was more "Handing Off Charlie" in 1950 with

Chapter 10. Giants Become Winners

Owen heavily stressing the running game. Conerly had some physical ailments, though he still started 11 of 12 regular-season games, but his overall statistics were limited. He threw just 132 times, completing 56, for 1,000 yards and eight touchdowns.

Rookie fullback Eddie Price, out of Tulane, carried the ball 126 times for 703 yards. Veteran Gene Roberts carried 116 times for 483 yards. And rookie Randy Clay, out of Texas, toted the ball 74 times for 254 yards. New York wasn't flashy but was good enough to score 268 points and average 22.3 points per game.

It was on defense, however, where the Giants truly shined. Owen always took more personal pride in the defensive side of the ball, and this year's crew made him beam. Overall, New York allowed just 150 points, a mere 12.3 points a game.

Emlen Tunnell, who intercepted seven passes, was still the main man on the defensive unit. Opposing teams feared throwing to his coverage area. But the defense was beefed up. Arnie Weinmeister, a future Hall of Famer at defensive tackle, joined the club. So did another defender by the name of Tom Landry, who became much more famous as the long-time coach of the Dallas Cowboys starting in the 1960s.

He may have been much less remembered in the long term because he only played four NFL seasons and retired at 28, but defensive back Otto Schnellbacher was one of the greatest ball-hawking defensive secondary players ever over a short stretch. As terrific as Schnellbacher was with eight interceptions in 1950, that was actually a comparative off-season for him. In 1948, as a 25-year-old rookie, Schnellbacher intercepted 11 passes for 239 yards and a touchdown for the Giants. In 1951, he also intercepted 11 passes, returning two for touchdowns. Seemingly inexplicably, Schnellbacher had just four interceptions in 1949.

Schnellbacher played college ball at Kansas and was the Jayhawks' first All-American in 1947. He was also a professional basketball player, suiting up for the Providence Steamrollers and the St. Louis Bombers during the 1948–1949 season. Illustrating just how poorly paid a professional athlete was in America in the 1950s, Schnellbacher retired from the Giants shy of his 30th birthday to become an insurance salesman.

In 1950, though, Tunnell, Schnellbacher, Landry and a fourth player named Harrison Rowe helped make the Giants' defense impregnable when Owen introduced the 6–1–4 umbrella formation. Opposing teams struggled to pass against the umbrella.

Landry the player was truly a coach on the field beginning with his first season on the Giants' roster in 1950. Landry the coach was almost always pictured on the sidelines wearing a fedora, but when he was still wearing a helmet, he was making coaching calls and interpretations for

New York. Landry was born in Mission, Texas, in 1924, and his high school team went 12–0 before he attended the University of Texas.

Like many athletes, including Charlie Conerly, Landry stepped away from college to fight for the United States during World War II. Landry served as a pilot for the United States Army Air Corps. After the war, Landry returned to Texas, resumed playing football, and in 1948 was drafted by the New York Yankees of the All-America Football Conference. He played one season for that club before joining the Giants. The Giants had previously chosen Landry in the 1947 NFL draft. When the Yankees folded, the Giants were able to take Landry in a dispersal draft of AAFC players.

While Owen may have invented the 6–1–4 defense, when it came time to implement it in training camp, he requested that Landry do the explaining to his teammates. As the star pupil, Landry did so, and his role kept expanding for the Giants, going beyond the field on Sundays.

"Steve Owen was not a great detail man," Landry said. "He'd just do things like that [create a new formation] and figure you would work out the details for yourself on the field. I learned much of my coaching by playing under him because I had to work out the details of what he meant."[1]

Lest anyone shake their heads at the seeming absurdity of such a scenario, Wellington Mara, one of the family of owners who have always operated the Giants, was an eyewitness to one occasion. "I can remember being in training camp and Owen would be up at the chalkboard, going over a defense," Mara said. "Suddenly, he'd just stop and say, 'Tom, come up and do this. You know more about this than I do.'"[2]

Whoever was directing the orchestra in 1950, the conductor did a first-rate job. The Giants were plenty stingy to opponents, right from the beginning of the season.

New York opened the 1950 season on the road on September 17 against the Pittsburgh Steelers at Forbes Field, then also the home of the Pittsburgh Pirates baseball team. Some 24,699 fans turned out to kick off the campaign. The Steelers would finish with a 6–6 mark that year. Probably Pittsburgh's most prominent player was defensive lineman Ernie Stautner, though he was a rookie out of Boston College.

Although Charlie Conerly got off to a lousy start, completing just three of 13 pass attempts, the Giants held down the Steelers, 18–7. Pittsburgh's weak point all season would be its sputtering offense. Tunnell intercepted two passes for New York, a reminder that his little corner of the field was a no-fly zone for foes. Indeed oddly, the Giants' defense accounted for all of the team's points. New York scored on two safeties,

Chapter 10. Giants Become Winners 79

Landry returned a fumble 37 yards for a touchdown, and Al DeRogatis recovered a fumble in the end zone.

New York had a bye in the schedule the following week, then traveled to Cleveland to take on the Browns on October 1. During a time of NFL history when attendance was not generally as large as it later became, the teams drew 37,647 fans to Cleveland Stadium. This was certainly a curiosity game for the Giants, seeing up-close the previous AAFC enemy which had dismantled the Philadelphia Eagles.

The most impressive part of this game once more was the Giants' defense. In winning over the Browns, 6–0, New York repeated a demonstration of its shaky offense but unleashed what was shaping up as a dominant defense. This was the first time in the history of the Cleveland franchise, dating to its origins in the All-America conference, that the Browns were shut out.

This was a second straight poor throwing day for Conerly, who went just four for 13 for only 61 yards. Cleveland's star quarterback, Otto Graham, wasn't much better. Although Graham was 12 for 30 for 127 yards, he tossed three interceptions. Halfback Ken Carpenter threw one, too. Four different Giants made picks. Eddie Price's two-yard rush for a touchdown was the game's only score. It wasn't pretty, but it counted, and the win ended up counting big-time in the standings.

The Giants won their third game in a row the next week by taking down the Washington Redskins, 21–17. Two of the three New York TDs came on the ground, one by Forrest Griffith and the other by Choo-Choo Roberts. Roberts registered a second touchdown on a 39-yard pass from Conerly, a completion that must have made the struggling quarterback feel good.

That heave did not drag Conerly out of his slump. While Conerly did complete a 33-yard touchdown throw to Joe Scott, he threw for just 59 yards in a rematch against the Steelers, this one won by Pittsburgh, 17–6.

Conerly did not even start the next week in a rematch versus the Browns, and he had no completions on three attempts in the game. Back-up Travis Tidwell handled things most of the time but was hardly a sharp passer, going two for nine for 17 yards. Two second-half rushing touchdowns and Ray Poole's foot, booting two extra points and a 22-yard field goal, gave New York a 17–13 victory. It also pushed the Giants a half-game in front of the Browns in the standings with a 4–1 record.

If the Giants thought that ended their problems, they were wrong. They came right out the next week with a lackluster 17–3 loss to the Chicago Cardinals. This was the forerunner squad of, first, the St. Louis

Cardinals and the now Arizona Cardinals. The Cardinals won the 1947 league crown and lost in the title game in 1948 but two years later were beginning to fade.

The only Giants points came on a 12-yard field goal by Ray Poole. Tidwell again played more than Conerly, though he did not do anything special. Conerly was three for nine for 23 yards and an interception. These were stressful times for Conerly. He began to hear boos from the Giants fans, critical of his erratic play. They were rapidly losing faith in him. Yes, he was singled out for the limited offensive output and for throwing interceptions.

"Charlie gets blamed for everything that goes wrong," said backfield mate Eddie Price, "and every criticism of him is absolutely wrong. There isn't a better passer in the league than Charlie, but he can't do it alone. Our offensive line is inexperienced and doesn't give Charlie any protection."[3]

Conerly did not throw his teammates under the bus, did not send blame in any direction. As little as he talked in the post-game locker room anyway, that would have been uncharacteristic. He could handle the boos at the stadium based on his performance.

"They got pretty rough at times," Conerly said of his home fan treatment. "But, hell, they were paying their money to see us play, and then, too, the booing didn't bother me none."[4]

Sometime later, though, he admitted to being irked when he was booed in public in a non-football setting. Once, he and some Giants attended a New York Rangers hockey game at Madison Square Garden. Unexpectedly, their presence was remarked upon by the public address announcer, who read off their names one by name. Sure enough, those other sports fans booed Conerly. "It was embarrassing out there in public," Conerly said. "But then, I was the quarterback, and they figured when things went wrong it was my fault."[5]

The loss to the Cardinals was a low point of the season. After that, things jelled and the Giants resumed winning. They won their next six straight games, on some occasions exploding for far more points than they had scored in any of their early games. In order, the Giants defeated the Washington Redskins, 24–21; the Cardinals, in a decisive rematch, 51–21; the Baltimore Colts, 55–20; the Philadelphia Eagles, 7–3; the New York Yanks, 51–7; and the Eagles a second time, in another war, 9–7.

The fourth quarter versus the Redskins was a turning point. Trailing 21–14 after three quarters, the Giants ran off 10 points in the fourth period. Ray Poole won it on a 40-yard field goal, but the score before that, a Conerly-to-Bill Swiacki 26-yard TD pass, was titanic.

In the stifling win over the Cardinals, a game so different from the teams' first meeting, Conerly threw a pair of 38-yard touchdown passes. A week later, when the Giants crushed the Colts by roughly the same score, the kudos went to Tidwell. Conerly didn't figure in anything. Poole booted seven extra points.

New York made a first-quarter touchdown hold up against the Eagles in their first showdown. It was an important victory, pushing the Giants to 8–2 and dropping the Eagles to 6–4. Otherwise they would have both been at 7–3. The Eagles were two-time defending NFL titlists and three-time Eastern Division champs. This Giants' win pretty much finished off Philadelphia's hopes for 1950.

What followed was the Giants' third 50-point game in four weeks, a sound thumping of the Yanks before 41,630 more enthusiastic fans at the Polo Grounds. Back in good form, Conerly threw touchdown passes of 23 and 10 yards and ran for another score on a two-yard run.

That led to the final game of the regular season. New York needed a triumph since Cleveland was hovering right there in the standings. Taking down Philadelphia for a second time was no gimme, either. At this time, the Eagles were coached by Owen's Toots Shor's drinking buddy, Greasy Neale. They had both been affiliated with the NFL for decades, so it was unlikely either man held any surprises in his game plan for the other.

The contest was played at Shibe Park in Philadelphia, the old baseball stadium, in front of 26,440 fans. The Giants put all nine of their points on the scoreboard in the first quarter on a 15-yard field goal by Randy Clay and a five-yard touchdown pass from Conerly to Bob McChesney. The Eagles spent the rest of the day trying to catch up but couldn't, cataloging one TD on a second-period pass from Tommy Thompson. The New York defense did the rest.

However, the Browns rolled over the Redskins, 45–21, leaving them with the same 10–2 record as the Giants. Ordinarily, during this era, the winners of the Eastern Division and the Western Division advanced to play one another for the championship without any preliminary playoffs. But because the Giants and Browns were tied, they had to face off in an extra game to determine the Eastern winner.

On a wickedly cold and blustery December 17 at Cleveland Stadium, with 33,054 bundled-up fans watching, the Browns held back the Giants, 8–3, to advance to face the Los Angeles Rams, who had outplayed the Chicago Bears in their own playoff. The Browns survived to win the title, 30–28, in their first season in the NFL after coming over from the All-America Football Conference and most definitely showing they were the real deal.

There wasn't a touchdown scored in the Giants–Browns game, only two field goals kicked by Cleveland's Lou Groza and a field goal kicked by New York's Clay. Also, the Browns scored a two-point safety when Conerly was tackled in his own end zone. Conerly threw for just 48 yards and tossed two interceptions, a low point in performance harkening back to the beginning of the season.

The 10–2 regular season was heartening for New York. The Mara management team and the players believed the Giants were back. Conerly hoped his 1951 would prove to be better individually than his 1950. Surrounded by better players than when he was a rookie, especially on the defensive side, he had to be optimistic about the Giants' future.

Chapter 11

Keeping It Going

The Giants slipped over to the dark side in the late 1940s, and they didn't like it. The 1950 season's 10–2 showing, even if it left the team one step short of playing for a title, was a resurrection. It was something coach Steve Owen wanted to keep going. The Giants brought the attitude of "we're back" into the 1951 campaign.

Owen didn't care much about how the Giants won, as long as they won. Make that as long as they played stiff defense, he didn't care too strongly how they acquired sufficient points on offense. If the defense held, the offense didn't have to play a high-octane style. Owen would adapt the offense to the personnel and the circumstances.

In 1948, when Charlie Conerly was a rookie, and in his second year, Owen assessed his lineup and determined that the strength of Conerly's arm was the strength of the offense. The running game was not capable. The receivers didn't excel, either, so Conerly was out on a limb. The team results were not good, although Conerly performed well.

In 1950 and again in 1951, when the Giants finished 9–2–1, the defense was so stout that Stout Steve did not have anything to worry about on that side of the ball. The running game was the best it had been in several years, which was critical because, for the second year in a row, Conerly did not play well. The confident leader of his first two seasons had some abysmal stretches where his passes could not find receivers' hands.

By 1951, Owen, who grew up in Oklahoma with the aim of becoming a jockey for Thoroughbred horses until he outgrew that notion, was a fixture in New York, more famously aligned with the football team than any of his players. He had played for the squad in its early years, coached the team to glory in selected years, coached the team through World War II, and persevered with the team during its shallow days in the late 1940s. Now he had the Giants back where he wanted them—in the hunt for championships again.

From the days when owner Tim Mara kept telephoning Owen to

ask him for advice on a new coach in the early 1930s, for the next nearly a quarter century, Owen filled the role—without ever signing paperwork with the team. "You see, Tim and I have never had a contract," Owen said many years after he began working as the head coach.[1]

Mara was a gambling man (a legal bookmaker) who paid just $500 to register the Giants with the NFL, and he pretty much chose Owen based on instinct. Mara used to say he was no football expert (something few owners admit), but he sensed Owen was the right man to fill the slot as coach. "[He] seemed to get along all right with the other boys and took his work very seriously," Mara said. "I just had a lot of confidence in him."[2]

That was old school carried forward in front office operations. But Owen was old school, too. The NFL itself was young when he competed in the 1920s, but Owen spanned eras and generations. When the NFL got rolling during the Roaring Twenties, the founders and stalwarts of the pro game bristled whenever critics or doubters argued that the college game was better, that college athletes still outshone the pros.

Harold "Red" Grange was the most famous football player in the United States, his brilliant gridiron exploits for the University of Illinois publicized everywhere. The pros were seen as more of a motley lot, affiliated with organizations that often quickly passed into the night rather than fielding players who were pure amateurs representing stable colleges such as Notre Dame.

Those in the know, such as Chicago Bears founder George Halas, and Green Bay Packers partisan Curly Lambeau, understood that the pros represented the best of the best among players, even if at the time they were paid paltry sums such as $100 a game. Some felt it was unseemly for college men to keep playing the rough-and-tumble game and to seemingly waste their college educations and degrees.

This ongoing debate was one reason for the creation of the Chicago College All-Star Game played between the reigning National Football League champion and a group of college all-stars. The game was established for the benefit of charity after *Chicago Tribune* sports editor Arch Ward pushed the idea, and results of the game essentially proved the point that the pros were superior. The game was played until the 1970s.

Over the decades, the professional team won 31 of 42 such contests, with two ties and nine victories going to the collegians. Those players basically were NFL draft picks on their way to training camps with their respective teams, some soon to be pro stars. Conerly was one of those selected for participation in that game before his first Giants training camp.

Demonstrating his old school leanings, Owen was still fighting this battle of perception, at least as late as 1950, espousing his belief that pro players were better than college players, even though only a comparative few were still making the argument.

> Anybody who maintains that the boys who play pro football are overstuffed athletes ought to come into the clubhouse and see them. They are as rugged a group of men as ever stepped onto a field. For some strange reason a few people seem to think that pro football players are not in good condition—in fact, are never in condition. Yet the reverse is true. I believe that pro football players today are probably the best conditioned in any sport.[3]

As for college football, sure they play the same style, Owen said, and the games may be exciting to watch, but "the colleges are the farm system, so to speak, for the pros. The pros' bones are harder, but more than that they know how to go with a blow—something like a good boxer."[4]

Pro football players' bones are harder? The world still awaits the scientific support for that statement. The players may have learned to roll with the punches but probably not in the classroom at Stanford or Michigan.

One thing Owen emphasized was how tough a man had to be to play and succeed at professional football. He referred to it as a game of collisions where one "can hear the leather popping like firecrackers."[5]

A college star, an All-American at the University of Mississippi, Conerly came into the NFL as a heralded passer. In his first two seasons, as the Giants faltered overall, he seemed to dodge trouble, both from any professional learning curve and from enemy pass rushers. Then, in his third and fourth seasons, it was as if Conerly was caught in an avalanche. He was buried in difficulties, from foes keying on him to fans booing him.

When the team was stymied, Conerly was singled out. Based on sheer numbers, the reading of statistics, he deserved some of the harsh treatment. In 1951, Conerly completed 93 out of 189 pass attempts for 1,277 yards and 10 touchdowns. However, he threw a whopping 22 interceptions. That was the problem area.

The Giants had a shortage of game-breaking receivers on the roster, as had been the case during his first few years with the team. The 1940s had begun ushering in a more free-flowing and free-throwing era of passing in the National Football League. Superstars for the ages emerged, such as Washington's Sammy Baugh and the Bears' Sid Luckman. In Green Bay, where Curly Lambeau had long been a long-distance dreamer, his quarterbacks, Cecil Isbell and Arnie Herber, were blessed with the world's greatest receiver in Don Hutson. Hutson virtually invented pass catching, tossing moves into his routes that never had been seen during his playing days between 1935 and 1945.

Neither New York nor anyone else had anyone like Hutson, but an addition to the roster in 1951 who would benefit the club and Conerly with his pass-catching style was Kyle Rote. Rote, who stood six feet tall and weighed about 200 pounds, was born in San Antonio, Texas, and was an All-American running back for Southern Methodist University after graduating from high school in 1947. He once booted a punt 84 yards for SMU.

Rote was the no. 1 overall draft pick in the 1951 NFL draft, when the Giants grabbed him. He did a bit of running in the pros but morphed into a reliable receiver, catching 300 balls over the course of a career ending in 1961.

The father of Kyle Rote, Jr., the most prominent American soccer player of his generation, Kyle the elder was slow to adapt to the passing game as a rookie, basically because he had knee problems and appeared in only five games. But he caught 21 passes his second year and improved from there. It was just too soon for him to make an impact in 1951.

Rote, the football dad, grew to truly appreciate Conerly's demeanor and his ability on the field.

"Conerly was quite a guy," Rote said.

> He had left college to join the Marines in World War II and fought in any number of battles in the Pacific. He was a laid-back kind of player, almost casual about the game. He showed little excitement on the outside, but there was a lot of it, I know, on the inside. He just never exhibited his emotions. But Charlie had an incredibly good touch when he threw the football and he was especially effective on the shorter ones.[6]

Although Conerly praised the individuals like Bill Swiacki and Gene Roberts, whom he aimed for during his early years with the Giants, he increased his level of gushing when it came to evaluating Rote and the soon-to-arrive Frank Gifford.

"Later, of course, Kyle Rote came up. And after him Frank Gifford," Conerly said. "You couldn't ask for better than those two."[7]

Still, Conerly said Rote was slowed by his knees throughout his pro career, and while Gifford was a terrific all-around player, the Giants lacked what he termed speedsters until 1961, his final year, when Del Shofner came over from the Rams.

"He was a great receiver, but he couldn't go deep because of his knee," Conerly said of Rote. "The players would often come into the huddle and tell me they thought they could get open, or this or that, Gifford and [Alex Webster] especially, and Rote, too."[8] Conerly listened to those players, but other players, lesser lights, delivered the same message and he did not take them up on the boast as often.

The Giants felt good about themselves in training camp under the hot August sun in Saranac Lake, New York, in 1951. Their 10–2 record of the previous season was a natural confidence-booster. There was strong faith in the defense, and that ferocious unit authored some pretty impressive history, limiting opponents to 161 points for the whole year and forcing 53 turnovers.

The Giants' regular season did not begin until October 1, and it started inauspiciously, with a 13–13 tie versus the Pittsburgh Steelers. The main quarterback for New York that day was Travis Tidwell, who did not particularly glow, and Conerly saw limited playing time.

New York cobbled together a three-game winning streak after that. Most of the upcoming games were close, but the Giants always held the other team down and prevailed 35–14 over the Redskins, 28–17 over the Chicago Cardinals, and 26–24 over the Philadelphia Eagles. Conerly was back in command against Washington and hurled three touchdown passes in what was one of New York's highest-scoring games of the season. Tunnell ran a punt back 81 yards for a touchdown against Chicago.

A 23-point third quarter gave the Giants the victory over Philadelphia. Conerly threw one TD pass, but Tunnell did it again, bursting free for a 71-yard punt return for a score. He was always dangerous when he got his hands on the ball. This was particularly notable because early in college, Tunnell broke his neck on a punt return and doctors told him he would never play football again.

"On account of my neck," Tunnell said much later, "I had three cracked vertebrae and there was a chance if something happened, I'd be crippled for life."[9]

The Giants lost their first game of the season on October 28 in another frustrating showdown with the Cleveland Browns. Cleveland won it, 14–13, dropping New York to 3–1–1 and moving to 4–1. Nearly 60,000 fans turned out at Cleveland Municipal Stadium. The Browns scored all of their points in the first quarter, and the Giants tried to peck away at the lead. The Giants scored on a 20-yard interception by Tom Landry and a 29-yard touchdown pass from Conerly to Bob McChesney. The difference was that Lou Groza made both of his extra points, and New York converted on just one. Conerly had one of his best games, completing nine of 13 pass tries for 117 yards. For Cleveland, Otto Graham completed two passes for touchdowns.

The Giants won two straight after that with their finest offensive production of the season. They topped the New York Yanks, 37–31, and the Redskins, 28–14. At 0–5–1, the Yanks were one of the weakest teams in the league. The Giants ran up points in a variety of ways. Conerly flung one TD pass of 57 yards to Joe Scott, Landry intercepted another pass, for 55 yards, running it all of the way back. Tunnell returned a kickoff 100 yards for still another special teams touchdown.

Landry was such a successful head coach with the Dallas Cowboys for so long, many forget what a tough player he was in the defensive backfield for the Giants. Landry intercepted 32 passes in his pro career, eight each in 1951, 1952, and 1954, putting him among the league leaders. He was also so passionate about helping his team in so many ways, he sometimes had to be restrained. He once chased Glenn Davis back to the Rams' bench after being beaten on a 10-yard pass play. Another time Landry was practically foaming at the mouth on the sidelines when the Giants met the Cleveland Browns.

"Tom was hollering and yelling and screaming when the offense was on the field," said Wellington Mara. "And he had tears in his eyes. When a Cleveland tackler hit one of our players who appeared to be out of bounds, and Tom interpreted this as a cheap shot, he rushed over and was all over the guy and ready to fight before they separated them."[10]

This was the second victory of the year over Washington. Conerly notched a touchdown pass, and remarkably, Otto Schnellbacher took his turn in the secondary, contributing a touchdown with 40-yard interception return. It was almost incalculable how helpful the Giants' defense was to the offense.

The problem for New York, sitting on a 5–1–1 record, was that the next team looming on the schedule was the Browns again. The Giants learned in 1950, when Cleveland joined the league, just how annoying the Browns could be. That would be a lesson that kept on being taught throughout much of the 1950s.

Still again, the Giants and Browns were fighting it out for the top spot in the division. This November 18 game lured 52,515 spectators to the Polo Grounds. In this meeting, a rare occurrence came to pass: Cleveland's defense was stronger. The Browns won, 10–0, scoring all its points in the first period. Conerly was sharp, a threat all day, attempting 23 passes and completing 13 for 140 yards, but the offense couldn't move the sticks often enough and could not cross the goal line.

Neither could the defense penetrate the opponent's end zone, though those nimble defensive backs gave New York chances. Schnellbacher picked off Otto Graham twice, and Landry intercepted one ball. But unlike their previous big runs after catch, they could not advance the ball much once stolen.

Groza kicked a 34-yard field goal and an extra point for the Browns, and Graham did pitch one good long ball to Dub Jones for a 68-yard touchdown. The win lifted Cleveland to a 7–1 record and left the Giants at 5–2–1. The division crown was slipping away.

The irritated Giants won the rest of their games, 10–0 over the Chicago Cardinals, 14–0 over the Steelers, 23–7 over the Eagles, and 27–17 over the New York Yanks. The back-to-back shutouts of the Cardinals and Steelers were showcases for the defense, especially the Pittsburgh game, when Landry ran a fumble home on a nine-yard scamper and Schnellbacher scored the game's only other touchdown on a 46-yard interception. They were virtually unsupported by the offense, but it didn't matter.

The big plays in the Philadelphia game were a 39-yard TD throw from Conerly to Kelley Mote and an 80-yard touchdown burst by Eddie Price. That was Price's career-long run in his career-best season. That year he led the league in rushes with 271 and in yards gained with 971.

There was very little interest in the Giants' season finale against the Yanks, as evidenced by an attendance figure of 6,658 people. Conerly hurled touchdown passes of 69 yards and four yards, but most astoundingly, Tunnell again broke free for another long punt return for a touchdown, this time going 74 yards. The man was a menace with the ball, a breakaway talent par excellence when he could catch those long punts and kickoffs.

Despite the Giants' fine season, when the gun sounded ending the season, they were looking up, in what was then called the American Conference, at the 11–1 Browns. New York's 9–2–1 record was worth second place in the conference and was better than any team's mark in the National Conference. But in an era when the only scheduled playoff game was the championship game, the Giants went home. Only the 8–4 Rams and the Browns played again. Los Angeles pulled off the upset, 24–17, winning the crown in the fourth quarter.

CHAPTER 12

The Old Man

No one ever asked. That was Charlie Conerly's shrugging comment when the topic of his age finally came up. It's not clear that people thought he entered the Marines when he was 15 years old or just what.

But the guy who lost a few birthdays during World War II in the middle of his college football career at the University of Mississippi was older than anyone outside his family thought. Eventually, football fans and sportswriters figured it out, but not for a long time.

Conerly's real birth date was September 19, 1921. That meant that right around the time the 1952 National Football League season was beginning, he was 31 years old. During that era of professional football, only a small percentage of players continued competing into their 30s.

Sports medicine was not what it would become, so injuries that in the future might not be so threatening were fatal to careers at the time, knee injuries in particular. Wiser nutrition was not widespread. Not only did athletes smoke, but they also endorsed cigarettes. Professional athletic salaries that would later soar into the millions of dollars were in the low thousands for most players. Conerly was well compensated for the time by being paid $20,000 annually. Overall, money was not necessarily an incentive to stick with a game if a different type of career beckoned.

Conerly's appearance also fit the image of an aging player. By the early 1950s he was starting to get some gray streaks in his otherwise black hair. His facial features, fitting to play a movie cowboy (something that would help him later), were getting craggier.

Still, no one bothered to ask, "Hey, Charlie, how old are you really?", and he was listed on roster sheets as being a few years younger than he was. When it finally came out that Charlie Conerly was roughly three years older than anyone had been saying, it was treated as breaking news in the New York newspapers.

Perian Conerly, who had become the first woman writing about pro football, had a humorous take on this subject. She suggested that despite

Chapter 12. The Old Man

Charlie being in the Pacific for the Marines for three years during World War II, the University of Mississippi sports information office merely transplanted his 1942 statistics, such as height and weight, and made only a minor alteration to his age without bothering to work it out.

"[They] charitably added but one year to his age," Perian Conerly said. When he signed with the Giants and joined that organization, New York picked up his statistics from the Rebels.[1]

Charlie Conerly never lied about his age, she said. "Now, Charlie has never made a secret of his age," Perian said. "It was just that nobody asked him what it really was."[2]

Until the mid–1950s, that is, when a sportswriter did get around to asking point-blank. One newspaper sported a headline that referred to Conerly this way: "Conerly—Amazing Old Pro at 33." Then someone asked, oh, by the way, when will you turn 34? Conerly's reply was "Been there. I'll be 36 on September 19."[3]

Charlie Conerly's response set off a mini-frenzy in the press corps. Perian said newspapers treated this item as if it was a major scoop, and once one paper reported it, others, including wire services, picked up the information, so every sports page reader in the country was learning Conerly would have a few more candles on his cake than they thought.

From a personal standpoint, Perian joked that this meant she could no longer deflect any stats about her own age. She was about five and a half years younger than Charlie, and she said she had planned to stop counting publicly when she turned 30. "Now they had me pegged, too," she said.[4]

Much later, when another sportswriter was examining Conerly's career in depth, he did note that after Sammy Baugh retired from the Washington Redskins in 1952 at 38, Conerly was the oldest quarterback in the NFL for the last eight years of his career. Over that stretch of time his hair turned grayer and his face more lined yet. The only thing that really mattered, however, was whether Chuckin' Charlie could still bring those passes with his strong right arm—and he could.

The key to his performance was an upgrade in wide receivers. It began with Kyle Rote. The highly publicized Rote had experienced a truncated rookie year because of a knee injury. In his second season, though perhaps not as fast as he had shown in college at Southern Methodist, Rote played a bigger role in the offense. He appeared in all 12 games, though he started just three. He caught 21 passes, averaging 11.4 yards per catch. That was a help to the passing game.

In some ways, compared to his SMU days, Rote limped his way through his pro career—a case of a knee injury derailing what he could really do. There was always some story following Rote around, some of it stemming from his sparkling college career, some from the earliest days of his relationship with his future wife, Betty.

When Rote showed up at school in San Antonio after a family move, Betty was already there. She was apparently a tough gal, having cowed everyone around. She greeted him by saying, "Wanna fight?" Rote, who had full confidence in his fisticuff ability, knew he could handle her and, instead of responding to a boxing challenge, he tied her to a tree and left her there. When the teacher inquired of classmates where Betty was, she discovered that yes, this escapade had really happened, and Betty was hitched to a playground tree. Later, she was hitched to Kyle.[5]

After Kyle flirted with playing for Vanderbilt and Betty spent some time at a nearby women's college, they both ended up at SMU and got married senior year. Rote had overlapped on the football team with Mustangs legend Doak Walker, who joined the Detroit Lions after college. Rote had not thought much about pro football until after Walker became a success. Then he thought about it in terms of a good job right out of school. "The main thing was money, more money right away than you could get somewhere else when you and your wife are trying to get started," Rote said.[6]

Compared to the glory of his college days, Rote was never quite the star with the Giants, but he was always a reliable, good-hands receiver for Conerly, collecting 26 passes here and 31 there in certain seasons. It was ironic that over his final two seasons, when he was in his 30s, Rote put together his two top pass-catching campaigns of 42 and 53 catches.

Rote had been robbed of speed but not sure hands. Also, in 1952, the Giants added a bigger threat in Frank Gifford to deflect defensive back attention. Frank Gifford was a golden-boy draft pick out of the University of Southern California, New York's no. 1 choice. He was movie-star handsome and had done some acting. On the field, he could do everything offensively, from rushing the ball to catching the ball, better than anyone the Giants had.

Just not right away. Gifford, who was eventually enshrined in the College Football Hall of Fame and the Pro Football Hall of Fame, accumulated 78 touchdowns for the Giants and had many famous moments, including some not-so-grand ones when he was knocked unconscious and lost a year of playing time.

The 6-foot-1, 197-pound Gifford played halfback and flanker and a little bit of defensive back, but the Giants needed him to be great immediately, and he was not in his first year, gaining just 116 yards rushing and catching only five passes. In the long run, Gifford caught 367 passes

Chapter 12. The Old Man

and became Conerly's best friend on the Giants. In the days when players did so, they roomed together on road trips.

Gifford was born in Santa Monica, California, and attended high school in Bakersfield before starring for the USC Trojans in college. His father was an oilfield roughneck, and Gifford's high school had 5,000 students, many of them described, as he put it, as "definitely the bottom of the socioeconomic ladder." The students were children of farmers and oil workers of all ethnic backgrounds, including "poor white kids like me."[7]

As a football glamor guy in college in Los Angeles and in the pros in New York, and later as a widely known sports television personality and the husband of Kathie Lee, a long-time television hostess on the *Today* show and on a show with Regis Philbin, there was an impression that Gifford always had it made. That was not true. He came from a modest background and ascended to heights financially and to fame and popularity through football.

Playing for Southern Cal uplifted Gifford initially, but as much as he was a hot property because of his football skills, he was not especially comfortable on campus at first.

"To begin with, USC was sort of a rich kids' playground, and I was poorer than a church mouse," Gifford said.[8] He lived in a converted garage across the street from the team practice field for two years.

One way Gifford stayed afloat was by taking part-time jobs. Unlike others who worked on campus, perhaps at the student union, or later students who worked summer construction jobs or had internships in offices, Gifford probably had the best gig of any student-athlete anywhere, although he always downplayed it. Frank Gifford, USC football player, appeared in Hollywood movies, many of them. He didn't even keep track, later estimating that he may have been paid for tiny parts in 20 or 30 films. That beat the heck out of other student jobs out there. His self-described work experience was referred to as "a highly exalted level." It wasn't clear if he was applying a self-deprecating notation there. He added, "Call it talking stuntman."[9]

When the recruiter who took a liking to Gifford to get those film jobs asked if he had anything to wear, Gifford owned just one sports jacket. His friend was spiffily dressed, and Gifford said, "I'd never seen a cuff link before."[10]

It was quite the introduction to Hollywood in the shadow of his caring friend, taken to parties with famous stars and starlets, calling studios for day work as an extra for $18.75 a day—a lot to Gifford at the time. He noted if he was visible on screen without saying a word, and just by shrugging his shoulders in response to a star's question, he could make $200.

"If a studio made a football film, I was sure to be in it," Gifford said, "and there were a lot of them then." In a film called *That's My Boy*, starring Dean Martin and Jerry Lewis, Gifford was the stand-in kicker for Lewis.[11] It took until 1953 for Gifford to earn enough points for a Screen Actors Guild card.

For sure, Hollywood in 1952 was more glamorous than pro football, even if Gifford was playing in New York. As Perian Conerly discovered, the home folk in Mississippi had no idea what she and Charlie were doing in New York when they were away for the fall. Gifford returned to Bakersfield and was more or less quizzed in the same manner. Friends asked, "Where've you been?" Gifford said. "In New York," he answered. "Really? Doing what?"[12]

It seems difficult to believe that people were so unaware of the pro game—and this was California—but except for the cities where the sport was played, the National Football League ranked behind other professional sports in following and did not have a national TV contract. Ultimately, TV would do more to boost the league's reputation than anything else. But somehow it was possible to play the pro game and be invisible in your home areas, as Conerly and Gifford were.

Gifford didn't like coach Steve Owen and was quite unflattering about the man when he wrote of his early pro days. This was many years, after Owen's death. "Steve Owen," Gifford reported, "was a fat, snarly Oklahoman who dipped snuff—the juice would dribble onto his dirty rubber jacket—and stuck rigidly to his 'old ways' of doing things." This included refusing to let the team fly to away games. "We dragged ourselves across the country so many times we felt like Lewis and Clark."[13]

For a guy who was being banked on to be a big part of the Giants' offensive future, Gifford got off to a poor start with Owen. Owen may have given birth to the A formation, now fading from prominence, but he was generally renowned as a defensive coach, and Gifford figured that out right away. Gifford carried a serious grudge against Owen.

"Because Steve either didn't understand the offensive game or couldn't have cared less about it, his best players could always be found on defense," Gifford said. "As for handling people, Steve believed in intimidation. You know, yell at 'em and they'll play better. As far as I'm concerned, that's ridiculous."[14]

Gifford always believed that many of the older veterans on the team resented his presence in the first training camp, looking to cut him down to size because of the hype surrounding his college success and his Hollywood background.

At that time, though, having recovered from the sad days of the late 1940s, the Giants were viewed as one of the top teams in the league.

Chapter 12. The Old Man

After 10–2 and 9–2–1 seasons, New York was back, right near the top of the conference. Owen seemed secure in his position, and it seemed likely the Giants would contend for the top spot again in 1952. Gifford had another bit part, away from Hollywood, with his limited time on the field.

But the Giants did not produce the expected season. They were pretty good, but that was all, going 7–5. It was not what fans and management were looking for.

Arnie Weinmeister, the defensive tackle who was a native of Saskatchewan, was kinder in his recollections of playing for Owen between 1950 and 1953, but he had some of the same criticisms as Gifford, from a football standpoint.

> Steve was a rotund, fun-type individual. He was a very down-to-earth guy, a great defensive coach. His only problem was that he spent almost all his time on defense and almost no time on offense. So we wound up having the best defense in the league, but we didn't score any points to speak of, and therefore we didn't win as many games as we should have.[15]

Weinmeister was protective of Charlie Conerly and felt badly when fans booed him or taunted him from the stands. Once, Weinmeister began yelling back at a heckler and made a move to climb into the grandstand to emphasize his point. The man disappeared in an eyeblink.

Two two-game losing streaks essentially cost the Giants a premium finish in the 1952 standings. It was a season that emphasized parity in the NFL. No team recorded a mark better than 9–3, one in the American Conference, the Detroit Lions, and the Los Angeles Rams in the National Conference. So the championship game opponents were easily delineated. The Cleveland Browns finished 8–4, and the Philadelphia Eagles and the San Francisco 49ers equaled the Giants' 7–5 record. There was no dominant regular-season team.

New York continued to be somewhat sluggish on offense, its 234 points ranking only 10th-best in the league. While the team's 231 points allowed rated as high as fifth-best, it was not enough to rescue the club when the total was almost dead-even with the offense.

Charlie Conerly was the lead quarterback once more, but the passing game was shy of devastating. He completed 82 of 169 attempts for 13 touchdowns and 1,090 yards. At different times, Owen asked a cross-section of players to toss the ball, including defensive back Tom Landry and rookie Frank Gifford, although the true second-stringer was Fred Benners.

Benners, who attended the University of the South and Southern Methodist, was no challenger to Conerly. He appeared in six games and was 25 for 58 while throwing zero touchdown passes and five interceptions. This was Benners' only NFL year.

The Giants' 1952 season opened on September 28 against a new team, the Dallas Texans, who were a warm-up for the Baltimore Colts of 1953 and an early attempt to place pro football in Dallas. In 1960, not only was there a new Dallas Texans club in the fledgling American Football League, but an expansion Dallas Cowboys team in the NFL. The AFL Texans gave it a good fight but became the Kansas City Chiefs.

The Texans of 1952 were the worst team in the league, finishing 1–11. The Giants began the season by thrashing Dallas, 24–6, a better showing for the defense than the offense, although New York scored in every quarter. Conerly threw one touchdown pass but only gained 78 yards through the air.

New York moved to 2–0 by thumping the Philadelphia Eagles, 31–7. Conerly threw one touchdown pass, and so did Gifford. Ray Poole's foot was quite helpful with four extra points and a 16-yard field goal.

The plurality wasn't as significant, but a third straight victory provided feel-good vibes for New York when the Browns were toppled, 17–9, in Cleveland in a game that attracted 51,858 spectators. The Browns' only scoring came from Lou Groza, who nailed three field goals. The biggest play of the game was a 70-yard TD pass from Conerly to Bob Wilkinson. In shades of Giants tradition, Tom Landry intercepted a pass that he ran back 20 yards for another touchdown.

Things were humming into mid–October—and then they weren't. The Chicago Cardinals squeaked past the Giants, 24–23, in a game that got away in the fourth period. It wasn't Conerly's fault. He heaved three touchdown passes, of 15, 34 and 18 yards, and he also ran the ball in for a two-point conversion. But Cardinals stars Ollie Matson, on a six-yard rush, and Charlie Trippi, on a one-yard run, made big plays that barely pushed Chicago past New York.

Worse, the Eagles recovered from the first beating and edged the Giants in a rematch, 14–10. The New York offense sputtered, and the only reason the game was as close as it turned out was a third-quarter blocked punt touchdown by New York's Bud Sherrod. There was the defense carrying more than its equal burden yet again. Now the Giants were 3–2.

The Giants started to get well again in a second match with the Cardinals, this time capturing the contest, 28–6. No late heroics were necessary. New York ran the show this time. Conerly hurled two touchdown passes, one to Bill Stribling for 52 yards and another to Bob McChesney that traveled 39 yards. The Giants were bolstered by a 75-yard TD run by Eddie Price.

Chapter 12. The Old Man

The next week brought a tough match-up with the 49ers. By then, San Francisco was quarterbacked by Y.A. Tittle, a future Hall of Famer and, ironically, the man who would eventually take over the Giants' controls from Conerly. New York won this one, 23–14. Tittle tossed two touchdown passes and Conerly one. Ray Poole's foot was the difference in the game. He kicked one extra point but was accurate on three field goals of 40, 25, and 25 yards. At the final gun, both teams held 5–2 records.

This presented the Giants with an opportunity to recoup lost ground in the American Conference, but then they presented little challenge to the mediocre Green Bay Packers, who would finish 6–6 that year. This 17–3 defeat hurt. The offense did little, and the defense didn't do enough, so it was a game easy to second-guess. Babe Parilli, who would later excel for the Boston Patriots, threw a touchdown pass and ran for another. The only scoring for New York was a Ray Poole field goal. Conerly had a forgettable day, gaining just 42 yards through the air. There were games like that when Conerly wasn't even asked to throw often.

Despite winning, 14–10, over the Redskins, to improve to 6–3, it was not an impressive victory for the Giants. Benners was the New York quarterback most of the day, but Conerly did score on a short run. Washington was only 2–7, so it was not a major triumph, but a W nonetheless.

Still, there was no reason to think the Giants were headed to a big-time shellacking the next week when they were crushed, 63–7, by the 4–6 Pittsburgh Steelers. This was a shocking defeat, one nearly as lopsided as the all-time most decisive NFL championship game of 1940, when the Chicago Bears destroyed the Redskins, 73–0. This was up there with the most embarrassing losses in Giants history. Of all things, the only New York score came on a 55-yard touchdown pass to Bill Stribling—from Tom Landry. Somehow, Owen got it in his head to try Landry at quarterback, and the regular defensive back also threw four interceptions.

Doing their best to regain their equilibrium, the Giants fell again the next week, this time 27–17, to the Redskins. Conerly didn't even play because of injury, and Landry was handed the ball again. He threw three interceptions this time, and it was pretty much determined that he had been playing on the proper side of the ball all along. This was the coming-out party season for Washington's Eddie LeBaron, who assumed the quarterback role from Sammy Baugh four games into the season. LeBaron threw 14 touchdown passes on his way to Rookie of the Year recognition, and three came against the Giants in this game.

A once-promising season had collapsed, and going into the final week of the year, the Giants were just 6–5 and facing a bruising battle with the rival Cleveland Browns. It was desperation time for New York to look good. And the Giants did, winning 37–34 before 41,610 fans at the Polo Grounds.

This was a fun game for spectators with the Giants building an early lead and withstanding a furious fourth-quarter rally by the Browns, who came up with 14 points to make the result close. Otto Graham passed for 279 yards and two touchdowns but was guilty of tossing three interceptions.

This was one of the greatest games of Charlie Conerly's career. He tossed four touchdown passes to carry New York to this victory. Four different Giants caught touchdown passes, Stribling, Rote, Joe Scott, and Bob Wilkinson. Allowed the freedom to throw more often, Conerly completed 16 passes for 184 yards and did not throw an interception.

After the up-and-down events that left the Giants questioning their status, the last-day win felt like something special. It was the team's third straight winning year, and there was a belief that the 1953 season would hold more than this one.

Chapter 13

1953: The Worst Year

When the New York Giants' offense stagnated, Charlie Conerly was booed. That had become fairly routine; even though he almost always had only limited protection from his offensive line, the blame fell on him.

In 1953, the boos and heckling became more widespread. Fans were upset with the whole team because it had reverted to the depressing days of yesteryear in the late 1940s, when the losses stacked up like cordwood. After the team had gone 10–2, 9–2–1 and 7–5, Giants supporters were prepped for a major success story in 1953. Instead, the season became as disastrous as the sinking of the *Titanic*. The team hit an iceberg early and took the rest of the fall to sink completely.

Charlie Conerly remained the starting quarterback, and there were no reasonable back-ups, even the pretenders of 1952 gone from the roster. As much as he was under siege from defensive rushers who constantly put the pressure on him in many ways, Conerly had a solid season throwing the ball. He completed 143 of 303 pass attempts for 1,711 yards and 13 touchdowns. The one glaring, unfortunate stat was interceptions—he tossed 25 of them.

Eddie Price and Kyle Rote each caught 26 passes to lead the team. There was virtually no complementary running game, however. The team's leading rusher, Sonny Grandelius, amassed just 258 yards on the ground. Two others topped 200, but that was for the entire season.

The Giants simply couldn't find the end zone this season, totaling just 179 points all year. That ranked them last in the league. Compounding the situation, the defense allowed 277 points, not as good as it had been. Those telling statistics added up to a dismal 3–9 record.

The tension was high in New York—and at home games—in the stands, before games, after games, whenever players passed through crowds. Loud displeasure was expressed, fans grumbling about the Giants' losses and booing players, and sportswriters criticizing the results.

"I don't mind being knocked when I deserve it," Conerly said of the newspaper content, "and there are plenty of times when I do. But I know when I play poorly and reading some reporter's description of it isn't going to help me improve. They have to write what they see, but I don't have to read it."[1]

Conerly had a post-game confrontation with a fan, someone who was young, likely in his teens, but built larger than Conerly. The individual blocked Conerly's path to the dressing room, began yelling nasty words at him, then pushed Conerly. Conerly responded, "Take your hands off me," and when the young man threw a punch, hitting Conerly on the shoulder, Conerly retaliated by slapping him in the face.[2]

Opening day in 1953 was September 27, and the tone was set for New York immediately with a 21–7 loss to the Los Angeles Rams. It was 21–0 before the Giants scored. A week later, New York dropped to 0–2, falling 24–14 to the Pittsburgh Steelers. Both Giants touchdowns came on passes from Conerly. The record devolved to an ugly 0–3 with a 13–9 loss to the Washington Redskins. The biggest play for New York was Frank Gifford scoring on an 18-yard lateral.

It was obvious after a brief three weeks that the Giants of 1953 were a flop and nowhere near the caliber of team that had been projected. They were not going to be contenders but hoped to be survivors. Depending on the definition, they probably didn't make it.

It was a relief when New York bested the Chicago Cardinals, 21–7, for its first win of the year. The capstone score came on a 60-yard Conerly TD pass to Ray Pelfrey. But that was a one-in-a-row winning streak, and the Giants followed up with a disappointing 7–0 loss to the unbeaten Cleveland Browns. New York gained just 67 yards on the ground and 95 through the air, and Conerly threw three interceptions.

The schedule was lucky enough to present the Chicago Cardinals again, and New York prevailed again, this time 23–20. The Cardinals, at 0–6, were worse than the 2–4 Giants. Kyle Rote grabbed two touchdown passes, one from Conerly and one from seldom-used Arnie Galiffa. With his 129 yards passing, this was the best game of Galiffa's career. The toss to Rote was a 70-yard play.

That was pretty much the high point of the year for the Giants, who went on a three-game losing streak afterward. It wasn't pretty. The November 8 contest versus the Philadelphia Eagles at Connie Mack Stadium produced a 30–7 loss. Philly quarterback Bobby Thomason threw four touchdown passes. New York's only score came on a TD pass from Conerly to Gifford, a 32-yarder in the fourth quarter. Philadelphia's excellent ends, Bobby Walston and Pete Pihos, caught two touchdowns apiece.

Chapter 13. 1953: The Worst Year   101

The bad news kept on coming after that. The next loss came at the hands of the Steelers, 14–10. Gifford's six-yard catch from Conerly was the only New York touchdown. Interestingly, Gifford kicked the extra point. After falling to the Redskins, 24–21, the Giants were 2–7 and dead men walking in terms of playoff hopes. Conerly tossed a touchdown pass to Kyle Rote, and Gifford scored a touchdown on the ground, but Washington rallied with 17 points in the fourth quarter to overtake the Giants.

Although many players took physical beatings, Frank Gifford always thought Conerly was disproportionately singled out for negative attention when the Giants lost. "The guy who really suffered, however, was poor Charlie Conerly," Gifford said.

> Charlie was a brilliant quarterback, but in those early years he had pitiful support. We had no really talented receivers and some of our offensive linemen were barely bigger than he was. Typically, the press and fans assumed the quarterback was responsible for everything wrong with the team. Charlie became the focal point for an incredible amount of anger, almost all of it unfair.[3]

Gifford said years later that the only fight he was in as an adult occurred as he and Conerly were exiting a stadium after a game. "After one defeat toward the end of the season, a couple of guys waited an hour or so outside our locker room just to heckle him," Gifford said. "I never have, and never will, understand people like that. They're like the ghouls who hang around a car crash."[4]

Gifford said "one of the idiots" began insulting Conerly, who kept on walking with Gifford a step or two behind. They had waited an hour for this? Gifford, tired from playing, dispirited from losing, lost his temper when one of the harassers "said something about 'your motherfucking quarterback.'" So Gifford "laid him out" with what he called a slap, but which he said dropped the man like a rock.[5]

If fans thought the Eagles loss measured the depths of the team, they did not anticipate the massacre handed down by the Browns on December 6 in front of 40,235 fans at Cleveland Municipal Stadium. The rejuvenated Browns, better than just good compared to 1952, moved to 11–0 with this dismemberment of their rivals. The final score was 62–14. Both New York touchdowns came on passes from Conerly.

This stunning and overpowering defeat spelled the end of the lengthy Steve Owen coaching tenure. He had taken the reins in 1931 when still a player, weathered some lean times, produced some championship teams, but he was under increasing flak for too many recent losses and a lack of offensive ingenuity. There was a mounting crescendo that Owen had to go to allow the Giants to start fresh.

Owner Tim Mara, who had hired Owen originally, and his sons, Jack and Wellington Mara, who had taken on increased roles in the operation of the franchise, called Owen into a meeting after the Cleveland debacle. They informed him he was being let go after the season, which had one more game to run against the Detroit Lions. Jack Mara gave Owen the bad news, with the proviso that the Maras would make room in the front office for him with some type of job. Owen was unhappy but decided he should coach the final regular-season game to complete his tenure.

When Jack Mara spoke to *New York Times* columnist Arthur Daley, breaking the news, there was sadness in his voice. "It was the toughest thing I ever had to do," Jack Mara said. "Steve was like family."[6]

The grim season ended on December 13 with a 27–16 loss to the 10–2 Detroit Lions. The Lions scored once in each quarter and were in control from the beginning of play. Conerly threw one touchdown pass of 49 yards to Gifford, and Gifford threw his own touchdown pass to Ray Pelfrey. The season ended at the Polo Grounds at 3–9 with a whimper, the Giants' future surrounded by question marks.

Gifford always remembered the post-game scene in the locker room. He sat for a long time in his uniform, bloodied and muddied. He was unprepared when Tim Mara approached him, shook his hand, and said, "We thank you." Then Mara put an envelope into Gifford's locker. "Then he was gone," Gifford said. "I discovered that it contained five hundred-dollar bills. It doesn't sound like much now and I don't know why T.J. did it, or whether he ever did it for anyone else, But I was very moved—and I also needed the money."[7]

No one knew who was going to coach the Giants in 1954. Everyone knew it was not going to be Steve Owen, who didn't want a front office position. He was bitter about his dismissal but returned to coaching for two seasons starting in 1956 for the Eagles, then moved on to the Canadian Football League. He spent four seasons in the CFL as a head man with three teams. Owen was 66 when he died in 1964, and he was inducted into the Pro Football Hall of Fame two years later.

Many kind words were written about Owen when he passed away from a cerebral hemorrhage. The loudest praise for Owen revolved around his invention of the umbrella defense and his emphasis on the A formation offensively, but he didn't brag about that kind of stuff. As evidence of his old-school connections, Owen declared, "You can put in a hundred systems, but football is still blocking and tackling."[8]

Most of the newspapers wrote nice things when Owen died, but they were also realistic about his overall characteristics and his unwillingness to embrace other changes in the sport when they became otherwise accepted.

"The game got away from him and people forgot how skillful he had been and reckless," wrote syndicated columnist Jimmy Cannon. "He was a creator of the sport, but it moved past him because he tried to keep football close to its origins. He made the kids play it as he had. He resisted the T and went with the A."[9]

Ultimately, that would be like a driver wanting to stick with the Model T Ford when the much smoother-riding, better-developed Model A succeeded it. That, as much as anything, probably cost Steve Owen his job as coach of the Giants despite a lifetime NFL regular-season record of 153–100–17, or a winning percentage of .598.

The Giants—and the Maras—planned to go on without Owen for the 1954 season. However, the team wanted to guarantee it wouldn't have to go on without its first-string quarterback, Charlie Conerly, too. The 1953 season wore Conerly down, physically by the constant pounding delivered by energetic defenses, and mentally, whether he admitted it out loud or not, by losing and maybe catching the blame for what went wrong. Friends and relatives insisted Conerly never complained about being taunted, that he shrugged insults off as if they were raindrops repelled by an all-weather jacket.

Conerly's level of self-confidence, self-awareness, and self-possession enabled him to dismiss unwarranted criticism. As he put it, he knew how he played and didn't need anyone else to give him grief about the off days.

As usual, after the 1953 season, Charlie and Perian Conerly departed New York for Mississippi and their off-season in the Delta, home where family resided and where Conerly had the 225-acre farm. Unlike the modern athlete, the pros who were underpaid in that era took on winter jobs, sometimes as car salesmen, sometimes as insurance salesmen, something to raise a little money or get their foot in the door for a second career after retirement. They did not spend all of their free time working out because they didn't have that much free time, especially if they had a wife and kids to support.

Conerly had a wife but no children (the Conerlys never did have any of their own), and the farm came under the supervision of his father. Conerly said he would have worked in Clarksdale in the off-season, but there was no real opportunity.

"There weren't any kind of decent jobs you could get for half the year," Conerly said, "so I just played golf every day."[10] Quite a few richer athletes these days who don't have to think about seasonal employment do the same thing.

The Conerlys enjoyed their free time in New York City, as long as Charlie wasn't being booed in public when they went out socially, but they also liked being home in Mississippi, on familiar ground. It provided a nice balance. But things were a bit different after the 1953 season. Conerly and the Giants were down, and he let it be known to team management that he might not come back for the next year, that he might retire and stay in Mississippi.

Perian had a good sense of humor and, while put off by the gossip, gradually got used to the beauty parlor talk about how Charlie and Perian had split up again because Conerly left in late summer for training camp. "The rumors are flying again," Perian heard from a friend. "I overheard Mrs. So-and-So in the beauty parlor telling her hairdresser, 'Well, he's left her again. I have it on very good authority she has instituted divorce proceedings. Can't much blame Perian, the way Charlie just runs off like that. I just don't see how she has stood it so long.'"[11]

Even into the 1950s, that outlook was still measuring the lack of nationwide attention pro football received, only to change later in the decade when more and more games were shown on national television. Another prominent Mississippi football player who joined the Giants was defensive back Jimmy Patton. By the time Patton arrived in 1955, there was more exposure.

> Well-meaning citizens of Greenville, Mississippi, no longer ask All-Pro safety Jimmy Patton, "Where are you stationed now, Jim Boy?" assuming that his periodic absences from his hometown could mean only that he was in the Army. What else? Today the local barber, or the milkman, or the preacher is more like to ask, "Say, Jim, is Big Daddy Lipscomb [a near-300-pounder] really as big as he looks on television?"[12]

There were several pluses to spending time in Clarksdale. Lulu Maness said her father, Tony Malvezzi, and Charlie Conerly were best friends since kindergarten, and for her, Charlie and Perian were like an additional set of parents.

"Our families were very close," said Maness, who is administrator at the Mississippi Sports Hall of Fame and Museum and the Conerlys' goddaughter. "They lived just a block from us." Sometimes, before the NFL was ubiquitous on television, she and her family would drive a couple of hundred miles to the closest city where they could rent a hotel room and watch the Giants play a game on TV.[13]

Lulu remembered as a little girl taking a trip to New York to stay with Perian in the Concourse Plaza Hotel, see the sights of the big city, and attend a Giants game in person. Another time she recalls taking the train from New York to Washington in Perian's care to see the Giants play the Redskins.

When Lulu was a youngster, she mingled with several of the

famous Giants players who were Charlie's teammates, like Alex Webster and Frank Gifford.

Lulu's family and the Conerlys made annual trips to Panama City, Florida's beach area, each summer. They went for two weeks, and "we would put Charlie on the airplane from there to go to training camp."[14]

Of course, that was all about rooting for Charlie, but for Perian and Charlie it was like having their own child for a while. Later in life, when Perian was in her 90s, Lulu was her caretaker. For a time, harkening back to the old days, Lulu joined Perian with season tickets in the stands for Ole Miss games.

Conerly had been through some hard knocks in New York in the Giants' backfield, including being a square peg fitted into a round hole as a quarterback-tailback in the A formation instead of always being the throwing quarterback he was in the T-formation. He had even less desire to run the football, or, especially, to be counted on for blocking now that he was in his 30s than he had been when he came out of Ole Miss.

He had been bruised, battered (and luckily not injured worse), and verbally pelted, and now the Giants seemed to be going backward. He let the Maras know he might just stay in Mississippi rather than return to New York City for the 1954 NFL campaign.

However, that year and almost every year, whenever Conerly felt he had performed well enough to be given a raise, he prepared his arguments and a speech to pitch his qualifications to Wellington Mara. He met with Mara face to face, ready to bargain, and yet he was spared much stress in negotiations because the Giants had already planned to pay him at least that much money. He didn't have to fight for raises; he was granted them.

Once before a season, Conerly arranged a meeting with Mara in a hotel room, completely ready to lay out reasons why he should be compensated more. He had declared as much to his wife, and the next day when he telephoned her with the result, Conerly said, "And you know what happened? I went to his room and before I even had a chance to sit down and light a cigarette, Well said, 'Charlie, you had such a good year we think you ought to have a raise.' And he handed me a contract already filled out for the exact amount I was going to ask for—down to the last penny. So I signed it!"[15]

Perian said this happened repeatedly over Charlie's career with the Giants, him having a figure for a salary demand ready in his head and then being blindsided by favorable offers from the Maras matching what he had in mind. It was so frequent, Perian said, "I began to wonder if they had our house bugged."[16]

The next season, after the disappointment of 1953, was once again a good year to be a Giant. There was a new regime led by coach Jim Lee Howell. Tom Landry was still honing his expertise as a defensive coach, on the way to his own greatness, and a new offensive assistant was on the scene. Vince Lombardi joined the staff, a man working his own way up to football genius status and someone who in many quarters became known as the greatest coach of all time for his leadership with the Green Bay Packers.

The Giants also beefed up the roster in 1954, picking up the kind of talent that leads to winning championships.

Chapter 14

New Look Giants

He was a known quantity but a surprising choice by management because Jim Lee Howell, like his predecessor Steve Owen, could also be defined as old school and because his football head coaching experience consisted of being the leader of tiny, nearby Wagner College.

Wagner is located in Staten Island, New York, essentially just down the street from the Polo Grounds or Yankee Stadium, but it wasn't as if the Seahawks had their names called to compete in major college bowls. Howell was from Arkansas and was a star football and basketball player at the University of Arkansas before joining the Giants as an end—and playing for Owen for several years.

Howell became a Giant in 1937, was with the club until 1942, spent parts of four years in the service during World War II, and played for New York again in 1946 and 1947 before retiring. He took over Wagner's team that same year and remained in the neighborhood through the 1953 season, when he wasn't operating a 700-acre pig farm back home in Arkansas.

When the Maras began a search for Owen's replacement, Howell was certainly conveniently located. He was neither on the lips of those nominating replacements nor any kind of favorite choice for the job. It was Frank Gifford who at first expressed concern about what type of leader Howell might be (too much like Owen) and then enthusiasm that he might bring needed change.

> We needed something different and Steve wasn't giving it to us. If anything, he [Howell] was a fair man and he knew a hell of a lot about football. We were sure there would be new things, a new concept. I, for one, almost fell over when I heard it was Jim Lee, but then I couldn't wait for training camp to start in 1954. I was really excited.[1]

The Giants' roster needed a shake-up, but that meant cutting the right people and keeping the right people. Chief among the keepers who was in jeopardy of departing was quarterback Charlie Conerly. Conerly turned 33 in 1954, though few knew that fact. His body certainly did.

His body reminded him constantly of one of the key Giants weaknesses—the offensive line and solid blocking. Conerly was in danger of retiring. Between Howell and the Maras, he was assured things would be different and he should stick around to experience the changes.

Howell's promise to Conerly was that he would sign tackles and guards who could protect him. "If you do that," Conerly said, "I'll try it."[2]

Conerly had reached a new plateau in terms of taking care of his future health and/or playing career. The man of few words had by then already played the latter part of one game with a separated shoulder without telling Owen or the trainers.

After the game, Conerly told Owen that he had been playing hurt. Owen was aghast and asked, "Why didn't you tell me?" Conerly stoically replied, "Why bother? I was the only quarterback you had. The others were injured, and I figured I was better than none at all."[3]

The Giants did come through on the promise of finding more and better offensive linemen. Some key linemen had previously been draft choices but had military service obligations. Some had not been tabbed to start. Among the keys for the 1954 season were such offensive line luminaries as tackle Roosevelt Brown (drafted in 1953), a future Hall of Famer, center Ray Wietecha (drafted in 1950), and guard Jack Stroud (picked in 1951). Like Brown, they became staples in the line for years, fixtures for the next decade. Just like that, whether it was giving those guys a chance to develop or recognizing their abilities, Howell had rebuilt the offensive line in a New York minute.

Tom Landry was still on the premises as defensive coordinator-defensive back, and at 30 years old in 1954, he had one of the finest years as a player. He was a holdover from Owen, but Howell did not want to tamper too much with a defense that had been a stronger point in recent years. The way things work in the present-day National Football League, Landry would have been ousted so a new coach could bring in his own man. But then, Landry would never be allowed to be a player-coach in the current NFL, either.

It was Landry who was a leading proponent of the 4–3 defense the Giants shifted to after Owen's creation of the umbrella's 6–1–4. Landry relied on two variations of the 4–3, an inside version and an outside version. Players covered zones more than individuals.

What set Landry apart from other active players was that he knew everything each of the 11 players on the field should be doing. It was one thing to memorize his responsibilities in the secondary, but he understood each player's role and what they should be doing when the ball was snapped.

Chapter 14. New Look Giants

One of the Giants' stalwart defensive tackles of the 1950s was Dick Modzelewski, whose brother Ed played fullback for the Cleveland Browns. Despite being fierce rivals on the field, the blood-is-thicker-than-water brothers talked football. One of those topics was how impressed Dick was with Landry.

"Most guys play ball and they know their position," Ed Modzelewski said. "But Dick said Tom Landry was so far ahead of everybody else. He reminded me of Chuck Noll. They were in-depth. They wanted to know about what this guy does, what that guy does, what's the reason for this, what's the reason for that."[4]

Noll, of course, became a highly successful head coach later, winning four Super Bowl titles with the Pittsburgh Steelers.

Everyone connected to the Giants realized the defense was in capable hands if Landry stayed involved in calling formations. There was much more worry about the offense. Howell was more offensively oriented than Owen, but that was easy enough to be. The Giants needed more explosiveness, needed to allow Charlie Conerly to throw the ball unmolested. Many of the needs were apparent.

With Owen gone, there would be a new, hopefully livelier approach on offense. Howell and the Maras concurred that fresh blood was a good idea. The man they brought in to orchestrate offensive innovation was known in the football world, but not someone who had a public visage among fans. That would change in the coming years in New York but would become much more magnified in the late 1950s and through the 1960s when Vince Lombardi emerged as perhaps the greatest pro football coach for the work he did leading the Green Bay Packers.

Due to his strong ties to Green Bay and the history written there, some people tend to forget Lombardi's roots. He was born in Brooklyn, New York, on June 11, 1913, and went to college at Fordham University. By coincidence, Wellington Mara was a member of the same freshman class in 1933.

The two men were not close friends in college, though they knew each other and shared some classes. Mara's future was linked to the Giants, and even in his 20s he did some scouting for the team. There was a college football legend in the making at Fordham. Although those days have long since passed, the Rams were a power in the 1930s under former Notre Dame exemplar Jim Crowley. The line coach was Frank Leahy, a future Fighting Irish leader of great teams.

During this period, it was the Fordham offensive line that stood out. One of the seven players highlighted for praise with the nickname "the Seven Blocks of Granite" was Vince Lombardi. The 1936 squad was the primary recipient of the nickname. Lombardi graduated in 1937 and spent one year playing minor league football for an outfit called the Brooklyn Eagles.

Then he began his coaching career. Initially, he was a great success in New Jersey high school ball. Steve Owen became aware of him and wrote a note to Wellington Mara, pointing out the potential of Lombardi.

Lombardi returned to his alma mater as an assistant coach for the 1947 and 1948 seasons and then left Fordham again to become an assistant for Army between 1949 and 1953. This was immediately after the heyday of Army football under the legendary leader Earl "Red" Blaik, whose teams won three national titles in the mid–1940s. By the time Lombardi went to work for New York, he was 41 years old.

Actually, when Lombardi received a phone call from the Maras asking him to interview, he thought it was for the head coaching position, to replace Owen. He was disappointed when he learned otherwise. Still, the assistant's job paid more than he was making for Army. He asked Blaik for a raise to stay but was turned down. Blaik said he was already at the top of the school scale.

Many may be surprised that Lombardi had been turned down for numerous college football head coaching jobs by then. He desperately wanted to run his own program. But openings had come and gone, and he had received recommendations from Blaik, one of the pre-eminent names in the game, and he still had been passed over.

The job in New York was still not a sure thing because Wellington Mara wanted to make sure Jim Lee Howell approved. He sent Lombardi to Arkansas for a meeting. Howell was enthusiastic and promised Lombardi he would have full say over offensive operations.

That was good enough for Lombardi, but the city boy in him, the New Yorker in him, could barely get over the environment of Lone Okie, Arkansas, and Howell's pig-farm operation. It seemed as if Lombardi could dine out on that story for the rest of his life, starting with his report back to Mara.

"I remember him laughing about all of the cow [crap] in Lone Okie, Arkansas," Mara said. "Lombardi told me he spent as much time dodging piles of cow dung as he did talking football."[5]

Howell, the head coach, became Howell, the manager, leaving Lombardi to boss the offense and Landry in charge of the defense. He was wise enough to shelve his own ego and spread the glory along with the responsibility. In newspaper analysis of the time, it was stated that this was a new way of running a football team. There was more delegation of authority than sports insiders and fans were used to seeing.

The more the setup was pondered, the less confusing it seemed to others. It was written off as a new corporate trend applied to a sports team rather than a regular business. In the broad picture, no one really cared much as long as the structure worked. As always, in sports, the bottom line was about winning, the antidote to problems in pro sport.

The timing was crucial in the careers of Landry and Lombardi, with both on the way up, ambitious men who hoped someday to run their own teams. They were still polishing their resumes and their own styles. They were handed laboratories where they could experiment and try out things. After an awful 3–9 season, they received a team aching for a fresh start. They were fortunate they had bosses who believed in their skills and who were counting on them. If they could execute, they could thrive.

Many who knew them felt Lombardi and Landry were very different personalities. Their outlook in producing success by their separate units could also be summed up in different ways. As a defensive leader, Landry, who demanded those on that side of the ball watch game film after game film, trained his players to anticipate and shut down what the other guys did best. Lombardi did not oversee fancy offenses. He was very much a fundamentals coach. The playbook was not complicated, but simple, featuring six or so plays with the expectation that they be perfectly executed, run so flawlessly the opposing defense could not stop them.

While Lombardi and Landry were granted extraordinary freedom, they were not free of ambition, so Mara's observation that Howell could handle men applied to his coaches as well. Everyone had to be on the same page. But Howell could also joke about the situation and how Lombardi and Landry were allowed to be mad scientists, developing and experimenting with their own formulas, with him as the head professor.

Howell even teased that despite holding the supervisory title of head coach, his main function for the Giants was to "make sure the footballs had air in them."[6]

The changeover in the coaching staff was good for Conerly. By then, the A formation was out, and he was installed as quarterback of the T-formation. No one expected him to run (Lombardi eventually picked up on that) and especially not block. The era of the big quarterback lay in the future, and Conerly, at 6-foot-1 and 185 pounds or so, was comparatively fragile.

Lombardi installed a play for the quarterback to run out of the split T, and it was worked on in practice. Then he ordered it called during an exhibition game. Frank Gifford came trotting in from the sideline with the coach's call, saying, "Lombardi wants you to run that play where you keep the ball."[7] Wishful thinking on Lombardi's part.

No telling exactly what Lombardi thought first when Conerly didn't signal for the play, probably figuring he saw something in the makeup of the defense that caused him to skip over the instruction.

That's not precisely what Conerly was thinking. "Well, I wasn't crazy, so I didn't do it," Conerly said much later. "He sent the play in a couple of other times, but I never did run it. After the game, Lombardi said to Gifford, 'How come Charlie won't run that play?' Gifford said, 'Hell, Charlie don't want to run the ball.'"[8]

Nope. By 1954, into his 30s, well into his NFL career, Charlie's body wanted no part of running the ball. Not unless he could avoid being tackled altogether on a short touchdown romp. Alas, in football, 95 percent of the time, the rule of law is much like the rule of gravity—whatever goes up must come down.

Chapter 15

The New Regime

While there were some skeptics about Jim Lee Howell, old Giant and new coach, being the right man to take over the New York Giants from Steve Owen for the 1954 season, most critics were prepared to be won over, as long as the Giants won. In that sense, if Walt Disney, Milton Berle, Harry Truman, or any other American luminary of the time ran the team and it won enough games, it would have been okay.

The key element as the 1954 season began with Howell in charge for his first season as coach in the National Football League was demonstration of significant progress after the dismal 1953 season. Nobody, not the Mara family or the fans, never mind quarterback Charlie Conerly, was going to put up with that again.

Essential for Howell was a better record, theoretically easy enough to come by, and just as important, an upgrade in the roster talent that promised more than a single season's worth of improvement, players capable of long-term growth. The two elements went together. Howell had to find some better guys or exploit the talents of players on the roster who were coming into their own and then win with them.

He did so. The Giants fought through the 1954 NFL season with a 7–5 record. That was not good enough to win a division title, but it was a four-win improvement, and newcomers and returning guys shone. In year one, Howell made believers out of observers, made them think the Giants were on the way up. It may have sounded harsh, but quickly enough after Steve Owen's long tenure, the prevailing mood was, "Who's he?"

Howell undertook a tenure that ran through 1960, a stretch of the 1950s that unlocked Giants potential and accounted for a record of 53–27–4, an overall winning percentage of .663.

The 1954 season started on September 26, with the Giants matched against the Chicago Cardinals. The game was played at Comiskey Park, home of the Chicago White Sox, and from New York's standpoint it deserved a bigger viewing audience than the 16,780 ticket buyers. The

Giants clobbered the Cardinals, 41–10, showing more offensive firepower than at any time during 1953. The Giants of that forgettable season did not crack 30 points in a game all year. The Cardinals result was a herald of what was to come in 1954—on both sides of the ball.

This was immediately taken note of by the daily sports pages covering the Giants. The scribes who watched the Giants regularly were not used to seeing such offensive explosiveness. "This team can go," went one comment. Howell and offensive coordinator Vince Lombardi were asked to promptly "take a long, deep bow" because the Giants now seemed to be "designed for deadly striking power."[1]

Conerly contributed two touchdown passes of 45 and 19 yards, both to Bob Schnelker. Kicker Ben Agajanian booted field goals of 41 and 38 yards and five extra points. Interestingly, the Cardinals' kicker was Pat Summerall. Soon enough, Summerall would be the Giants' kicker.

As the tight end, Schnelker was one of the new faces in the Giants' lineup after being a 29th-round draft pick for the Cleveland Browns in 1950 out of Bowling Green and making his NFL debut with the Philadelphia Eagles in 1953. By then, Schnelker was 25; he served in the Marines first. Including his many years as an assistant coach with several teams, Schnelker spent 27 years in the NFL. This debut year with New York made a splash. He caught 30 passes for 550 yards and eight touchdowns.

A savvy coach later, with his own skills, Schnelker recognized the key attributes in a receiver.

> A receiver has to have speed, hands, size, agility, quickness and the intelligence to run patterns and recognize defenses, which is one of the most important things in our league. So, they have to know what to look for. You just can't go out and run a line here and a line there. You've got to be able to adjust to the defenses.[2]

Smarts and tenacity are what Schnelker brought to the Giants rather than speed. He wasn't going to outsprint the defense, but he had ways to come up with the ball. He was one of those receivers who could fake a defensive back to get open but also outfight a smaller secondary player if it was a jump ball.

Schnelker was a needed fresh receiver for the Giants and Conerly. He was 6-foot-3 and 214 pounds and played tight end for New York through the 1960 season before completing his active career with the Minnesota Vikings and Pittsburgh Steelers in 1961. Schnelker caught 211 NFL passes, most of them for the Giants. The most impressive Schnelker statistic was running with the ball after the catch. He averaged 17.4 yards per grab during his career.

Schnelker and Lombardi developed a rapport with New York and later, when Lombardi needed another assistant to handle the passing game in Green Bay, he thought of his old pupil. "The majority of what I know about the passing game, I learned from Coach Lombardi," Schnelker said.[3] That started in 1954, when they connected for the first time.

Given that Schnelker and Conerly clicked twice in the opening game, it was apparent that the arrival of a new receiver in the mix, to complement Kyle Rote and Frank Gifford, would aid the quarterback. Don Heinrich arrived on the scene from the University of Washington and emerged as a permanent backup, although he saw very little action, and another player, Bob Clatterbuck, started two games in 1954 with Conerly out.

The defense wasn't in as much need of bulwarking as the offense, but the Giants picked up linebacker Cliff Livingston, who became a long-time contributor, out of UCLA. It was Cliff's older brother, Howie, who had been swapped to the Washington Redskins for the rights to Charlie Conerly when that club drafted the quarterback while he was in the U.S. military.

The euphoria and the high scoring lasted just one week. New York fell to the Baltimore Colts, 20–14, the first week in October. Both Giants touchdowns were scored on rushes by Frank Gifford.

Unlike the previous season, however, this defeat did not throw the Giants into a tailspin. They won their next three contests, 51–21 over the Washington Redskins, 31–17 over the Cardinals again, and 24–7 over the Redskins again. They were sitting on a 4–1 record, which already bested the entire 1953 season.

The first Redskins triumph represented one of the great recent passing games for the Giants and Conerly. Chuckin' Charlie gained 237 yards through the air and heaved four TD passes. Three of them, on throws of 27, 20 and six yards, went to Schnelker. Ken MacAfee scored on the other touchdown pass of 23 yards. Agajanian added three field goals and five extra points. He was running up as many points as a pinball machine.

For the second time around versus the Cardinals, the passing game broke out in a tricky manner. While Conerly threw one touchdown pass, supporting members of the backfield also got in on the passing action, with Gifford throwing for two TDs and Kyle Rote one. Conerly totaled by far the most yards with 123, but he also threw three interceptions.

After the Giants were through with the Redskins the second time, they were 0–5, and people in D.C. were ready to bronze Conerly's arm. In this contest, he fired three more touchdown passes, three yards to

Schnelker, 36 yards to Buford Long, and 26 yards to Eddie Price. The offensive total was 185 yards through the air.

By this point in the season, with the four wins, it was apparent that the Giants' offense was a different animal than it had been. For the first time in a while, the offense helped create excitement. Much of the success could be attributed to a stouter offensive line.

This season marked the beginning of the influence of Roosevelt Brown, Jack Stroud, and Ray Wietecha in the offensive line, a literal addition of Grade A beef and some of it unexpected.

Wietecha, a fixture at center, was born in East Chicago, Indiana, in 1928 and attended both Northwestern University and Michigan State before joining the Giants for his entire pro playing career between 1953 and 1962. He had played minor league baseball and realized he would never reach the majors. In New York, Wietecha gained so much respect playing on Vince Lombardi's Giants unit as a four-time All-Pro that Lombardi later hired him as offensive coordinator of the Packers, and he was serving in that capacity when they won Super Bowls I and II.

Once Wietecha moved into the starting lineup in 1954, he never moved out. He did not miss a game for 10 years, and the only time in that decade he missed a few minutes of playing time occurred in 1959 when he volunteered to sit down so another player could get onto the field for a change. A fan joked that a Wietecha appearance on the gridiron was a certainty like death and taxes.

Injury is much more common in football than in other pro sports, but Wietecha was never seriously hurt during a regular season. "Just the regular bumps and bruises," he said. "I've been lucky that way."[4] Once, Wietecha did injure a knee, but that happened during exhibition play, so when he sat out three games it didn't count against his consecutive games streak.

Wietecha played when linemen were larger than the average man on the street but nowhere as big as they are in the NFL now. In the modern game, centers are humongous compared to what they were like in the 1950s.

Wietecha said he was just over 195 pounds when he showed up at Giants training camp, spurted to 215 pounds, and finally topped out in the 230 range. "When I joined the Giants, I went up fast," he said.[5]

As time passed and Wietecha established himself as a force in the NFL, spilling over into his 30s, he gained verbal respect from teammates and coaches. Kyle Rote, for one, expressed his feelings in teasing fashion as Wietecha approached his 10th season rooted to his position. "Most fellows stay in pro football a couple of years until they learn what it's all about," Rote said of the sport of so many hard knocks. "Then

Chapter 15. The New Regime

they quit. It merely indicates that it's taken him longer to learn than others."⁶

Maybe not. Allie Sherman, who followed Jim Lee Howell as head coach of the Giants, inherited Wietecha and gave him credit for being smarter than others all around.

"Ray is as bright a lineman as I ever saw," Sherman said of Wietecha. "He has such perceptions and football intelligence that he can call changes in blocking assignments on the line of scrimmage. It's like having a second quarterback out there. Because of his resourcefulness and adaptability, we can plan plays we wouldn't dare use without him."⁷

One reason Sherman may have thought so highly of Wietecha's brain was how he perfected the no-look hike to the quarterback, something people credited him with introducing as a regular thing. Kicker Pat Summerall, who came over from the Cardinals, said Wietecha's excellent long snaps, a skill more challenging than many believe, made Summerall a superior kicker.

> Kicking field goals requires perfect timing and a good snap from the center and then a good hold, and, of course, a good kick. What helped was that Ray may have been the only center who could snap the ball without looking. That way he was looking up when he snapped the ball and was ready to block. And Charlie [Conerly] has such quick hands that as soon as he gets the snap he spins the ball so that the laces are facing forward and not toward me. In my time with the Giants, I never once saw the laces.⁸

Jack Stroud was drafted out of Tennessee in 1951 and also spent his entire NFL career with the Giants between 1953 and 1964, a period of tremendous success. Stroud, who was 6-foot-1 and weighed 235 pounds, not only played football for the Volunteers, but he was also an esteemed member of the track team. Twice he won the Southeastern Conference title in the javelin.

In some ways, despite becoming a three-time All-Pro for the Giants, Stroud was one of those anonymous linemen who were hardly ever mentioned by sports commentators and were recognized only among peers or when awards were handed out for entire elevens. He understood the ways of publicity, too, and the way it goes in the trenches at the line of scrimmage.

"They've got to have two offensive guards on every team every Sunday," Stroud said. "If you didn't show up, they'd know you weren't there. When you're pass protecting for the quarterback, like you do half the time, you're just holding off the man opposite you, letting him get all the licks. So, once in a while I like to rap him."⁹

Stroud was undersized when he came out of Tennessee as a tackle at 215 pounds and had to pound the weights to get playing time after

Steve Owen initially belittled his chances. A bulked-up Stroud made himself more valuable after Howell took command. He had to keep fighting through repeated knee injuries to stick with the Giants into the 1960s.

While all linemen are brutally strong, the ones who get ahead, as Wietecha said and Stroud echoed, use their brains as much as their brawn. "I've noticed that the boy who is the best thinker does the best job," Stroud said. "If he knows what he's doing, he has the best punch."[10]

Even later in his career, after he had been battered, Stroud still drew compliments from the best who made a living on the other side of the line. Baltimore Colt Gino Marchetti, a Hall of Fame defensive end, was one of those who admired Stroud. "He's the greatest Giant tackler I've ever faced," said Marchetti, who essentially meant blocker, since blocking was what Stroud did to him, "and one of the best I've ever played against."[11]

Despite the supposed knowledge rattling around in scouts' heads, despite what they have seen with their own eyes on the playing fields, making professional sports team draft picks of young talent, whether the athlete is just coming out of high school or college, is as much luck as science. The number of sure-thing players who don't make it is legion. The number of overlooked players who worked themselves up to starters or stars is uncountable.

There are occasional extreme exceptions, but whether it is baseball, basketball, hockey, or football, it is difficult to match the story of Roosevelt Brown. Brown was the New York Giants' 27th-round draft pick, the 322nd player selected in the 1953 NFL draft.

Las Vegas doesn't make odds on such long shots in terms of not only making the team but also of becoming a Hall of Famer. Brown, fondly called Rosey, was a 6-foot-3, 255-pound tackle out of Morgan State, an historically Black school in Baltimore. Brown developed into a nine-time Pro Bowl choice as one of the great offensive linemen of all time.

Representatives of NFL teams were tiring and just about ready to cease selecting new faces when the Giants' turn came up on the 27th round. Someone suggested they all quit, but Wellington Mara wasn't finished. The story goes that he took note of a copy of the *Pittsburgh Courier* newspaper open to a story about the previous season's "Negro All-American" team and saw a picture of Brown. The photo provoked Mara to draft the player.

It was a remarkably accidental coup. Brown became the anchor of the improved offensive line, a bodyguard for first Charlie Conerly and then Y.A. Tittle into the 1960s. Brown nearly amazed the Giants with his ability, which was also a commentary on how Black players could be overlooked by major colleges and the pros in the 1950s. After all, it was purely by chance that Brown was drafted at all.

An indication of just how a Black player of such talent could slip through cracks was the circumstance of Brown's arrival at training camp that year. Unlike more prominent draft picks, Brown, who grew up in Charlottesville, Virginia, was not well supplied for his journey to St. Peter, Minnesota, at Gustavus Adolphus College. He had $5 in his pocket and traveled with a box lunch made by his mother. There was no big advance signing bonus for a 27th-round draft choice.

At that time, All-Star Emlen Tunnell was the only other Black player on the roster. Brown made a favorable impact on him from the start. "He looked like a real football player," Tunnell said. "He was big and rangy, and he wore glasses and he was very quiet."[12]

Brown came from a predominantly Black school with all Black teammates. Now he was trying out for a team that was almost all White. He took notice of the situation. "It made me feel a little funny," Brown said. "I had never played with, or against, White players, or a White coach."[13]

Brown was somewhat naïve. He had never seen a pro game in person. He had only listened to the 1951 championship game on the radio. He thought when the Giants brought him to camp that he had the team made because he didn't know they cut players. But he learned, and learned fast, first under Steve Owen, then under Howell, when he blossomed.

As it has always almost been, offensive linemen hardly ever get featured in the news clips compared to the quarterback and receiver who combine for passing touchdowns or the running back who bursts free for long runs. Coaches used to say commonly that they couldn't tell how so-and-so did until they watched the game films. The Giants had a practice of looking at those films and then presenting the best blocker of the game with a monetary reward—$10. Otherwise, the offensive linemen could often be overshadowed.

"Glory?" Brown was asked once. "No, there's not much glory in it. But there is self-satisfaction and we have to do with that. When the newspapers say somebody ran 50 yards to a touchdown and they don't tell who made the blocks, it hurts a little. We know we sprung him and everybody else on the team knows. We made it possible."[14]

The improved offensive line in 1954 made winning more likely, made it possible, if not guaranteeing it. The 4–1 start was encouraging, and the Giants were playing at a higher level than the year before.

After the solid start, the Giants ran up against the Cleveland

Browns, who had maintained their excellence under coach Paul Brown and with stability on the roster. Quarterback Otto Graham wanted to retire, but Brown kept persuading him to stick around one more year. This time the Browns were a little bit better—not enormously so as they had been the year prior. Cleveland won, 24–14, by scoring once in each period. Charlie Conerly scored on a one-yard run, but the showcase play for New York was an 83-yard pass for a TD from Frank Gifford to Eddie Price.

The loss did not throw the Giants. Rather, it sparked a two-game winning streak. In early November, New York overpowered the Pittsburgh Steelers, 30–6, at Forbes Field. This was a grand game for Conerly. He threw three touchdown passes, one each to Ken MacAfee, Kyle Rote, and Bob Topp.

A week later, the Giants polished off the Philadelphia Eagles, 27–14. Still again Conerly tossed three touchdown passes, 35 yards to Gifford, 19 to Topp, and 17 to MacAfee. The Eagles did move the ball, mostly through the air, but their one TD pass was offset by three interceptions. This left New York at 6–2 and thinking a division crown was possible. That idea lasted about one more week and was certainly dead within two after consecutive losses, 17–16 to the Los Angeles Rams and 16–7 to the Browns.

Against Los Angeles, Conerly fired a 68-yard touchdown pass to Bob Schnelker, but all other New York scoring was produced by Ben Agajanian's foot on three field goals and an extra point. It was a close defeat and it hurt, emotionally and in the standings. The Giants could not find the end zone after the first-quarter score.

The Browns damage was worse, in both ways. The only New York score came on a 48-yard punt return by Herb Johnson. Meanwhile, Graham ran for a touchdown and Lou Groza booted three field goals and an extra point. That moved Cleveland one and a half games ahead of New York in the standings.

The Pittsburgh Steelers came around on the schedule again, and the Giants thrashed them with the same vehemence as they had earlier in the season. They did so without Conerly's help. He was out with an injury, and back-up Bob Clatterbuck threw two touchdown passes.

That brought New York to the end of the season and a difficult game versus the Eagles, who were lying in wait after an earlier loss. The Eagles took this game, 29–14. Clatterbuck played again and threw two more TD passes. The loss enabled the 7–4–1 Eagles to slip ahead of the 7–5 Giants in the Eastern Division standings for second place. The Browns won the division title with a 9–3 record, then crushed the Detroit Lions, 56–10, for the league crown.

Chapter 15. The New Regime

The Giants hoped for better but showed more flash on offense all year, and although it was under the radar somewhat, the defense was better, too. Boss Jim Lee Howell had delivered. Assistant coaches Vince Lombardi and Tom Landry delivered. When the season was over, Howell felt he had to defend the defense because everyone had focused so much on the gradual improvement of the offense.

"Tom took a green defense and transformed it into one of the best defenses in the league," Howell said of Landry's work, citing the squad's 33 interceptions.[15]

The offense totaled 293 points, a 24.4 average, and the defense allowed just 184. No one could argue with those comparative numbers. They would only get better as the 1950s wore on, but Gifford believed they may have let an opportunity get away as they were coming together. "I think we could have won our conference title in the first year of our new regime," Gifford said. "We'd gotten rid of all of our locker room lawyers and kept the guys who truly wanted to play."[16]

Then he and Rote got injured on the same play. Rote incurred a concussion and missed two games. Gifford harmed his right knee and said it bothered him the rest of his career. Gifford blamed those circumstances for losing three of their last four games.

Chapter 16

Charlie and Perian

It would be an exaggeration to suggest that Charlie and Perian Conerly were the king and queen of New York, but it would not be an exaggeration to say they were athletic royalty. From frequent appearances at Toots Shor's to being spotted at other nightclubs out on the town, Charlie's stature as quarterback of the New York football Giants conveyed status on them.

They liked to go out and take advantage of New York's cultural opportunities. Although the Giants ran behind the baseball clubs in a ranking of most prominent teams—this was the heyday of New York baseball with the Yankees, baseball Giants, and Brooklyn Dodgers all excelling and fighting it out among themselves for World Series supremacy—compared to the New York Knicks in pro basketball and the New York Rangers in the National Hockey League, the football Giants mattered more.

As quiet as Charlie was (and one must wonder whether, if he was a single guy in the big city, he would have ever stepped out anywhere except a conveniently located tavern), Perian made up for it. She was outgoing and wanted to mingle with whoever was out there, from other athletes and their spouses to actors and actresses. She wanted to have fun in New York. The pro football schedule made it easy enough to do so. Teams only played once a week, and while practice filled weekday days, Charlie could always be available for dinner.

Then the most unusual of things happened. Perian became a celebrity on her own, in an unlikely way. The 1950s was the decade of the homemaker, the stay-at-home mother who cooked, did the dishes, and took care of the kids. Only a tiny percentage of married American women held jobs outside the home.

There was not much room in the job market for women. The chauvinistic outlook was that women would be taking needed jobs from family men if they competed for positions. They were patronized whenever they did work. They were underpaid compared to men's salaries. This was all routine.

Chapter 16. Charlie and Perian

Perian Conerly ended up with a job. She didn't just waltz out of the Concourse Plaza one day to go door to door to find work. She played to her strength, her ability to write, and her uniqueness. She wryly noted how people back home in Clarksdale, Mississippi, did not seem to grasp the nature of Charlie's responsibilities in New York. There was that lingering gossip about how he deserted her for several weeks late each summer and how it was that the couple spent so much time in New York. It seems absurd in retrospect that this knowledge gap existed, but she decided to fill it.

While at Mississippi College for Women, Perian was the editor of the school newspaper. She had a passion for writing, but she had no outlet. One day she was approached by the local *Clarksdale Press Register* to see if she would be interested in writing some stories about her life with Charlie in New York, immersed in the pro football world.

The opportunity became a once-a-week article, first for the Clarksdale paper. A Jackson, Mississippi, newspaper became interested in running stories. Then the *New York Times* heard about Perian's work, and she became a syndicated columnist. This was unheard-of—and it was unique to her combination of abilities, interest, and access as an insider.

When Perian first went to New York in Charlie's second season with the Giants, she was one of several player wives who shared time and appreciated the excitement of being in the big city where they could take advantage of Broadway shows and other cultural activities. The wives sat together in the stands at home games and shared the ups and downs of winning and losing with their husbands and each other.

Once she began writing, Perian offered different perspectives to readers who might be curious about life away from the field, what life was like in New York, and what happened the other six days of the week apart from game day. There were no other female football writers around, covering the Giants or almost surely not in the rest of the country.

Eventually, Perian Conerly became the first woman accredited by the Pro Football Writers Association of America. Hers was such an unusual role that the producers of the popular television show *What's My Line?* sought her out for an appearance. After she stumped members of the panel, Charlie popped out from behind the curtain to share the stage.

Perian was keenly aware that some people resented women writing about this sport and doubted her credentials. She always had a retort. Ultimately, she wrote a book called *Backseat Quarterback*. In the book, she said some people "exhibited more curiosity than tact" when quizzing her about what made her qualified to write about pro football.[1]

She explained that her father gave her heavy-duty instruction in football, and she followed the game closely in high school and college. She called her approach to the column more like color commentary for a broadcaster than a play-by-play report.

Perian didn't even tell Charlie she was going to write a football column until she finished one and then asked him to check it. She mentioned a Broadway show and meeting Ernest Hemingway and said she had picked up some gossip from back-up quarterback Don Heinrich. She didn't even know if the Clarksdale paper, which had a circulation of 4,400, would print it. Right away she termed the column *Backseat Quarterback*. The editor sent a telegram that read "Keep them coming" and said he planned to run the stories every Saturday.[2]

From there, Perian expanded to the *Jackson Clarion-Ledger News* and then the North American Newspaper Alliance. The Mississippi reader and the national reader constituted different audiences. While Perian observed that she had always loved to write, she discovered that meeting deadlines was a different animal and ratcheted up the pressure.

Over time, while always relying on Charlie as a copy editor, she picked up different sources. After he came over from the Cardinals, Pat Summerall filled Perian in on some team news. Periodically, Charlie advised her not to put something in the paper that was private within the team.

Freelance writers in such a position were not highly paid, but Perian appreciated being someone who was working for her own money. Calling these paychecks "mad money," she jokingly said, "For the first time in my life I was independently wealthy."[3]

One humorous aspect of Perian's new relationship with the quarterback of the New York Giants, after being married to him for years, was gaining access to his football thoughts. Charlie Conerly was renowned on his team and among sportswriters as a taciturn guy, someone who would never utter a lengthy sentence when a single word would do.

He was a man who carried himself with dignity, and he projected that to his teammates. He was not a rah-ran guy who exhorted them with fiery speeches, but he led with his actions more than his words. "Charlie commands respect with quiet confidence," receiver Kyle Rote said.[4]

When asked another time by a different sportswriter, Rote expanded that same viewpoint. "He never yelled or berated anyone in the huddle," Rote said. "But there was always a strength and a determination in his manner that made us believe in him."[5]

That was one way of saying Conerly didn't say much, a theme

enunciated over and over by coaches and teammates, who at the same time watched Conerly endure physically demanding times in games and not complain about them. Sometimes he was seriously beat up and ignored it to the point where he didn't even realize it until he was in the locker room after a game.

Following one victory over the Cleveland Browns, who were always hard on him, Conerly retreated into the dressing room with cuts on his legs and bruises all over his body and on his face. He looked in the mirror and said, "Doggone, ain't I a mess?" Jack Mara, one of the team owners, passed by, stopped abruptly, and said, "Charlie, I know now that they had you in mind when they wrote that song, 'You've Gotta Have Heart.'" Pal Frank Gifford said, "Hurt much, Charlie?" Conerly formulated an answer with a small laugh. "Never hurts much when you win," he said. "It's when you lose that it hurts something fierce."[6]

That amounted to a full-blown speech for Conerly. Anecdotes like that indicate just how tough Conerly was without bragging about it or even acknowledging it. He just was. Physically, Conerly endured a lot, especially in Giants down years. He was a tackling dummy for defenses when his own men could not provide the protection necessary to keep him upright and give him time to throw. Other times, he just played hurt.

On one occasion when Steve Owen was still coaching and Conerly didn't bother telling anyone he was hurt, Owen came to realize the situation during the game just by watching. He recognized that Conerly was not his normal self. "I could see him wince when he threw," Owen said. "He knew I had nobody else. And I could only thank him from the bottom of my heart."[7]

As the Giants' roster shifted, as the team was rebuilt and grew stronger, Conerly was a constant. He rode the waves, as uneven as they were, taking the fan abuse when things were going poorly, hanging in there as things improved, and leading the team to high points after no one believed the low points would ever go away.

"Charlie Conerly of the New York Giants is a winner when it counts," wrote Jimmy Cannon. "Crisis improves him."[8] Another time Cannon wrote, "In this town, Conerly was the Giants. He was for a long time a special man like Joe DiMaggio or Pee Wee Reese, or Carl Hubbell. He was a Giant when that didn't mean much. No one I've ever covered was more of a football player than Charlie."[9]

Few of the sportswriters elicited much in-depth analysis from Conerly's lips, but once in a while his wife did. She recounted an occasion in her book when she began interviewing her husband over dinner, then shoved the dirty dishes aside and kept right on going after the meal—until she burst out laughing. "I was just thinking that a stranger who happened on this little scene would have no idea we even knew each other," Perian said. "We're both being so business-like."[10]

Generally, despite his proofreading and overall interest, Charlie was not a source for Perian's column material.

> Charlie would read it over and say either it was fine, or that I couldn't tell that so-and-so did this or that. I enjoyed it [writing the column] immensely. Of course, times were so different then. There were no women in the locker rooms, and honest, my articles were more personal public interest stories. I was the first woman in the Football Writers Association. Someone submitted my name as "Perry," and they thought I was a man. I broke the glass ceiling by accident.[11]

Perian offered the once-in-a-while insight into what Charlie was thinking, but mostly she offered her own insights into the world of pro football, aiming for a broader reading audience than people who fixated on Xs and Os. Among some of her chapter titles in the book were "The Wives Arrive," "New York Is a Winter Festival," "The Game from the Stands," "Boos," and "Cheers."[12]

In the chapter called "Boos," Perian did address the times when things were going badly for the Giants and fans took out their frustrations on Charlie, including, as she put it, a sign reading, "Back to the farm, Conerly." Yet on this topic, she is not terribly revealing about Charlie's emotions.

The man who kept them hidden from sportswriters apparently applied the same rule to his wife the sportswriter. "I am sure the expressions of disapproval left their scars," Perian wrote.

> But Charlie is a master at hiding his feelings ... even from me. Describing him as stoic would not be far from the truth. He never complains. He never offers an alibi. He rarely allows disappointment to affect him. [She exempted golf and playing cards.] He accepts undeserved criticism and valid censure with equal calm—and without expressing malice toward his detractors in either case.[13]

To whatever degree of satisfaction it gave hecklers, Conerly admitted that he heard the insults hurled his way, even if he did not let them interfere with his performance. He said he was certain pro athletes had sensitive hearing, with all negative words caught on the breeze. "But it gets to some fellows," he said.[14]

The flip side of booing is cheering, but Perian said the most intriguing aspect of positive reinforcement came in personal letters by mail, many from junior high school boys looking for football advice, from supportive fans, and from people asking for autographed pictures.

Charlie did reply to his mail, and the Conerlys did send out autographed pictures upon request.

One of the most memorable letters Charlie ever received, Perian said, came from a teenager in Minnesota who, after praising Conerly by saying, "I think you are the greatest quarterback in the world," asked to come stay with him for a summer in Mississippi so he could learn how to be a better quarterback. He would even stay in the barn on the farm. Nothing was worked out on that front except urging the young man to seek extra help from his high school coach.[15]

Charlie Conerly being quarterback of the New York Giants in the 1950s gave him and his wife entrée into high society and opened doors to good times and events they would never have experienced by staying in Mississippi. But Perian held up her end with her writing. She became a "name" as well, through her pen.

Perian's personality was more vivacious than her husband's, and her words won fans and drew attention, too. Rick Cleveland, a long-time Mississippi sportswriter who got to know both Conerlys, praised the caliber of her newspaper writing. "Perian could write," Cleveland said.

> In her columns and in her book she wrote intelligently and with much wit. She took a complicated sport and broke it down in the simplest of terms. She wrote cleverly in terms even a novice fan could easily digest. And she had great sources, people named Gifford, Rote, Summerall and "Chunkin'" Charlie Conerly.[16]

Chapter 17

Not Quite There

After the 1954 debut season of Jim Lee Howell as head coach and the posting of a 7–5 record, there was a strong feeling that the Giants were on the way to prominence, that in 1955 they would be contenders for an NFL title. Players felt good about their chances. Fans were excited. Team management thought the Giants were on the edge of a breakthrough.

They were all wrong. Instead, the Giants were the not-ready-for-primetime players. It turned into a frustrating season, characterized by close losses, but for that matter, also close wins, with one exception. The 1955 Giants did not quite jell.

It turned into more of a vamp-till-ready season. A couple of players who had been on the fringe of the roster increased their roles, and several significant players began long-term tenures with the team. Some of the best-known and key players of the era joined the Giants as rookies. There were at least six fairly new and brand-new faces who became regulars or stars who had been overlooked somewhat in 1954 or who were added in 1955.

The addition of defensive tackle Roosevelt Grier, linebacker Harland "Swede" Svare, and defensive backs Jimmy Patton and Dick Nolan sealed any cracks in the defense. Running backs Alex Webster and Mel Triplett added talent and depth to the backfield. Webster would become one of the team's legendary heroes and a Giants head coach later on. Grier and Triplett, both Black, added to the diversity of the roster as professional sports continued to change and embrace more African Americans.

Webster, Triplett, Patton, and Grier were officially rookies. Nolan was with the team the year before. Svare came over from the Los Angeles Rams after two seasons on the West Coast. The Giants had their all-star cast of coaches, but even Howell, Vince Lombardi and Tom Landry seemed to have difficulty fitting all these pieces into the lineup with the holdovers. New York was third in the league in scoring and third in the league in defensive points allowed, but the Giants had only the third-best record in the Eastern Division.

For seven years, the Giants counted on Charlie Conerly to start at quarterback. They rode his right arm and his judgment, game after game. Now, all of a sudden, the brain trust tried something new. Conerly played in all 12 regular-season games, but he started just four of them. Relying on a new look, New York started second-year man Don Heinrich most games.

It was never quite clear what the Giants were trying to accomplish with this game plan, but Conerly still ended up throwing more passes, completing 98 of 202 attempts for 1,310 yards and 13 touchdowns. Heinrich was 31 for 67 for 413 yards with two touchdowns. Overall, it was not a terribly potent passing attack this season. Frank Gifford caught 33 balls, Bob Schnelker grabbed 25, and Webster, who was the top rusher with 643 yards, caught 22 passes.

The two-quarterback approach was Vince Lombardi's idea. Heinrich was given the role of feeling out the foes before Conerly, who was supposed to be the attentive pupil on the sideline studying the action, was inserted with the goal of picking apart the enemy later. There are very few instances of an NFL team achieving great things by alternating quarterbacks.

As terrific as he turned out to be, Gifford did not feel Lombardi made a good first impression, and it took time in 1954, his first season in New York, and into 1955 for the players to warm up to him. "When Vince arrived in 1954 to take over our offense, we didn't like him at all," Gifford said. "He was loud and arrogant, a total pain in the ass. We had a lot of nicknames for him, most of them unprintable."[1]

When players gathered in a bar after practice, they did Lombardi imitations and made fun of him. They did not feel his football knowledge, accumulated from high school and college coaching, was strong enough for the pros—at first. Then the coach and the players connected, and Lombardi asked for help from older players.

"That changed the whole tone of our relationship," Gifford said. "We discovered that he was a real guy, a warm, funny guy. In terms of offensive strategy, Lombardi and the Giants learned from each other."[2]

The 1955 season opened on September 24 in Philadelphia at Connie Mack Stadium against the Eagles. The Giants were undefeated for 59 minutes, falling 27–17. New York started the season well enough, with Gifford catching a 31-yard pass from Conerly for the first touchdown. The Eagles stunned the Giants, though, when Jerry Norton returned the following kickoff 96 yards to tie the game. Ben Agajanian kicked a field goal and linebacker Cliff Livingston pounced on a fumble in the

Philadelphia end zone for another New York score. The Giants had all 17 of their points in the first half and then watched the Eagles come back and take control in the second half.

A week later, the Giants lost similarly to the Chicago Cardinals, 28–17, again scoring all of their points in the first half before an anemic crowd of 9,555 in Comiskey Park. Bob Schnelker caught a TD throw from Conerly, and Webster scored his first Giants touchdown on a run. It was 17–14 at the intermission, but the Cardinals scored all the points in the second half.

New York followed that up with a 30–23 loss to the Pittsburgh Steelers on the road. The Giants scored in every quarter this time, but just a little bit less than Pittsburgh. Conerly threw two touchdown passes, one of 34 yards to Buford Long and a long one of 71 yards to Kyle Rote. Conerly (125 yards), Heinrich (92) and Gifford (one throw for 25) combined for just shy of 300 yards through the air. That was a rarity at the time, but also a rarity that such proficiency didn't produce a victory. So the Giants, hopeful of a playoff-caliber season, were already 0–3. Their season was almost surely dead less than a month in.

Playing other teams tough wasn't satisfying. The Giants needed the Ws. Not necessarily acknowledged at the time was the value of the younger guys finding niches and assuming bigger roles on the field.

Alex Webster was a sleeper get. He grew up in New Jersey and played well for North Carolina State in college as a tailback and a defensive back. Webster was brought to North Carolina by coach Beattie Feathers, the first player to gain more than 1,000 yards rushing in a season in the NFL.

At 6-foot-3, 225 pounds, Webster turned into an excellent NFL fullback, just not right away. The Washington Redskins saw enough in him to make Webster an 11th-round draft pick in 1953 but not enough in him to keep him on the roster. The Montreal Alouettes of the Canadian Football League liked him better, and Webster spent two seasons playing in Canada, including an appearance in the Grey Cup game, although on the losing side.

Ex-Giant Al DeRogatis was scouting for the team and watched Webster shine in Canada, cajoling him into a deal with New York. Webster made a serious impact from the start in 1955. He led the team in rushing that season and established himself quickly in that early-season loss to the Cardinals when he gained 139 yards.

Webster played all 10 of his National Football League seasons for the Giants, gaining 4,638 yards rushing and scoring 56 touchdowns. Later inducted into the team's Ring of Honor, Webster also spent five seasons as head coach.

Chapter 17. Not Quite There 131

"The Giants in 1955, when I arrived, were just coming into their own," Webster said. "Jim Lee Howell had taken over from Steve Owen and instituted a more modern game. He had a lot of very good ballplayers who were coming into their own. I got off to a good start in the regular season and was playing a lot."[3]

Webster was initially used as a halfback but spent more time at fullback later. He understood his own strengths and weaknesses. Webster was a savvy football man, but he was no track speedster coming out of the starting blocks or in the backfield.

"I was not the fastest of ball carriers," Webster said. "Long yardage was not my plan. Hell, if I could get ten yards on a play I was ecstatic. Everything else was a bonus. I think I probably hold the record as a running back of getting caught from behind. The open field was not my country."[4]

For a guy who couldn't make it with the Redskins, the two years in Canada must have done Webster considerable good. During his official rookie year with the Giants, he drew rave comparisons with former running stars, including Washington's Cliff Battles and New York's Tuffy Leemans and Ward Cuff.

Sometime later, after he had watched Webster perform in key capacities for the Giants, Charlie Conerly wrote a rave-review column for a New York newspaper about Webster.

> Webster is the ideal back. He's big and sturdy. He can run. He can catch. He can block. More importantly, he is an inspirational symbol to every man who wears a Giants uniform. Watching Alex Webster run the ball is always a thrill for me and I've handed off to him a thousand times since we got together in 1955.[5]

Given Conerly's iffy history with pass protection and all of the black and blue marks he accumulated over the years, it was no small thing for him to take note of Webster's superior blocking. How many other times over previous years did Conerly yearn for a blocking back for company in the backfield? "Speaking selfishly, it's nice to have Webster blocking for me when I'm back to pass," Conerly said. "Al knows all the tricks of picking up red dogging linebackers and storming ends. Not many guys get past him."[6]

Another perspective on Webster was uttered by one of the NFL's toughest defensive players, future Hall of Fame defensive end Gino Marchetti of the Baltimore Colts.

"Tell you what," Marchetti said in a vivid description, "if me and Alex are in a bar and get jumped by a dozen guys, we'll walk out without a scratch and he'll be the one who got ten of them."[7] That was flattering coming from such a renowned rugged player, though those who knew Marchetti might have doubted his failure to credit himself.

Concurrent with Webster's arrival in the offensive backfield was that of another long-time contributor in Mel Triplett. Triplett, another fullback, was from Ohio and competed in college for the University of Toledo. In 1955 he began a six-year stint with the Giants, then finished his NFL career with two years for the Minnesota Vikings during the early years of the expansion franchise.

There was always a sense that Triplett, nicknamed "the Human Bomb" by some because of his power, might break out and be more productive, but he could never get ahead of Webster in the lineup.

Triplett was a fifth-round draft pick of the Giants who gained 2,857 yards as a runner during his career. He always wore no. 33 for the Giants and later, Lew Alcindor, aka Kareem Abdul-Jabbar, who grew up in New York and became perhaps the greatest player in National Basketball Association history, said he chose to wear the same number because Triplett was his favorite player.

New York's secondary had been the strongest department on the team in the early 1950s, but Tom Landry had retired as the defensive coordinator in favor of full-time coaching, and fresh blood was needed. That came in the way of two critical additions, Dick Nolan and Jim Patton.

Nolan was a 6-foot-1, 185-pound, fourth-round draft pick out of Maryland in 1954 who began seeing more time. His 1954–1957 stay with the Giants was just the beginning of a very long NFL career that included playing stops with the Chicago Cardinals, the Giants again between 1959 and 1961, and the Dallas Cowboys, and then a lengthy coaching career as an assistant and also as the head man for the San Francisco 49ers and New Orleans Saints.

When Nolan shifted to the Cowboys, he played for old teammate Landry and then coached for him before taking over his own team. Three times, Nolan's 49ers lost to Landry's Cowboys in the playoffs, twice in the National Football Conference championship game.

Nolan said Landry was very influential when they were both with the Giants, and things he picked up helped him as a player and later as a coach. "Landry was a really good teacher and he taught me how to tackle," Nolan said. "He was a very detailed guy who didn't miss anything, and he was very organized."[8]

Pro football statisticians played with Jimmy Patton's height and weight as if he were a basketball player and they didn't want to tell the truth. He was possibly just 5-foot-10, or maybe 6-foot, or possibly 6–1. He weighed as little as 175 pounds or as much as 190 pounds.

Chapter 17. Not Quite There

Like Charlie Conerly, Patton had been a star at the University of Mississippi, in his case after growing up in Greenville. As good a player as Patton was, the only explanation for him being drafted by the Giants as low as the eighth round in 1955 was a question about his size.

During his career, all with the Giants, Patton excelled in the secondary as a weak-side safety, five times chosen first-team All-Pro and once selected for the second team. He was a magnet to the ball, one of those buzzing bees in the Giants' defensive backfield who always seemed to get their hands on opposition throws. He collected 52 interceptions during his NFL career.

The better Patton got, the more often his size was ignored, though it seemed to shrink to smaller proportions. One writer, for *Sport* magazine, called him the smallest player on the Giants' roster for years (he was referred to as 5–11, 175 in this piece) and said in Patton's rookie year an unnamed coach commented, "He'll kill himself the way he tackles." Presumably, Patton was attacking like a dive bomber and putting his fragile body at risk.[9]

This was not a joke. Patton was so aggressive in his first training camp, Jim Lee Howell and other New York coaches did worry about his health. "Jimmy is a little tiger," Howell said. "He thinks he's better than everyone and he just about is, you see, but he's a very vicious, mean-type little fella and he was trying to knock all of those 230-pound fullbacks out. So as a rule he'd be lettin' 'em have it with all he had and we'd be carrying Jimmy off."[10]

In the pre-season and early going of the season, the Giants lost track of how many times Patton was knocked out on the field, guessing three or four. Landry benched Patton and ordered him to alter his tackling strategy to stay in one piece. Patton learned.

"I'd always been drilled to get my head in front of the runner and hit him with my shoulder," Patton said. "Tom taught me to get my head behind the runner. Of course, you go for the easiest shot, but you don't go head-long all the time. You protect yourself and still make the tackle. I learned not to be reckless about it."[11]

Harland Svare played a role in making the Giants' defense tougher after he came to New York from the Los Angeles Rams for the 1955 season. The linebacker stayed with the Giants for the rest of his playing career through 1960 and then immediately went into coaching with New York. Svare eventually had two chances as a head coach, with the Rams and the San Diego Chargers, but he never recorded a winning record in seven seasons, partial and full.

On the field, Svare was listed as six feet tall and 215 pounds, and although he retired at 30, he was somewhat opportunistic, grabbing nine interceptions and recovering five fumbles. Svare was surprised to be traded from the Rams to the Giants and initially wasn't sure how to take it. The deal ended up being fortuitous for him. "At the time, the trade was devastating," Svare said. "I was shocked. I thought I was going from a good team to a team I didn't know a thing about."[12]

Later in life, Svare was more connected to West Coast football, but among fans and the team, he was always seen as a Giant. Not only did he play a key role with the defense when he was active, he became the successor to Landry when the defensive coordinator departed for the Dallas Cowboys job.

It can be reasonably suggested that one of Charlie Conerly's new teammates with the New York Giants for the 1955 season had one of the most unusual, colorful, even funky all-around lives of any pro football player. Not only did Rosey Grier become a sterling member of the Giants' defensive front four, but he kept on making intriguing moves in other endeavors after he retired from the field.

Roosevelt Grier, born in 1932, attended Penn State and was a third-round pick of the Giants in the NFL draft of 1955. As a player with the Giants through 1962 and then with the Rams through 1966, he was measured at 6-foot-5 and somewhere between 285 and 300 pounds. He became a three-time All-Pro and a member of two famous defensive units.

To read Grier's biography these days, one could be forgiven for overlooking that he even played professional football because it mentions he was also an actor, a singer, and a Protestant minister; was present as a bodyguard with U.S. Senator Robert F. Kennedy when Kennedy was assassinated while campaigning for president in 1968; and was a sideshow of sorts widely associated with the hobbies of macrame and needle work, pastimes not associated with big, burly men. Grier even authored a book called *Needlepoint for Men*.

On the day of RFK's assassination in California, Grier was guarding Kennedy's wife, Ethel, a few steps to the rear of where Sirhan Sirhan shot the candidate. Grier grabbed the gun away from the shooter and helped subdue him. Grier appeared on dozens of television shows and in numerous movies. He recorded songs for many years.

Rosey's nephew, Mike Grier, a former player in the National Hockey League who competed in more than 1,000 games, was named general manager of the San Jose Sharks over the summer of 2022, becoming the first Black GM in league history.

As a player, Rosey Grier developed a pre-game ritual of lying down in front of his locker on a bed of towels, absorbing some moments of peace, it might be said, before the gridiron war began. "Sometimes I

Chapter 17. Not Quite There 135

think," Grier said. "It's a fine way for thinking, laying there with your eyes closed and pushing the rest of the world away from you. Sometimes I pray. Very often thinking and praying are the same thing."[13]

Grier was an All-Star from Penn State in the annual college contest in Chicago, but he was not a ready-made pro. Few are. The shift to the demands of training camp under a broiling sun with the demands of coaches who want to make sure the new guy understands the difference between college and the big-time is a strain.

Grier recounted his first day of running sprints on a summer day along with fellow rookie Mel Triplett. "Mel, do you think we are going to make it?" Grier said as he ran and ran. "They can't kill us, Rosey," Triplett responded. "They can't kill us." Soon enough, by the end of practice, Grier speculated that Triplett's statement was not a sure thing.[14]

Grier did wonder how he would be treated as a Black man with the Giants. He noted that Jim Lee Howell was from Arkansas, quarterback Conerly was from Mississippi, Kyle Rote was from Texas, and linebacker Ray Beck was from Georgia. Would he encounter prejudice from the Southerners? "But I didn't," Grier said.[15]

There was keen disappointment when New York started the season 0–3. It was definitely unexpected, especially with the addition of fresh talent. Perhaps it was underestimated how challenging it would be to work the new faces into the lineup as smooth cogs in the machine.

Finally, in mid–October, the Giants won a game. It was the second contest versus the Chicago Cardinals. This time New York won, 10–0. The defense was sharp, the offense nondescript. Giants scores came on a run by Frank Gifford for six points and four points on Ben Agajanian's kicking. It was a poor-weather day and nobody did anything through the air. Light rain fell throughout the 60 minutes, with wind speeds in the mid–20s mph range limiting passing accuracy. Conerly was four for seven for 55 yards. Chicago was nine for 21 for 32 yards. Only 17,264 fans showed up at the Polo Grounds.

The victory was pleasant enough but did not set a trend. The Giants next met the Steelers for a second time in 1955, and while the game was closer, the result was the same—another loss. Pittsburgh prevailed, 19–17. Don Heinrich and Conerly threw one touchdown apiece. Conerly was 13 for 15 for 141 yards, but Pittsburgh out-threw New York behind Jim Fink's 212 yards. The Steelers ran up 359 yards on the Giants' defense.

By this time the trio of coaches, Howell, Lombardi and Landry, were likely maxed out on fresh ideas, but the Giants concluded the month of October with a sound 35–7 beating of the Washington Redskins. It was a desperately needed win, and Conerly was a marquee player in making it happen. He threw a 42-yard TD pass to Alex Webster and a 36-yarder to Kyle Rote.

The most dangerous weapon on the field, however, was Jimmy Patton. As a rookie, before he became a full-time safety, Patton was deployed to return kicks and punts. In this game, he exploded for a 98-yard kickoff return in the first quarter and a 69-yard punt return in the fourth. In a rare twist, Conerly booted the extra point after Patton's second touchdown.

At 2–4, the Giants were sunk deep in the standings, but at least they were no longer winless. Were they ready for the top-rated Cleveland Browns? No. Cleveland took down the Giants, 24–14. Conerly and Gifford connected on a six-yard TD throw, and Gifford found Rote open for a 71-yard touchdown in the first half, when New York led. The Giants couldn't keep it up in the second half, though.

Five games remained in the regular season, and the Giants were 2–5. Who were these guys? They were searching for their own identity, convinced they were better than the record on paper, but not playing consistently and not proving in real life what was going through their minds. It was too late in the season to make a run at the playoffs, but it was not too late to show they were capable of much more right this minute but also in the future.

The November 13 game against the Baltimore Colts, another team on the rise, brought 33,982 fans to the Polo Grounds. The attraction wasn't completely clear, but it may have been because certain fans, on this date and over the next couple of weeks, wanted to see one last game at the old park. Starting in 1956, the Giants shifted their home field to Yankee Stadium, so this began a long goodbye to the Polo Grounds. Rosey Grier observed that some 6,000 Baltimore fans showed up waving Confederate flags as well, padding the attendance.

Baltimore came to New York with a 4–3 record and led by a rookie quarterback named George Shaw out of the University of Oregon. He was the first player taken in the NFL draft in 1955 and was touted as a star of the future. Shaw was in the middle of a solid rookie year, but by October of the next season he would be on the sidelines with a broken leg that allowed the legendary Johnny Unitas to take the controls.

This Giants contest was not one of Shaw's finest of the year, though he did throw one touchdown pass. New York handled the Colts, 17–7. Conerly fired a 28-yard touchdown pass to Ken MacAfee, and Webster scored on a two-yard run. The win changed everything for the Giants. "That turned out to be the day the New York Giants came alive and started playing the kind of football we would soon be famous for," Grier said.[16]

Chapter 17. Not Quite There 137

The win was an awakening. The next week, the Giants crushed the Philadelphia Eagles, 31–7, also at the Polo Grounds in front of 22,000-plus spectators. A 21-point New York third quarter was decisive. Conerly threw one touchdown pass. Emlen Tunnell returned a punt 66 yards for another TD.

That set up a rematch for the 4–5 Giants with the 7–1 Browns. This was the last scheduled game for New York at the Polo Grounds, and attendance suited the occasion with 45,699 ticket-holders present. This was a wild game, ending in a 35–35 tie with New York coming from behind in the fourth quarter with the final touchdown on a Conerly 23-yard pass to Gifford. Conerly also found Rote free for another touchdown pass. Otto Graham threw three touchdown passes for Cleveland and gained 319 yards through the air.

That was the end of the Giants' home season, but they had two games remaining. They seemed to be on a roll and downed the Redskins, 27–20, and then the Detroit Lions, 24–19. Conerly and Rote connected on a 27-yard TD throw in the Washington game. Gifford scored twice on the ground versus Detroit as the Giants held off the Lions.

The two triumphs gave New York a winning record of 6–5–1, not at all what the Giants were looking for the preceding August in training camp, but bringing some satisfaction after the ghastly start.

Conerly did not sugarcoat the performance, thinking of what might have been if the Giants had played up to their potential from the beginning of the year.

"We were the best damned 6–5–1 team you ever saw," Conerly said. "We lost games we should never have lost. We tied the Browns and we should have killed them. The damned Cardinals even beat us and that was my fault. But we were coming strong. We all felt it. The next year was going to be ours."[17]

After these years of a rebuild, Conerly was right. It was time for the Giants to flex the muscles of giants.

Chapter 18

Their Turn

Over the final month of the 1955 season, the Giants realized how good they could be and how good they might become. They were irritated they hadn't done better on the field overall. Charlie Conerly put it best when analyzing the team's skills. But there are no do-overs when things go sideways.

Going forward, Conerly was not the only one in the organization who recognized the value of the 1955 close-out and what it could mean for the new season.

"What a difference it made for us at the end of the 1955 season," said coach Jim Lee Howell.[1]

The Giants were a hungry team, and the New York fans, spoiled by the repeated all-around brilliance of the three Major League teams in the boroughs, wanted the same kind of satisfaction produced by the football team. By the time the 1956 season began, the Giants had recorded uneven seasons, some good ones and some lousy ones, for a long time. The last time New York had won the National Football League crown was 1938, some 18 years earlier.

While 6–5–1 did not automatically tab the Giants as a contender for 1956, it was the excitement generated by the strong 1955 finish, the attitude of veterans who determinedly wanted to end a championship drought, and the inner workings of management, emphasizing wise personnel moves, that uplifted New York's outlook.

What an off-season haul, from draft picks to trades. New York added five new players who were difference-makers, most of them immediately, but all of them long-term, players who live on in team history as big-time contributors. Four of them were major additions to the defense, two of them future Hall of Famers. Such a collection of new players scooped up simultaneously was nearly unheard-of, a crop so impressive, looking back it is incredibly unlikely a team—and a fairly good one not picking at the top of the draft heap—could outsmart the rest of the league so thoroughly. It was almost as if the Giants said,

Chapter 18. Their Turn

"We'll take one from Column A and one from Column B, and, oh, by the way, the rest of you guys just get out of the way."

The NFL conducted a 30-round draft in 1956. The Giants did not have a first-round pick, but it hardly mattered. In the third round, New York selected Sam Huff from West Virginia, in the fourth round they took Jim Katcavage from Dayton, and in the fifth round they grabbed Don Chandler from Florida.

Andy Robustelli, who attended tiny Arnold College (which became the University of Bridgeport), was drafted in the 19th round by the Los Angeles Rams in 1951 and played his first seasons with Los Angeles. New York, which had made a recent habit of picking the Rams' pockets in deals, traded for Robustelli after he had already been named a two-time All-Pro. Dick Modelewski, who had starred at Maryland with his brother Ed, had also been in the league for three seasons, with the Washington Redskins and Pittsburgh Steelers, when the Giants traded for him. Dick won the Outland Trophy as the best college lineman in the country in 1952.

Although the 6-foot-2, 215-pound Chandler later became equally well known for his place-kicking, especially with the 1960s champion Green Bay Packers, he walked right into the starting role of punter for the Giants. Chandler was a member of the Giants from 1956 to 1964. Twice with New York in the early 1960s, Chandler scored more than 100 points in a season. Several times he averaged more than 44 yards per punt. At a time when the NFL record for the longest field goal was 56 yards, Chandler booted one of 53 yards.

Once, Chandler kicked four field goals in a game to help beat the Philadelphia Eagles, 19–14, but that was after he warmed up by missing 20 out of 25 practice kicks, making holder Ralph Guglielmi quite nervous when he trotted out on the field for the real thing. "Before the game, I found the field was rough because of the steady rain and I shortened my stride," Chandler said.[2]

Defensive coordinator Tom Landry was pretty proud of what he had accomplished with his defensive personnel, his creativity and innovation. His secondary had been nonpareil with such luminaries as Emlen Tunnell, Jimmy Patton, and Dick Nolan, and he already had such other stalwarts in his lineup as Rosey Grier, Cliff Livingston, and Harland Svare. That did not mean he was not open to suggestions when gifts were bestowed upon him or he was so stuck on his returners that he wouldn't give fresh guys a chance.

The reason why the Giants did not have a first-round draft pick that year was their investment in the trade for Robustelli. Robustelli was a 6–1, 230-pound defensive end who, remarkably for a defensive lineman, had scored six touchdowns for Los Angeles in his first four seasons in the league. Defensive linemen get sacks and create safeties. They don't score touchdowns. That is like catching a bison swimming laps in a pool. It just doesn't happen. Robustelli was from Stamford, Connecticut, a short distance from New York City, and he kept his residence in Connecticut. He enrolled at Arnold College, which had just 300 students at the time, because its specialty was physical education, and Robustelli's ambition was to become a high school coach and teacher.

Robustelli seemed to be just about as good a prospect in baseball as football, and after playing college ball and batting .400 as a third baseman, he was given a tryout with the other New York Giants, the National League team he had grown up supporting. Robustelli showed well enough to be offered a Class B minor-league contract. Still, he pondered making the right move.

Robustelli was already married to his high school sweetheart and had a baby. One advisor told him to steer clear of pro football because it was an iffy world and to stick with the teaching-coaching idea. His father convinced Robustelli to go after his California chance so he would not wonder for the rest of his life if he could have made the cut.

Even though Robustelli himself realized that ultimately he was only recognized as a New York Giant, his time with Los Angeles was both successful and special. The 1951 Rams were beloved in L.A., and they won the NFL crown in Robustelli's rookie year. While in Los Angeles, Robustelli made the first two of his All-Star teams.

"We were seen as something special away from the field, as well," Robustelli said. "While Hollywood celebrities abounded, none held more esteem and popularity than the Rams player, and whenever we went to the same clubs and restaurants in the Los Angeles area that were frequented by such stars as Frank Sinatra, Dean Martin and Don Rickles, we got the most attention."[3]

You could almost say that Robustelli lived the Toots Shor life on the opposite coast. That feeling soured a bit during the off-season following the 1955 campaign. Robustelli and his wife had their fourth child, and in a less sensitive era, Rams coach Sid Gillman not only refused to permit Robustelli to report to training camp a few days late due to the birth, he was rude about it. "I don't care whether it's a couple of days or not," Gillman told Robustelli. "You get your ass out here, that's all I can tell you."[4] It took only a matter of days before Giants owner Wellington Mara telephoned Robustelli to see if he wished to play for New York instead.

Robustelli was one of two new defensive ends. Katcavage was the other. He was a Giant all the way, playing 13 years for the team and then becoming the defensive line coach. He was a superb pass rusher, unofficially credited with 91½ lifetime sacks, unofficially because the sack was not defined by the league until after his career began.

Robustelli was so good and already so established that Katcavage played a chunk of his career in the shadow of the older guy at the same position, if on the other side of the line. Katcavage, who seemed to sport a Marine-style brush-cut on top forever, was not especially large for a defensive lineman, even during that era. Members of the 2021 Giants at his position weighed 30 to 40 pounds more than his regular 237 pounds.

"I really haven't found anybody who can overpower me," Katcavage said. "The minimum weight for a defensive end is 220. Lower than that, you lose efficiency. Then they can double-team and you can't hold your ground. If I'm double-teamed by an end and a tackle, I'll hit into the end. I don't try to beat them both. The end is generally weaker."[5]

Katcavage could speak to that because when the Giants chose him in the draft, that was about what he weighed. He bulked up quickly through bigger portions of food. Yet one of his primary attributes was speed, and he did not lose a step with the bonus weight. While Katcavage's nickname was "Kat," it was applied more because of his name than his ability to move like a cat, even if the idea was not misplaced.

Robustelli got more attention, the first defensive end All-Star selectors thought of connected to the Giants, but eventually, Katcavage got their attention, too. He was three times chosen first-team All-Pro and three times chosen second-team. Team achievements aside, Katcavage said probably his best single performance came against the Cardinals when he amassed five sacks. "For a defensive end, getting to the passer that often in one game is like Mickey Mantle hitting four home runs in four times up."[6]

They called Dick Modzelewski "Little Mo," but it wasn't as if he was little. It was because he was the younger brother of Ed, who beat him into the National Football League and who did outweigh him when they played football in high school. A defensive tackle, Dick weighed 250 pounds, distributed over a 6-foot frame. In fact, Ed, who was two years older, was smaller, weighing 217 pounds and playing fullback, primarily with the Cleveland Browns. This set up some interesting showdowns in the 1950s when the Browns and Giants battled for first place in the NFL's Eastern Division.

Dick was a second-round draft selection of the Washington Redskins in 1953 and he played two seasons in the nation's capital, but he could not get along with coach Joe Kuharich. So Modzelewski signed a deal with the Calgary Canadian Football League team to escape. Washington fought to keep him, initiating litigation. That halted Dick's move to the Stampeders, and the Redskins responded by trading him to the Steelers. For a moment, it seemed, Dick and Ed would play for the same pro team, but Pittsburgh swapped Ed to Cleveland, so their parallel careers went on. In the spring of 1956, Dick Modzelewski was sent to the Detroit Lions, but four days later he was traded to the Giants.

It was quite the odyssey, but Dick literally and figuratively found a home—in New York and with the Giants' starting defense. At that point, the addition of Modzelewski gave New York the formidable front four in a 4–3 defense of Dick, Rosey Grier, Robustelli, and Katcavage. Although quartets of other NFL defensive fronts earned snazzy nicknames (or even the same one), the Giants in 1957 were the first to be referred to as "the Fearsome Foursome."

A few years later, other teams, such as the San Diego Chargers and Detroit Lions, briefly adopted it. Most notably, the Los Angeles Rams, after they acquired Grier, assumed the designation in the 1960s.

No matter which team Modzelewski represented, he suited up ready to play. A big deal was made in newspapers when he played in his 175th straight contest near the end of his career—he played in 180 games before retiring. Modzelewski was always recognized as a key Giant during his eight years with the team, but there were only so many honors to go around when picking All-Star defensive linemen, and "Little Mo" was often overlooked.

"I don't mind, though," Modzelewski said. "I do my job and as long as the coaches are satisfied, that's what counts. Publicity? Sure, I like publicity, but I guess I'm just not the type who attracts attention."[7] The odd part of that self-analysis is that Modzelewski often entertained his teammates with jokes and did imitations. Guys like that usually get plenty of attention from sportswriters, but Modzelewski's comedy routine apparently stayed within the confines of the team.

The fifth big addition to the Giants of 1956 may have been the most important of all. Sam Huff became a Hall of Fame linebacker and often the most identifiable player on the defensive side of the ball. Huff, who became one of the most famous middle linebackers in history, was initially an offensive lineman at West Virginia. It was Landry who saw the potential in Huff to assume his new role in the Giants' defense.

At first, Huff belonged to Vince Lombardi, and the Giants were trying to shape him into a professional guard at 235 pounds. Huff had experience on both sides of the ball, and he realized in training camp that at his size, he would have trouble keeping bigger rushers out of the backfield and off of Charlie Conerly.

One day, Landry approached Huff and asked, "Son, have you ever thought about playing linebacker?" Huff replied in the best possible

Chapter 18. Their Turn

manner, saying, "I could play wherever you want me. Fine. I'm a rookie. I'm trying to stay alive."[8] In some ways, the position shift was like moving from outfield to pitcher in baseball, but it took for Huff.

Blocking and tackling, the fundamentals of football, were night and day, land and sea, and being able to play one way did not guarantee someone could play the other way. But almost instantly, it was realized Huff was more valuable on defense than as a scratching-at-it offensive lineman.

"So now, I can see everything," Huff commented later about that moment. "I have terrific peripheral vision, even to this day. So now I can see everything, and boy, I made tackle upon tackle. It was the best move for me in my life."[9]

The irony was that Huff and Don Chandler were so frustrated with their early experiences in training camp, sick of being yelled at, and convinced they were doomed to be cut, that they planned to quit, return to the real world as non-athletes, and make new lives for themselves. Their chances were not sugar-coated, but Vince Lombardi caught up to them and unleashed tirades, cowing them into staying. Huff would make 30 interceptions over the course of his career and 17 fumble recoveries, and he was selected All-Pro as a linebacker four times.

He also gained a national profile through a television documentary narrated by Walter Cronkite. It was a 1960 reality film titled *The Violent World of Sam Huff*, bringing fans inside the game.

By the time the Giants exited from training camp to start the 1956 season, Landry was the supervisor of a quicker, smarter, stronger defense that was about to establish itself as a special unit in New York football lore. The Giants' offense had been retooled since the start of the decade while featuring Conerly at quarterback and Frank Gifford and Alex Webster in the backfield, and Kyle Rote and Bob Schnelker receiving, with a solid, stable offensive line.

The coaching staff stuck with the oddball approach of starting Don Heinrich at quarterback. Conerly watched games unfold from the sideline early to soak in the tendencies of the opposing team. There were Conerly cheerleaders on the team.

Conerly, then 35, completed 90 out of 174 pass attempts for 1,143 yards and 10 touchdowns. Heinrich was 37 for 88 for 369 yards. Gifford had an extraordinary all-around year, catching 51 balls for 603 yards while also rushing for 819 yards with an average of 5.2 yards per carry.

Yet Gifford said of Conerly's strategic importance, "I think of Charlie as the personification of leadership. The Giants had a sellout every game because of what we did in 1956, and Charlie was the biggest reason for that." Similarly, Andy Robustelli said, "All of us looked up to

Conerly in one degree or another. He was as unflappable in those good times as he was when he was getting worked over by the fans. He was tough, methodical, and dependable."[10]

The 1956 regular season opened September 30 on the road against the San Francisco 49ers, and the Giants resumed winning, just as they had concluded 1955 with wins. They took out the 49ers, 38–21, at Kezar Stadium. Heinrich actually threw two touchdown passes in this one. Mel Triplett caught one of the six-pointers and ran for two more scores. Gifford scored on one catch and also booted a field goal and four extra points, more evidence of his versatility.

A week later, the Giants got a surprise, falling to the Chicago Cardinals, 35–27. Triplett remained on fire, scoring three TDs on short runs. Conerly threw one touchdown pass. This was somewhat of a shocker for a team with grand aspirations. But it was the last blip for some time. In what was a must-win game for a team that hoped to rule the division, in the third game, New York defeated the Cleveland Browns, 21–9, at Municipal Stadium. Alex Webster scored all three Giant touchdowns and Don Chandler performed the role of kicker. The 60,000-plus home fans did not help the Browns. New York's defense strangled Cleveland's running game, permitting just 40 yards in 25 rushes.

This was one of those satisfying wins that Conerly relished for the rest of his life. For much of the 1950s, the path to Eastern Division supremacy meant outplaying the Browns. The Giants and Browns met twice a season, so it was imperative to hold an edge. Conerly said that so many of those Browns showdowns determined how the teams ended up at the conclusion of the season. This one fit that description.

The Giants manhandled the Pittsburgh Steelers, 38–10, the next week to move to 3–1. It was the first home game of the year, and the Giants were christening their new home stadium—Yankee Stadium instead of the Polo Grounds. Attendance was good at 48,108, and the Giants put on a good show. The spotlight was on Conerly. If this was Broadway, he would have been nominated for a Tony Award for leading man in a drama. Conerly completed three touchdown passes, to Ken MacAfee, Alex Webster, and Kyle Rote. Ben Agajanian was back in the kicking role, scoring a field goal and five extra points. The defense held the Steelers to 91 yards rushing and 98 yards passing. A trend was forming.

During this regular season, the Giants' defense held seven of 12 opponents to two touchdowns or less, dramatically increasing opportunities for the offense to win. Used to rooting for touchdowns, the Giants audience in Yankee Stadium developed a new habit. The fans began shouting a new chant: "Dee-fense! Dee-fense!" This spectator

Chapter 18. Their Turn 145

Giants fullback Mel Triplett (33) lying on the ground in the end zone after scoring the first touchdown in New York's championship game rout of the Chicago Bears on December 30, 1956. The referee at right raises his arms in the air to call the touchdown (Associated Press).

involvement became an institution and was also adopted by other fan bases as time went on, often called upon at select moments for teams around the league. The shout is still employed today, though it has become something of a cliché, or at least a staple, of fans bellowing out their feelings to stop the opponents. But it was new in 1956, and members of the defense took note.

"That chant made us feel great," Katcavage said. "It gave us more incentive to play." He said the noise did actually help the psyche of the players, particularly when the foe was the Browns.[11]

Roars like that beat getting booed. Winning beat losing, too, and the New York streak went on with another home victory, 20–3, over the Philadelphia Eagles on October 28. There were 40,690 fans present for the encounter. New York football fans were catching on that this team might be something special. Conerly threw a 20-yard touchdown pass to Gifford, and Webster scored on a short run. The New York defense slammed the door to the end zone, permitting only a 15-yard field goal by Philly's Bobby Walston. In 30 rushes, Philadelphia gained just 65 yards.

That Giants spirit was contagious. Attendance for the next week at Yankee Stadium was 62,410. One might have thought a World Series game had broken out. New York came after the Chicago Cardinals. The teams brought matching 5–1 records into the game, but the Giants controlled play on their way to a 23–10 triumph. Andy Robustelli gave New York a 2–0 lead in the first period on a safety. Conerly reached Gifford on an 11-yard TD pass, and Heinrich threw one also.

Then, for whatever reason, the Giants spaced out for a game. Playing at Washington's Griffith Stadium, they were beaten up by the Redskins, 33–7. The Giants were never in this one. The only New York touchdown came on a Conerly pass of 12 yards to Schnelker. This was an outlier, a performance for which there was no good reason, dropping New York to 6–2.

The next contest was nearly as disruptive. The Giants faced the Chicago Bears, leaders in the Western Division and bearers of a 7–1 record. Inspired by their sloppiness of the week before, New York moved out to a 17–0 lead by halftime. Agajanian kicked a 17-yard field goal. Rote caught a 17-yard touchdown pass from Heinrich. Webster scored on a two-yard run.

However, the rest of the game belonged to the Bears, not intimidated by the 56,836 fans in Yankee Stadium. Future Hall of Famer George Blanda, who made his reputation in the 1960s with the Houston Oilers, kicked his own 22-yard field goal. Bill McColl and Ed Brown both completed touchdown heaves to end Harlon Hill, McColl's covering 79 yards. The game concluded 17–17, the Giants more disappointed by the result than the Bears.

Emlen Tunnell remembered the feeling of rolling along and containing Hill. In some ways, Hill was one of the least-heralded great football players of his time. A native of Alabama, he so excelled in college that the NCAA Division II Player of the Year trophy is named after him. It is the equivalent of the Heisman Trophy for Division I. In 1954, he was the NFL's Rookie of the Year, and in 1955, he was the league's Most Valuable Player. In 1956, Hill made 47 catches for 1,128 yards. He compiled a league-leading 24 yards per catch as the most dangerous man with the ball after a grab.

Early in the game, Tunnell noted, "Harlon Hill, who had been having the most sensational year in the history of forward pass catching, hadn't hurt us yet. The Bears hadn't hurt us at all. We were leading 17–3 and Chicago just couldn't seem to do anything about it. We'd stopped them running. We'd stopped them passing."[12] Until they didn't anymore. Hill basically earned the tie for Chicago.

The Giants could not afford to brood about the result. If they kept winning, they could still win the division title and advance to the championship game. A 28–14 victory over the Redskins, good revenge for the unexpected slaughter in D.C., was pretty much the Frank Gifford show.

Gifford threw a 29-yard touchdown pass to MacAfee, rushed for touchdowns of six and 11 yards, and caught a 14-yard score from Conerly.

Now New York was 7–2–1 with two games remaining. This was a somewhat odd year in the Eastern Division. There was no dominating team, and the Browns were nowhere near the top of the standings. If only the Giants could maintain, they could take the crown and move on. But they stumbled.

In the season's 11th week, the Giants faced the Browns again, a Browns team that for the first time in the decade was completely out of the picture with a 5–7 mark in its first season after quarterback Otto Graham's retirement.

Yet the Browns beat the Giants in this crucial game. Easily. The final was 24–7. Conerly threw a touchdown pass to Gifford, but that was all the offense New York mustered, and the defense did not stop Cleveland. The defeat did not ruin the Giants' hopes, but it did put on the pressure entering the final weekend of the season.

Most of the division was bunched—with the exception of the Eagles, who had the worst record. The Giants traveled to Philadelphia for the finale and romped, 21–7. Gifford was outstanding again, throwing a touchdown pass and running for another, and the defense bottled up the Eagles. New York's rushing game amassed 291 yards, and the Eagles totaled just 73 yards in 23 carries. Philadelphia finished the year 3–8–1, and the Giants posted the reverse record, 8–3–1, good enough to stay ahead of other contenders, including the second-place 7–5 Chicago Cardinals.

New York won when it had to and won the crown for an automatic berth in the NFL championship game. It was Gifford, the heart of the team in the statistics that winning year, who said the true secret of the Giants' 1956 success was the bond between the players.

> If there's a single explanation, it may be the team members meshed both on and off the field. There was incredible togetherness. We ate at places like Jack's Delicatessen on Manhattan's West Side and a lot of us lived in the same hotel, the Concourse Plaza in the Bronx. On Monday nights, we'd do New York as a group. That closeness paid off on the field.[13]

The closeness helped the Giants win throughout the fall of 1956 and earn the right to play one more game before the end of the calendar year. The Bears won the Western Division with a 9–2–1 record, barely edging the 9–3 Detroit Lions. The championship game would be a rematch of a regular-season tie.

Chapter 19

World Champs

Twice the New York Giants snookered the Chicago Bears. That was even more remarkable because the circumstances should have been once in a lifetime.

In 1934, the Giants faced the Bears for the National Football League title in the Polo Grounds. A freezing rain rolled in and coated the grass in a sheen of ice. When the Giants were warming up, they realized how slippery the going would be. End Ray Flaherty was heard to say something on the order of "Gee whiz, I wish we could wear sneakers." The light bulb went on in coach Steve Owen's head. He sent a Giants sideline worker to Manhattan College to round up some sneakers for his men.

While the Bears slipped and slid all over the field, the Giants ran with confidence and crushed Chicago, 30–13. In 1956, as unlikely as it seemed, when the teams woke up to compete for the title on December 30, the situation was essentially the same as it had been 22 years earlier. Yankee Stadium was the site of the game this time, but the field was frozen, icy, and the air temperature was around 20 degrees.

Whether it was an issue of the Giants possessing long memories or just making a quick analytical call of the circumstances, New York team personnel set out to find a few dozen pairs of sneakers once again. This game became known as Sneakers II.

Actually, coach Jim Lee Howell did recall the past history ahead of time, and he thought it possible that a change of footwear might be warranted on this occasion, too. As it so happened, defensive end Andy Robustelli was in the sporting goods business with friend Ed Clark, and they owned such a store in Connecticut. Howell asked Robustelli to provide the secret weapon. He and Clark delivered four dozen pairs of sneakers manufactured by U.S. Rubber, a brand called "Big League." They definitely were this day.

Robustelli later claimed credit for the idea to possibly use sneakers because earlier in the week a Keds salesman had been in his store, raving about a new type with excellent rubber soles and firmer grip. Robustelli said he brought enough pairs to Yankee Stadium for the entire team, just in case.

Howell's pre-game preparation extended to much more than Xs and Os. Prior to kickoff, he performed his own science experiment. Rookie kick returner Gene Filipski tried on a pair of sneakers and ran out onto the turf. Defensive back Ed Hughes donned the regular cleats. Filipski discovered he had pretty good traction. Hughes was slipping on the ice. The call went out for everyone to accentuate their uniforms with the sneakers.

There may have been some dispute about who thought up the sneakers plan, but the tryout was Howell's plan alone, and the decision to go ahead wearing them was also his. Bears coach Paddy Driscoll later said the footwear did make a difference. Robustelli said, "I don't know whether the sneakers did it.... I believe we could have played in bare feet that day and beaten the Bears because we were a dedicated team."[1]

New York Giants teammates Frank Gifford (left) and Charlie Conerly celebrating in the locker room after New York defeated the Chicago Bears, 47–7, for the 1956 NFL title on December 30, 1956 (Associated Press).

More reliable footwear aside, this was a Giants team peaking for the moment, with a lot to prove, and carrying a grudge against the Bears because of the 17–17 regular-season tie. Fullback Alex Webster was one player who felt the tie gave a false impression and believed the cohesiveness and confidence of the Giants would make a difference in the title game. "[We] were really up for them in the championship game," he said, "and we just walked all over them that day."[2]

It didn't seem to matter much to the 56,836 fans just how cold and uncomfortable the weather was in the seats at Yankee Stadium. It was 18 years since the Giants won a title, and if they were going to do it again, rooters wanted to be able to say they were there.

The way the game unfolded, it was an afternoon-long celebration for Giants fans and players alike. There was no suspense about the result, and the 60 minutes of playing time served as a stage for a New York coronation. It was long in coming for such veterans as Charlie Conerly and Emlen Tunnell, a welcome reward for shorter-serving players who joined up later.

Fullback Mel Triplett scored the first points on a 17-yard run at two minutes, 40 seconds of the first quarter. Ben Agajanian's foot added six more points on two field goals, one of 17 yards and one of 43 yards. When Webster scored on a run in the second period, it was already 20–0 Giants. The Bears, who had been favored, were finished, although they did post their only score on fullback Rick Casares' nine-yard run in the second quarter. That touchdown was set up by a New York mistake, a fumbled punt on the Giants' 26 yard line. Otherwise, the game might have been a shutout.

The game literally favored the Giants from the first moments. Filipski, who had tried out the sneakers on behalf of the team and liked their feel, got a chance to exercise their usefulness on the contest's first play. He gathered in the opening kickoff on his own eight yard line and ran the ball back to the Bears' 39. The 53-yard return gave New York excellent field position, and the Giants' offense played with precision, culminating in that Triplett burst.

Sensing the way the game might be shaping up, the Bears gambled on a fourth and one early on, but Tunnell dropped J.C. Caroline to hold Chicago down. The Giants took over deep in Bears territory and turned that into a score, too. A 13–0 deficit became a 20–0 deficit.

As was their habit, the Giants started Don Heinrich at quarterback. Charlie Conerly took command in the second period and picked apart the Chicago secondary. He ended up completing seven of 10 pass attempts for 195 yards and two touchdowns, with a quarterback rating of 152.1. Third-stringer Bob Clatterbuck played the fourth quarter. For Conerly, who had survived so many hard times with the franchise, this win was almost too easy. Fittingly enough, Kyle Rote, on a nine-yarder, caught one of Conerly's touchdown throws. And Frank Gifford, on a 14-yarder, caught another. The Giants just kept pounding away on the Bears till the end, running up a 47–7 final score.

"I was particularly pleased to see Chuck play one of his finest games because so many people seemed to think we couldn't win with him," Howell said. "He showed everybody what a poised, skilled pro he is in his biggest game."[3]

Given that the Bears were slight favorites, by three points, going into the game, surprise was expressed at the margin of victory by sportswriters, and Howell was asked if he had done anything special to get the players ready, as if he or the other coaches had served some kind of elixir or something special at breakfast.

"We did nothing to try to get them up," Howell said.

> They are all good pros and we decided that we couldn't gain anything trying to needle up spirit. In fact, we tried to play down tension by practicing only six days in the two weeks before the game and in refraining from coining slogans and pasting things on the board. There was one exception that we couldn't help pinning on the clubhouse door.

It was easy to see why the item was made an exception. This was a postcard sent to the Giants and signed "A Bears Fan." It read: "Merry Christmas, but you won't have a Happy New Year."[4]

Certainly that was worth a chuckle, especially because as a forecast it proved untrue. Howell had given the team four days off around Christmas, a contrast to pro football these days, when teams compete on Christmas Day if the league schedules games. The Bears practiced hard just about every day. Were the Bears weary? Were the Giants fresh and bursting with energy?

Most assuredly, Howell felt the team was raring to go. No one was going to say the Giants came out listless. "When it came time to play the game," he said, "we just opened the door and got out of the way. No one and nothing could have stopped the Giants that day."[5]

Once again, the Giants' defense stifled a team's running game. Chicago gained only 67 yards rushing on 32 carries. The Giants themselves rushed for 126 yards, and their total offensive yardage was 348.

"They were up," Bears coach Paddy Driscoll said. "We were down. When you run up against some fellows playing like that, there's just nothing you can do."[6]

Robustelli was particularly proud of the work the defense did in ruining Chicago's game plan and overwhelming the Bears' offense. This was a rise-to-the-occasion moment for New York's defense. "We sacked their quarterbacks a half-dozen times and their work netted them just five yards per passing attempt," Robustelli said. "There was no doubt after that game that the New York Giants' defense had an orbit all its own."[7]

The 1956 season was something special for the New York football Giants. The local sports scene had been dominated by the three big-league baseball clubs, the baseball Giants, the Dodgers, and the other tenants in Yankee Stadium, the Yankees. They were their sport's glamor teams, and they traded off winning pennants and World Series championships as if the rest of the American League and the National League were mere sandlot clubs.

People wanted to love the football Giants, and the Maras invested and invested and built and built, acquiring more and more talent, until in 1956 they were big enough winners to win the Eastern Division and qualify for the championship game. There were famous enough names on the team, players who were celebrities on the social scene, but they were just starting to bust out beyond Toots Shor's and the other fancy watering holes into mainstream social figures. Winning this crown solidified the Giants' status.

The fans adopted that catch-phrase "Dee-fense! Dee-fense!" and that aided in establishing an identity. The players who won it all put in the time and the work. They were not unknowns but established names in the big city who had sacrificed and won big. If you followed football at all in New York City, you knew Charlie Conerly, Alex Webster, Frank Gifford, Kyle Rote, Sam Huff, Andy Robustelli, Emlen Tunnell and several others.

Gifford had a spectacular season and won the Most Valuable Player Award for the league at the same time his team won the championship. "As for me, 1956 will always be a magical year," Gifford said. "The lowly, downtrodden, hapless Giants won it all. I went into 1956 in the greatest shape of my life. Whatever the reason, things began happening to me that hadn't happened before."[8]

That was the regular season, and it was a spectacular year for Gifford, from start to finish, running, passing, and catching the ball—and, of course, winning it all.

Gifford long remembered the team celebration the night of the triumph. The grand party moved out of the stadium to exactly where it belonged: Toots Shor's, the prime team hangout. Toots was ready to receive them, no matter how many players came through the door. It was the Giants' night. Gifford called the scene "a major blowout. There were so many of us Toots had to set aside the entire back of his restaurant. God, we were on a high."[9]

As they had every right to be. Some snippets of the evening stuck with Gifford forever. Tackle Roosevelt Brown, who by then was as good an offensive lineman as there was in the NFL, at one point lifted Gifford off the floor, instead of blocking for him. He hugged him and shouted, "We're the champions! We're the champions!" Everyone else chimed in with the beautiful chant. "It still took a long while to sink in," Gifford said.[10]

For many, the 1956 victory was super sweet, a culmination of years of sweat first under Steve Owen and then Jim Lee Howell, with his partners Vince Lombardi and Tom Landry. In reality, this was a team built to last, one that should stay a contender for some time and had every chance to repeat as champion. This was not supposed to be a one-off. It wasn't, either; beginning with 1956, the Giants would become Eastern Division champions six times in eight years. They were now a league power.

Gifford and Conerly were best friends and roommates on the road, and they had lived through years of wins and losses together. Naturally enough, they were together at Toots Shor's on the night of the championship party, sharing a celebratory drink, toasting one another, the team, and its hard-won accomplishment.

Conerly had put in four years with the Giants before Gifford even arrived on the roster, some of them painful years. No one besides wife Perian realized all the tribulations Conerly faced.

"The best part was watching Charlie's joy," Gifford said of that party night. "He'd gone through so much incredible crap, the physical poundings every Sunday, the abuse from the fans and the writers. I was the official hero that year, but my roomie was the one who made it happen, who subordinated his ego, who did everything he could to make me look good."[11]

Forever after, Perian Conerly said this win, beating the Bears, being no. 1 in 1956, was the biggest thrill of Charlie Conerly's career. If Gifford read the party moment correctly, it sounded as if Conerly knew immediately how special topping the Bears was, being given free rein to drink to themselves at Toots'.

The way Gifford recalled the scene, late that night, Conerly lifted a glass of Scotch in a toast to Gifford and said, in his Mississippi drawl, "Giff, ah luv yew."[12]

Whether Gifford captured that inflection just right or not, at that moment Conerly and the Giants loved everything about life. They couldn't have been living any larger on the day they became the undisputed football champions of the world.

Chapter 20

Trying to Do It Again

By the start of the 1957 National Football League season, Charlie Conerly was 36 years old. After his true age had become known—and with his aging visage and graying hair available for viewing as supporting documentation—Conerly was repeatedly asked if he was going to retire.

Conerly was not particularly coy on the topic. But as each additional off-season arrived, he did not have an answer. He would return to Mississippi for the break after the last Giants game to evaluate his body and mind, reviewing aches and pains carried over from being so often tackled during the preceding season. He gave thought to his state of mind and whether he was still up for playing football.

Also, each year Conerly dealt with the New York front office in contract negotiations, wondering if he would have to haggle for a raise or a paycheck he believed he deserved. There are many famous cases of professional sports hold-outs who became fodder for off-season press attention. In the days prior to free agency, when players gained a much stronger foothold in the bargaining process, even the biggest of stars engaged in highly publicized arguments with the front office.

This was also true in New York, and it was true even with the perennial champion New York Yankees. Even Babe Ruth and Joe DiMaggio fought over money with management and they were responsible for dynastic success. Since players had no options besides retiring—they couldn't force a trade or jump to another team—management always flexed its muscles and sometimes heedlessly seemed to purposely humiliate their most important players.

In the 1950s, it was considered bad form for athletes to go public with how much they were making, and the front office did not want players comparing earnings. In Conerly's case, the Mara family seemed to appreciate his contributions and value. This was an era when a top-flight quarterback might only make $30,000, certainly not a salary approaching $100,000, although the first Major League Baseball stars were beginning to reach those stratospheric amounts.

Chapter 20. Trying to Do It Again

Future Hall of Fame first baseman Hank Greenberg was traded from the Detroit Tigers to the Pittsburgh Pirates in 1947. The Pirates paid Greenberg $100,000 not to retire, though he did a year later.

Although Red Grange came out of the University of Illinois and went on a professional barnstorming tour in the 1920s to reap $100,000, in the 1950s, the average NFL salary across the 33-man roster was $6,000 a year. Conerly signed his remarked-upon original rookie contract to join the Giants instead of with Branch Rickey's alternative opportunity, but he was not the type to speak about money matters any more than he was prepared to divulge other personal secrets.

It seemed to become a bit of a joke in the Conerly household just how hard Charlie would have to negotiate—or would be willing to negotiate—in order to obtain a raise. Essentially, the Mara family was generous to him in relation to that time. Conerly might prepare for his meeting with the front office about a new contract with the intensity of someone preparing to take final college exams, but when he showed up in the New York office, he was almost always pleasantly surprised to be offered at least as much as he intended to ask for and sometimes more.

Conerly had outlasted his initial five-year contract signed in 1948, so after that, his play was subject to fresh terms. One year, Conerly was going to rendezvous with Wellington Mara at the Senior Bowl in Mobile, Alabama, to hammer out a new deal. The night before he left home, he told Perian that he believed he had had a good year and deserved a raise. He hinted that if he did not get it, he might step away from pro football.

An illustration of how Conerly was esteemed by the Giants followed. After meeting with Mara, he called home and informed Perian,

> And you know what happened? I went up to his room and before I even had a chance to light a cigarette, Well said, "Charlie, you had such a good year, we think you ought to have a raise." And he handed me a contract already filled out for the exact amount I was going to ask for—down to the last penny! So I signed it.[1]

Perian said this type of thing happened time after time, Conerly calculating his worth and the Giants meeting or exceeding his price without bargaining. She referred to Conerly's waffling on retirement as his annual "'This is my last year' avowals."[2]

Nineteen fifty-six had been the Giants' greatest moment of glory during his tenure with the team, and it was not going to be Conerly's last season. He was back for 1957, a centerpiece in the game plan to repeat the title.

No doubt every single professional sports team that captures its league championship believes it has the goods to do it again. Yet repeats are rare. There have been dynasties in all major professional sports leagues in North America, such as the Boston Celtics in the National Basketball Association, the Montreal Canadians (as well as the New York Islanders and Edmonton Oilers) in the National Hockey League, the New York Yankees (more than one stretch) in Major League Baseball, and to a lesser degree in the NFL. In various decades, the Green Bay Packers, Chicago Bears, and New England Patriots have dominated, though never to the extent of the teams in the other sports.

The last back-to-back NFL champion dates to the 2003 and 2004 Patriots. Football has been marked more by periodic powers rather than consecutive title winners. Whether it is football, baseball, basketball, or hockey, fans can be sure something major will be different in the season following a championship. The reigning champion may have a change of coaches, be undercut by the retirement of key players, have athletes play out options and leave for other teams (at least in the more modern era), suffer a crippling injury, or see another team surpass the champion in talent, ability, or even pure luck.

One more thing can haunt champs. They have proven themselves and can feel so fulfilled by achieving a long-sought goal that they may bask too long in the pleasure of it and may not attack foes with the same aggressiveness the next year.

Winning it all certainly meant a great deal to long-time Giants. It was a prize won dearly with a price paid, and the 1956 title would be a shared experience never forgotten. "This was the game Charlie and I had been waiting for through nine seasons," said Emlen Tunnell. "This was the championship that Mr. Mara [Wellington] had awaited through 19 long years."[3]

The year 1956 was special for the Giants and Charlie Conerly. The team and the player had waited a long time for vindication and recording the singular accomplishment of capturing a championship. The 1956 team was a mature version of the early 1950s clubs, ready to win. Players felt they were just entering their prime and could repeat, could keep on winning.

They should have been. The gang was all there. Every single important starter on offense and defense and in the kicking game was back. On offense, New York had Conerly at quarterback, Frank Gifford and Alex Webster in the backfield, Kyle Rote, Ken MacAfee, and Bob Schnelker catching passes, and Ray Wietecha, Roosevelt Brown, Jack Stroud, Bill Austin, and Ray Beck blocking, plus Mel Triplett. On defense, Sam Huff was the middle linebacker, flanked by Harland Svare and Cliff

Chapter 20. Trying to Do It Again

Livingston, with Rosey Grier, Jim Katcavage, Andy Robustelli, and Dick Modzelewski as the front four, and Tunnell, Jimmy Patton, Dick Nolan, and Ed Hughes in the secondary. Don Chandler was punting and Ben Agajanian was placekicking.

They were all known quantities with experience, veterans of the title run, all capable men, or All-Star–level players. Did they become self-satisfied overnight, or were they just as hungry as they had been, ready to devour another multi-course meal?

Close to the beginning of the 1957 season, the nation became embroiled in a racial crisis in Little Rock, Arkansas, an example of the growing tensions surrounding the Civil Rights movement and one of the opening salvos in the 1950s–1960s unrest due to discrimination against Blacks.

Nine African Americans attempted to enroll at Little Rock Central High School on September 4, but Governor Orval Faubus ordered the Arkansas National Guard to prevent the students from enrolling, and a crowd of angry protesters sought to keep them away.

On September 20, a federal judge ordered the National Guard to step back and allow the students to enter and integrate the school. When the students attempted again to begin their high school education on September 23, some 1,000 protesters turned out, and the nine were evacuated by police. President Dwight Eisenhower responded by sending in 1,000 U.S. paratroopers and federalizing the National Guard to enable the Black students to join the student body.

This had become national news, and it was a topic that Giants teammates and friends Emlen Tunnell and Charlie Conerly addressed. Theirs had always been an easy companionship despite Tunnell being a Black man from the North and Conerly being a White man from the South.

As one of their regular entertainment habits, Tunnell and Conerly frequented night clubs in Harlem, places at the epicenter of Black night life in New York. The Little Rock situation was so highly publicized and so incendiary, it became a topic of discussion in these establishments. As members of the New York Giants, Tunnell and Conerly were known attendees of shows and were known as compatriots.

"When the trouble started out in Little Rock, people would stop at our table in Harlem and start talking to him about it," Tunnell said.

> Nobody abused him, you understand. They respected him too much for that. What they were interested in was the reaction of a White man they admired. They didn't seem to understand that they were being thoughtless, that they were making things uncomfortable for Charlie, who had come there to relax, not to discuss sociology.[4]

It was unlikely Conerly had uttered a controversial statement in his life. He was known for not making waves. Neither did he voice strong sentiments on any topic. He was not about to start. Once, Tunnell and Conerly left a restaurant more quickly than planned because the attention and conversation heated up around them.

"Whatever I'd answer, I'd be wrong," Conerly told Tunnell. "No matter what I might say, people would think I didn't mean it."

Tunnell said, "Honesty and sincerity are everything to Charlie, and now he was taking a pounding that couldn't be shaken off like the beatings he took on the field. He hoped the questions would end, but when they didn't, Charlie stopped going up to Harlem."[5]

The implication, unspoken by Tunnell, was that Black people in the clubs in Harlem wanted Conerly to take a stand, tried to corner him into staking out a who-is-right position in Arkansas, and he chose not to do so.

The Giants received a head-slap from the Cleveland Browns on opening day, September 29, when they traveled to Ohio and lost, 6–3. The tough, low-scoring game sent a very important message from their Eastern Division rival. It was a game of all field goals, two by Lou Groza, one by Ben Agajanian. This result let the Giants know that the rivalry with Cleveland still existed. And it introduced a new combatant to the series.

Playing fullback for the Browns was rookie Jim Brown, a 230-pound, chiseled star who before he retired would be called the greatest football player of all time by many. Brown made his debut out of Syracuse University with an 89-yard rushing day. He rushed for 942 yards that season, was Rookie of the Year, won his first Most Valuable Player Award, and before retiring to become a Hollywood actor and a civil rights leader, totaled 12,312 yards rushing, a record that lasted for years.

In the coming years, Brown and Sam Huff would be portrayed as rivals—and to some extent they were. However, Brown was so good he was always the focal point of Cleveland's offense, a nearly unstoppable force who created havoc for the Giants' defense. The Browns and Giants faced off twice a season, and those contests could decide the division crown. It was obvious from the beginning that Jim Brown was a difference-maker, and Sam Huff later said that during that season, defensive coordinator Tom Landry set up the defense to single out Brown when the Giants met the Browns.

"And my assignment was to key on him," said Huff, who called Brown "the greatest runner in the history of professional football. Wherever Brown went, I'd be right there with him. That's really how

Chapter 20. Trying to Do It Again

Brown versus Huff started, and as the years went on, it was a rivalry that kept getting built up and up."[6]

In defense of their title, the Giants started 0–1. The wake-up call came a little bit late, but New York followed with a three-game winning streak, taking down the Philadelphia Eagles, 24–20, the Washington Redskins by the same 24–20 score, and then the Pittsburgh Steelers, 35–0, the first time that season they resembled a juggernaut capable of winning another championship.

New York needed some grit to outlast the Eagles in a game that was close all the way. It was 10–7 Philadelphia after one quarter, 14–10 Giants at the half, and 21–20 Giants after three quarters. Ben Agajanian kicked a breathing-room field goal for the only score in the fourth quarter. Conerly was 10 for 16 for 121 yards.

The Washington game was similar, with New York tallying one touchdown per quarter in the first three and kicking a field goal in the fourth. Conerly tossed one touchdown, but the Giants' biggest offensive splash was a 66-yard TD throw from Gifford to Schnelker.

The Steelers had no answers for the Giants, who scored a touchdown in each quarter and two in the fourth. Conerly heaved two TD passes to Schnelker. Gifford threw another to Rote. Jim Patton ran back an interception 50 yards for a touchdown, one of three picks by New York in the shutout. Pittsburgh managed just 54 yards rushing.

Just when the Giants seemed to be cruising, the Redskins turned things around on them, making up for the previous loss with a 31–14 thrashing. New York did not score in the second half. One of the early touchdowns came off Conerly's arm on a 10-yard throw to Webster.

The 3–2 record did not feel terribly good at that point, but then the Giants won November. They went on a four-game tear that altered the look of the season and reminded opponents who they had been a year ago. They played their best football of the season.

The defense did more than its share in a 31–17 victory against Green Bay on the road. Huff began the scoring by recovering a blocked punt in the end zone in the first quarter. Later, Tunnell intercepted a pass and ran that back 52 yards for a touchdown. In between, Conerly clicked on a three-yard pass for a score to MacAfee.

Okay, better. The Giants got off to a fast start against the Chicago Cardinals and held them down when they tried to rally late in the game, winning 27–14. New York led 10–3 at halftime and 17–7 after three periods. Conerly threw a 32-yard touchdown pass to Schnelker and a 13-yarder to Rote. Conerly threw for 185 yards, and the team ran for 170, Gifford collecting 126 of those yards.

Round two with the Eagles came next, and the defense posted its second shutout in a 13–0 victory. The offense was tepid this week with a Gifford run and Agajanian kicks accounting for all of the points. The defense protected the end zone as if it was the team castle.

Challenge no. 2 from the Cardinals was disposed of successfully as well, by a 28–21 final. Conerly passed for two TDs, and Webster ran for two more. Two Cardinals quarterbacks, Ted Marchibroda and Lamar McHan, kept Chicago in the game, each finding future Hall of Famer Ollie Matson with long throws of 75 and 62 yards for scores.

As the calendar turned to the coldest month of December and the regular season's conclusion loomed, the Giants were 7–2, very much in control of their fate and positioned to take the division title again—as long as they kept winning. They did not. New York seemed to be a team ready for any type of opponent, wore their champions' stripes with pride, and seemed to have all the necessary weapons on both sides of the ball to keep winning. Taking all three remaining games would be a lot to ask for, but winning two out of three would likely win the division. Instead, the Giants lost all three. They pulled an embarrassing fold.

There were more than 54,000 fans at Yankee Stadium to watch the Giants lose to the San Francisco 49ers, 27–17, making no real inroads in the second half. Conerly threw for 215 yards and one touchdown, and still it wasn't enough. Patton, Tunnell, and Bill Svoboda intercepted Y. A. Tittle once each, and that wasn't enough, either.

On December 7, roughly six weeks after the October 20 meeting that ended with a 35-point Giant victory, New York faced the Pittsburgh Steelers again and this time lost, 21–10. A 40-yard Conerly-Gifford touchdown connection was the main bright spot for the Giants.

For the last regular-season game, the Giants entertained the Browns at Yankee Stadium. Unlike the low-scoring inaugural game of the year, this one had much more action. The game ended the same way, though, with Cleveland ahead, 34–28. New Browns quarterback Milt Plum threw for 229 yards, and Jim Brown rushed for 78 yards and scored a touchdown. For New York, Frank Gifford put two scores on the board.

This discombobulating New York season ended with a 7–5 record, second in the division behind the Browns and their 9–2–1 mark. This time the season did not end with everyone's favorite drink at Toots Shor's. If players imbibed, it was probably too much beer, drinking to forget.

Chapter 21

Redemption Tour

For the most part, the New York Giants would have preferred to pretend the 1957 season never happened. They would have been content to erase it from the record books, eradicate it from memory or reality.

Many teams in the league would have been satisfied with the 7–5 record, but the Giants were gunning for much more and believed they had another title in them. The roster had all of the pieces, and the pieces had experience, and the Giants ended up running in sand.

That made 1958 a "We owe you one" for the fans and management, and for themselves. The Giants had the ingredients to win and win big. They knew it, too. No one was going to put more pressure on the players than they did on themselves. The front office had provided the tools. It was up to the players to use them.

There were some issues. Rosey Grier went into the service, though he would play all but two games in 1958. Jack Stroud, the iron man who was one of the first players in the sport to employ weightlifting to build his strength, got hurt and missed five games. Frank Youso became an offensive line starter instead.

Although they either didn't realize what they had or he wasn't ready yet, Don Maynard was a new receiver on the scene. Ultimately, Maynard would have a Hall of Fame career, with his key production in the American Football League in the 1960s. He was only a ninth-round draft pick out of lightly regarded Texas at El Paso.

Al Barry moved into a starting spot on the offensive line. Lindon Crow came over from the Chicago Cardinals and became a regular in the secondary. The same team yielded placekicker Pat Summerall, who replaced the venerable Ben Agajanian.

They were still around, but assistant coaches Vince Lombardi and Tom Landry were creating buzz with their knowledge, and other teams began thinking of them as head coaching material. Things might soon change in that area.

Top to bottom, the Giants were sound. Top to bottom, they had all the necessary ingredients to become a big winner. The same thing could have been said the previous year, yet it was on everyone's mind how that turned out.

The rock in the middle of the offense remained quarterback Charlie Conerly. He was in for his 10th season at age 37. The back-up was still Don Heinrich. A third quarterback on the roster, Tom Dublinksi, out of the University of Utah, was an insurance policy after putting in some time with the Detroit Lions.

Most people say the NFL exhibition season means nothing, wins and losses are irrelevant. The Giants lost five of six pre-season games in 1958, looking every bit like a team nursing a hangover from 1957, but as the public and league came to see, that stretch was meaningless.

"Despite our awful record in the pre-season," linebacker Sam Huff said, "a lot of us felt that Wellington [Mara] had really improved the football team in the off-season."[1]

Conerly was the center of the offensive scheme, the old wise man who read opposing defenses. Some thought he looked fairly old when he was a rookie. Now he was a 10-year man, and he had physically aged in appearance. Frank Gifford was his best friend on the team, and the men had been in close quarters, in hotels, at celebrations, and at work, for half of Conerly's time with New York.

The more time passed, the more Gifford appreciated what Conerly brought to the team, in terms of knowledge, athleticism, and especially leadership. As the sportswriters had long before learned, Conerly never pumped up his stats and his performances or craved the spotlight. He just showed up and clocked in at the office.

"When I first set eyes on Charlie Conerly," Gifford recorded many years later, "I thought, 'My God, he's got to be a coach. No son of a bitch that old could be playing football.' Charlie had gray hair and a gnarly, banged-up nose and he spoke with a kind of wheeze." More people characterized it as a whisper. "His facial expression suggested that he was either entering or emerging from a deep slumber."[2] And this was his friend talking.

Gifford said he pondered Conerly's appearance and seeming age—until the quarterback threw him his first pass. Instantly, he recognized that Conerly "was something special. He had this beautiful, graceful motion and an amazingly soft touch. As I discovered later, Charlie's touch perfectly reflected his personality."[3]

Gifford made Conerly sound like a refugee from the story *The Old Man and the Sea*, but he actually said, "Tennessee Williams could have created Charlie."[4] That linked Conerly to his Southern Mississippi roots. Gifford said Conerly was usually soft-spoken and stoic or responded to

Chapter 21. Redemption Tour

matters with a distinctive half-smile.

Rare enough, since Conerly kept quiet about his Marines experiences around most people, even those closest to him, Gifford said one time when they were sharing a beer-drinking session, Conerly told him some stories from World War II. They were events that led Gifford to conclude that Conerly was fortunate to come out of the war alive after being part of fighting on Guam, Iwo Jima and Tarawa. One soldier right next to Conerly was killed violently, Gifford said.

These were the kinds of experiences that made it difficult to rattle Conerly on the football field, whether defenses were charging him or fans were booing him. He had seen worse and survived it. It became fashionable somewhat later to compare football to war, but Conerly was one player who knew the sport was not life and death.

Charlie Conerly in 1958 football collector cards (author's collection).

Even if Conerly was loathe to reveal his inner feelings to newspapermen or to others in the locker room, Gifford formed his own conclusions about the man's character that was mostly hidden. "He only did it for a living," Gifford said of Conerly's connection to football.

> You could never tell from the expression on his face whether he'd just tossed a 50-yard touchdown, or been intercepted. I've always suspected that Charlie's emotional reserve was shaped by the horrors he witnessed in the war. A few of us, however, saw through Charlie's act. We knew he was a sensitive, thoughtful man who desperately hated to fail.[5]

The Giants were desperate not to fail in 1958, and Conerly was ready for another chance at a ring. During this season, Conerly threw for 1,199 yards and 10 touchdowns, while missing two games. The offense was not the main strength of this club, but Conerly made things happen when needed.

New York's season began with a 37–7 shellacking of the Chicago Cardinals. Gifford scored three touchdowns on runs from inside the 10 yard line, and Alex Webster scored two more on short runs. The game marked the regular-season debut of Pat Summerall with the Giants, and his foot was welcome. Summerall kicked a field goal of 28 yards plus four extra points.

By the end of the season, Summerall would be a pivotal figure in one of the most famous plays in team history. But he was no callow rookie with New York. He had been around the league since 1952, when he broke into the NFL with the Detroit Lions. He played just one season with that team before moving on to the Cardinals. Summerall was born in Lake City, Florida, and represented Arkansas collegiately.

Remarkably, given Summerall's athletic profession, when he was born in 1930, he had a club foot on his right side, what he referred to as "a bum leg." The leg was twisted backward. Summerall said his parents' marriage ended when his mother was pregnant, and in his small town, sophisticated medical care wasn't available. Summerall later said, "There wasn't much hope that I'd be able to walk normally."[6]

Summerall underwent risky surgery—still as an infant—and his leg was successfully repaired. Neither of Summerall's biological parents chose to raise him, so he lived with relatives growing up, on his way to becoming a tremendous athlete and eventually one of the best-known sports faces in America as a national broadcaster. The shift to New York to play with the Giants after competing for the lowly Cardinals lifted Summerall's profile, beginning with this 1958 season.

Joining the Giants represented a whole different world for Summerall. In his first season with New York, the team's training camp was about as far from the big city as possible while still in the United States. For some reason, management chose Salem, Oregon, as a summer visitation locale. Summerall was surprised, noting it was "a long way from the neon lights of Broadway and Times Square. It was more like the land time forgot."[7] It may well be that was the effect the team sought to establish in order to focus on a rebound from the disappointment of 1957.

This was Summerall's first up-close involvement with Vince Lombardi. Summerall was considered a back-up end as well as placekicker, but he caught just three passes in his entire pro career and none until 1959, so describing him as an end was window-dressing. His initial impression of Lombardi was intriguing. Summerall called him their "General Patton. He spoke with complete authority."[8]

Summerall got to say hello to many old friends on the Cardinals roster during the rout, but mostly the Giants thought they were waving goodbye to Chicago in the standings. It was a good start that was quickly negated by a 27–24 loss to the Philadelphia Eagles the next week. Conerly tossed touchdown passes to Gifford and Kyle Rote, but the backbreaker that gave Philadelphia a huge lift was a 91-yard TD pass from Norm Van Brocklin to Tommy McDonald. That hurt since the Giants slammed the gate on the Eagles' running game, allowing just 70 ground yards in 32 carries.

Starting 1–1 was not in the game plan, but at least the Giants won their next game, 21–14, over the Washington Redskins. Conerly and Don Heinrich each threw a touchdown pass. Gifford, Schnelker, and MacAfee each scored a TD. Once again, the New York defense was formidable, a stone wall, against the rush, permitting just 69 yards on the ground on 32 Washington carries. Those defenders really were living up to the home fan pleas of "Dee-fense! Dee-fense!" And the men were reveling in the attention. Huff said, "Our defensive unit was really something special. We'd been together for a few years, we were all close friends, and we were developing into the crowd favorites of Yankee Stadium."[9]

The good news was followed by bad news. New York threw in a very obvious clunker, falling to the Cardinals, 23–6, in their second meeting, an inexcusably massive turnaround from the 37–7 opener. A Mel Triplett short touchdown rush was the only New York moment worth remembering. This could have been a pivotal point in the season. The record was 2–2, and the Giants had to be more consistent or watch high hopes slip away.

New York moved over .500 with a 17–6 victory over the Pittsburgh Steelers. There was nothing flashy about the win. Defensive back Carl Karilivacz scored on a 23-yard fumble return, Heinrich scored on a one-yard run, and Summerall's foot accounted for the other points. The defense was voracious, allowing the Steelers just 45 yards rushing in 25 tries. Conerly did not play, and Heinrich was just two for 10 passing.

Next up was the season's first contest against the Browns in Cleveland's cavernous Municipal Stadium. The Browns were 5–0, and the 78,404 home fans sensed a renewal of championship form. A loss in this one and the Giants might be dead in the standings. The 1950s Giants–Browns head-to-head games were usually important. The tenacious defense the Giants brought to opponents' running games was neutralized by the immense talent of Jim Brown. Brown alone collected 113 yards rushing, double or more what some entire teams had compiled versus New York. He scored a touchdown on a 58-yard burst. However, Conerly had the response, throwing for 197 yards and three touchdowns, two to Alex Webster of 15 and 10 yards and one of 39 yards to Bob Schnelker. New York trailed at the half, but the Webster catches represented the only second-half scoring as the Giants rallied from behind.

It had taken almost no time for Jim Brown to establish his supremacy in the league. He was a tank with feet, strong and fast with terrific running instincts. In no games were his performances more magnified than those against the Giants.

"Tackling Jim Brown was the toughest task in football," Summerall said.

> He was a hulk of a man who made the rest of us look like weenies. To stop most ball carriers, you'd hit and wrap around them, then hang on till your sheer weight made them collapse That didn't happen with Brown. He'd just keep running while you and the rest of your team dragged along like so many tin cans on a string. He was stronger, faster and bigger than any other back in the league.[10]

The Cleveland triumph was huge, leaving the Giants with a 4–2 record and the Browns at 5–1 but with lots of time to catch up. The next foe, the Baltimore Colts, was a team moving up in the NFL, the product of a steady rebuild guided by coach Weeb Ewbank. The Colts were ready to bust out. The Giants were beginning to stir fan energy again, and 71,164 fans showed up at Yankee Stadium. George Shaw was still Baltimore's quarterback, and he tossed three touchdown passes in a tight game that was decided by a Summerall 28-yard field goal in the fourth quarter. Conerly threw one touchdown pass. Webster, Rote and Gifford each contributed a touchdown.

This was another valuable win over a tough team, accomplished in rugged fashion. Then the Giants promptly went walk-about again, blown out 31–10 by the Steelers in a loss that made little sense. It was a bravura performance by future Hall of Fame quarterback Bobby Layne, who had the gift of leadership. Layne threw one TD pass and twice ran in on one-yard scores.

Four games remained, and if the Giants wanted to make something out of this season, they had to win and win often. Test no. 1 in this stretch was versus the Washington Redskins on November 23. The Giants were not going to enjoy their turkey and cranberry sauce for Thanksgiving unless thy gobbled up a victory. They did so, convincingly, winning 30–0 in New York. It was a crush job from start to finish, two touchdown passes by Charlie Conerly, three field goals by Pat Summerall, and a defensive whitewash with Jimmy Patton and Harland Svare each making a pick.

Chapter 21. Redemption Tour

Game two against the Eagles was next. After Philadelphia's early-season win, the Eagles hadn't done much all season. Nor did they on this day, New York pulling away 24–10. Conerly did not play in this game, but Heinrich threw a couple of touchdown passes. Now New York was 7–3.

The Detroit Lions encounter was a fierce fight in front of 50,115 fans in Briggs Stadium. Desperate to stay alive for a shot at the crown, the Giants won, 19–17, with Gifford's one-yard rush in the fourth period giving New York the W.

Appropriately, and not surprisingly, the Eastern Division title came down to a showdown on December 14 at Yankee Stadium. New York fans got up for the game. With the Browns 9–2 and New York 8–3, the best the Giants could hope for was a tie in the standings that would necessitate a playoff game.

Jim Brown and his 148 yards rushing aside—it was apparent that he was playing in his own league—the entire contest was a defensive battle. Brown gave Cleveland a 7–0 lead in the first quarter with a 65-yard touchdown run. The Giants' lone touchdown came on a pass from Gifford to Schnelker. Summerall booted a 46-yard field goal in the second quarter after Lou Groza kicked a 22-yarder.

As the game wound down in the fourth quarter, with the score 10–10, the weather devolved into a raging snowstorm. Nonetheless, coach Jim Lee Howell huddled with his coaches, and they decided to take a long shot. Literally. Summerall was sent out into the blizzard-like conditions to attempt a field goal. The Giants' offense was on the Cleveland 24 yard line.

Everyone realized a tie game would do the Giants no good. If the game ended even, the Browns would clinch the division. If the Giants won, their season would continue.

Summerall's attempt in blowing snow missed wide from 31 yards. He was crushed, feeling he had let his team down and doomed it to defeat. Yet the Giants got a last chance late. Conerly found Webster open in the end zone, but Webster dropped the ball. Conerly was preparing to throw a Hail Mary when Summerall appeared in the huddle on directions from Howell.

"What are you doing here?" Conerly asked Summerall. "They sent me in to kick the field goal." Conerly replied, "You're kidding!"[11]

This loomed as an impossible task, at a time when 49-yard field goals were rare and the odds against making such a kick in absurd conditions were large.

Many years later, when Summerall recounted the moment of the biggest kick of his life, he sugarcoated neither the scene nor the difficulty of the challenge. It was the only chance the Giants had for a win, and the weight of New York was on his shoulders.

Summerall's recounting of the situation is both dramatic and vivid. Doubting Conerly was Summerall's holder for the kick, his soft hands the most trusted on the team. "I made the mistake of looking toward the distant goal shrouded in a heavy curtain of falling snow," Summerall said. "The wind was howling. My breath was a vapor cloud hovering in front of my face. Lacking ice picks, Charlie and I kicked out a little clearing for my feet."[12]

The snow had obliterated yard makers and, looking half the length of the field, Summerall had the impression the goal post had shrunk. He was disoriented by the snow blowing into his face. The hike was clean, and so was the hold. Summerall's boot sailed into the mists—far enough and straight enough to count for three points and the Giants' triumph.

"A mob of teammates hit me like a runaway snowplow," Summerall said. When Summerall swam his way through other players to the sideline, assistant coach Vince Lombardi, who had argued for going for a first down, uttered the famous line that stuck: "You son of a bitch, you know you can't kick it that far!"[13] Well, it turned out Summerall could.

The suspenseful finish extended the season. There was no Eastern Division winner. So for the third time this 1958 season, the Giants and Browns played, this time with matching 9–3 records. Winner goes on and loser goes home. This was quite the task facing New York. The Giants had beaten the Browns twice already. Summerall's kick—probably the most famous in franchise history—could have been for naught.

The third New York–Cleveland game took place on December 21, just a week later, at Yankee Stadium, the contest this time attracting 61,254 fans. Howell had been criticized, even as his plan worked, for going with Summerall for the winning points in such demanding circumstances. This time it was difficult to find anyone who had anything much to dislike about what played out.

Conerly, who almost never ran the ball from farther away from the goal line than a single yard, scored a New York touchdown on a 10-yard play in the first quarter, and Summerall kicked another key field goal in the second quarter from 24 yards. That was all of New York's scoring, and the Giants didn't even need that much. The defense clamped down brilliantly in a 10–0 win. That defense prevented Cleveland from doing anything offensively, and that included Jim Brown. Brown rushed for just eight yards in seven attempts, the lowest production of his career. Linden Crow made two interceptions.

The Conerly play was a once-in-a-decade call from the sidelines by Lombardi. Conerly received the snap from Ray Wietecha and handed

Chapter 21. Redemption Tour

the ball off to Webster. Webster made as if to run around the end, but Gifford was coming the other way and took the ball on a reverse, with Conerly trailing.

"Well, Frank got about 10 yards and was about to be tackled when he wheeled around and lateraled the ball to me," Conerly said. "Everybody was on him, and I just took it on in for the touchdown." Conerly noted that Cleveland coach Paul Brown said afterward, "What the hell was he doing there?" Conerly said the trick play Lombardi chose did call for him to be there, and the old QB got a hoot out of making the run. "I don't know how long it'd been since I scored a touchdown, but it was great for an old guy like me to run it in."[14]

Conerly's 37-year-old legs did not fail him in the clutch, sending the Giants into the 1958 NFL championship game against the Baltimore Colts. Baltimore and New York were about to engage in what has been called the best game in league history.

Chapter 22

Greatest Game

The 1958 National Football League championship game between the New York Giants and the Baltimore Colts has been termed "the Greatest Game Ever Played" by coaches, broadcasters, other observers, and even some participating players who didn't think about the description much at the time.

This nickname may have been a misnomer. "Greatest" is almost never indisputable and is buttressed by opinion. A more accurate substitute word for this title game's impact would be "Most Important Game Ever Played" or "Most Significant Game Ever Played." It would be difficult to generate arguments to challenge that.

Circumstances, competition, and long-term meaningfulness reflect the situation better, although books have been written about this single contest, one with the declarative title *The Best Game Ever.* No doubt, winners or losers aside, it was probably the most memorable pro football game of all time.

The Giants had to outfight the Cleveland Browns (for the third time that season) in an extra playoff game to qualify as the Eastern Division representative in the championship game. The Colts had to survive their own tight race to claim the Western Division crown, also with a 9–3 record. The Chicago Bears and Los Angeles Rams tied for second with 8–4 records. Both divisions had down-to-the-wire races.

Baltimore had been reshaped and retooled by coach Weeb Ewbank and was finally ready for the bright lights of the national stage. The average football fan may not have been familiar with the Colts lineup then, but Baltimore was loaded with talent.

Members of that 1958 Colts team eventually inducted into the Pro Football Hall of Fame in Canton, Ohio, were receiver Raymond Berry, defensive tackle Art Donovan, coach Weeb Ewbank, defensive end Gino Marchetti, running back Lenny Moore, offensive lineman Jim Parker, and quarterback Johnny Unitas. The country was just about to meet Unitas.

Meanwhile, Giants assistant coaches Tom Landry and Vince Lombardi would reach the Hall of Fame (mainly for their jobs leading other teams as head coaches). They were joined by players Emlen Tunnell, Roosevelt Brown, Andy Robustelli, Sam Huff, and Frank Gifford. Receiver Don Maynard made it, too, but this was his only season with the Giants, and he was recognized for his performance in the 1960s in the American Football League. Giants team founder Tim Mara and son Wellington Mara are also members of the Hall of Fame. Another Giants back-up was quarterback Jack Kemp, who did not excel until he also went on to the AFL and other endeavors as a United States congressman.

That was a cast of luminaries, and it did not even include the number of players like Charlie Conerly, Alex Webster, Ray Wietecha, Rosey Grier, and Jimmy Patton, multiple-time All-Stars on the New York side, and Gene "Big Daddy" Lipscomb, Alan Ameche, Art Spinney, and Andy Nelson on the Baltimore side.

Giants kicker Pat Summerall was glad the game was scheduled for New York. He was worn down from the grueling season-ending schedule, and he knew the Colts would be a tough opponent.

"We were at home again, which was a good thing because our butts were dragging," Summerall said. "I don't think I had the strength to pack. By nearly every assessment, we were the underdogs. The book on us was that we'd gotten some lucky bounces in our defeat of the Colts earlier in the season."[1] That was the 24–21 victory on November 9.

The game was set for Yankee Stadium on December 28, and 64,185 fans showed up for the entertainment. In those days, pro football was not ubiquitous national television programming, and color TV could best be described as being in its infancy. This was pre–cable TV, and the networks were still feeling their way without the aid of six, eight or 10 camera angles.

When it came to screen clarity, the weather did not help: it was a gray, chilly, damp winter day after brief sunshine at the 2 p.m. kickoff. Those in the stands may well have carried an abundance of hip flasks, as was the stereotypical image of college football fans. No one counted raccoon coats, but definitely the attire involved warm layers.

The first quarter evidence indicated a possible low-scoring result. Neither team moved the ball well, and both teams turned the ball over. On a play with Unitas fading back to pass on the first Colts possession, Huff shot through the line, sacked Unitas, and caused a fumble, which was recovered by Patton on the Baltimore 37 yard line. Good field position.

New York hoped to capitalize quickly, but the Giants paid for

Charlie Conerly (42) holds on a field goal try by Pat Summerall (88) in a playoff game victory over the Cleveland Browns on December 21, 1958 (Associated Press).

sticking with the iffy strategy of starting Don Heinrich at quarterback instead of Conerly. On the first play, Heinrich fumbled when hit by Marchetti, and the ball went back to Baltimore. Opportunity squandered. The situation remained all defensive showmanship, however. The Colts moved the ball a bit, but when Unitas aimed downfield and threw, defensive back Lindon Crow intercepted. The Giants were once again stagnant, handing the ball back to the Colts, but when Steve Myhra lined up for a short field goal, Huff blocked it.

That was it for Heinrich. Conerly entered the contest and led the Giants into Colts territory, sparked by a 36-yard run by Gifford. Webster was open on third down but slipped on the wet field, and the pass was incomplete. That set up Summerall for a 36-yard field goal try, and he made good on it—conditions were not great but were far superior to when he made his clutch 49-yarder earlier in the month. That made it 3–0 New York. So far, the game, plagued by turnovers and a lack of offensive action, was about as far as possible from the greatest any kind of game anyone would rank.

The Giants' defenders did not have time to stand around congratulating themselves on what a great job they were doing pitching a shutout. By the end of the second quarter, Baltimore led, 14–3. Alan Ameche was a solidly built, six-foot, 220-pound runner who attended Syracuse University and had been the NFL Rookie of the Year in 1955, when he led the league in rushing with 961 yards and added nine touchdowns on the ground. Crunching over the goal line on a two-yard run, Ameche gave Baltimore a 7–3 lead.

New York could have retaliated quickly, but after recovering a fumbled punt on the Baltimore 10, Gifford fumbled the ball back. The Colts added to their lead with a Unitas-to-Berry 15-yard TD. That culminated an 86-yard Baltimore drive for the solid 14–3 halftime lead. It was a worrisome situation, exacerbated by a sequence early in the third quarter. "They threatened to put the game away early in the second half when they drove for a first down at our 3-yard line," Robustelli said.[2]

Possibly with the game at stake, the Giants' vaunted unit turned in a goal-line stand, stopping Ameche on third and fourth downs. Linebacker Cliff Livingston shut down Ameche on the five yard line. That still left the Giants with 95 yards to paydirt.

Going for the sting, Conerly ducked back in the pocket and heaved a long throw to Kyle Rote, connecting about mid-field. Rote broke a tackle, kept churning his legs, and then to the horror of home fans was hit and fumbled on the 25 yard line. However, Alex Webster was trailing the play, scooped up the ball, and darted all the way to the one. New York promptly scored on a one-yard run by Mel Triplett—critical points at that juncture.

That sequence put the Giants back in the game as the clock ticked on with Baltimore ahead, 14–10. At the same time, outside the stadium, around the region, throughout the country, something peculiar was happening. This was just the third time the NFL championship game had been nationally televised. The league was battling for public legitimacy, to move up in the hierarchy of important big-league sports in the United States. Major League baseball was king, the national pastime. Boxing and horse racing were popular. The NBA was a fledgling league, and hockey was very much a regional sport, its best teams competing in only six large cities, two of them in Canada.

Bert Bell had been painstakingly trying to increase NFL visibility and public acceptance since becoming commissioner in 1946. When he woke up that morning, not even he could have realized his moment was at hand. The weather in many of the most populated communities in the North grew worse and worse. Snow increased. Nobody wanted to go outside except perhaps for kids seeking to build backyard snow forts. So they turned on their television sets to see what was on, and many stumbled across a championship football contest that was a close game and drew them in. Eventually, it was believed that some 45 million

Americans tuned in as the game went on and became even more suspenseful. The NFL offered a taste of its best to even those who had no interest in cheering on a New York team or a Baltimore team.

Son of a gun if, early in the fourth quarter, after all of their miscues and errors earlier in the game, the Giants didn't take the lead. Conerly directed the traffic and the offense, moving the team down the field on the Baltimore D. On this day, Conerly turned in an exemplary performance. Effectively mixing up his short game and deep balls, Conerly completed 10 out of 14 pass attempts for 187 yards and a quarterback rating of 137.5.

On this drive, Conerly fired a 46-yard completion to tight end Bob Schnelker and followed up with a 15-yard touchdown pass to Gifford. When Summerall kicked the extra point—and it seemed likely every point would matter—New York led, 17–14. Now the Giants had to hold it, relying on the defense.

"But with Unitas around, everyone in the stadium knew it was hardly the time to breathe easy," Huff said.[3] He was right. Borrowing from what Yogi Berra did or did not utter, "It's not over 'til it's over."

Huff may have made that comment about Unitas later, but the quarterback had not yet established himself as a star and a clutch comeback king. This game, and what was to come, did that for him. Giants players didn't even know who the free agent was when they faced him in a 1956 exhibition game. When that game concluded, Gifford asked Conerly who the other team's quarterback was. Unitas did not make an imposing presence, partially because he was stoop-shouldered. "'Who is this guy?' I ask Charlie. "He goes off to find out, comes back and says, 'U-na-tis.'" Gifford replied, "Sounds like a Greek drugstore chain."[4]

The Giants and other NFL players learned how to pronounce Johnny U's name soon enough. By the 1958 title game, Ewbank, the Colts, and Unitas' teammates looked to him as their leader, as their rescuer. Unitas ended up completing 26 of 40 passes for 349 yards in this game, high totals that were extremely rare for the era. He relied heavily on Berry, one of the greatest possession receivers and precise route runners ever, who caught 12 passes as the Colts moved the ball and assaulted the Giants' defense.

For much of the fourth quarter, the Colts came at the New York unit, penetrating into the New York side of the field but then facing stiffened opposition. Baltimore could not get into the end zone. Twice, the Colts threatened. On the first try, Bert Rechichar, who owned the league record for longest field goal at 56 yards, missed a 46-yard attempt. On another possession, Baltimore reached the Giants' 27, but Unitas was sacked by Robustelli and a second time by Dick Modzelewski. The two losses threw him back 20 yards, and that shoved Baltimore out of field goal range.

The Giants got the ball and did their best to kill the clock. This was one day, however, when the New York running game was not clicking on all cylinders (Gifford was the best rushing weapon with 60 yards, but he also fumbled twice). Gino Marchetti tackled Gifford on third down, and the referees placed the ball shy of a first down. Some Giants were furious, convinced he made it to the marker.

"I was certain I had it," Gifford said. Although coach Jim Lee Howell also believed Gifford had crossed the line for a first down, he did not make a major stink at the time. Gifford added, "Our team didn't argue about it too much. That's because there was more discipline among the players. Today they would have been charging the officials and creating a scene."[5]

Marchetti stayed on the ground with a broken ankle. Doctors wanted to evacuate him from the field for medical treatment, but once on the sidelines, Marchetti refused to leave until the game was over. There is an iconic photograph of Marchetti propped up on a stretcher, watching play.

The Giants had the ball on fourth down at their own 40 yard line with about two minutes left. The Colts had been moving the ball steadily but had not breached the Giants' defense to reach the end zone. Howell made the decision to punt. It was up to the defense to control Unitas, and when the Colts were stuck on their own 14 yard line, it seemed as if Howell's gamble was a secure one.

As the clock wound down, it came to Perian Conerly's attention that her husband was going to be announced as the Most Valuable Player and the winner of the automobile awarded with the prize. "After the third quarter, the journalists voted Charlie as the most valuable player, but after the teams went into overtime, they re-voted and Johnny Unitas was the winner," Perian said. "He received a Corvette. I always said Barbara Unitas was driving my Corvette."[6]

That was how quickly the atmosphere in the stadium switched. As improbable as it was, Unitas led the Colts on a last-ditch drive down the field, defying the tackling arms of the Giants and the taunting voices of the fans screaming for their players to stop them. This last-minute push began slowly, with incomplete passes, until Unitas completed a third-down 11-yarder to Lenny Moore, followed by three straight passes to Raymond Berry. Berry masterfully used the sideline as an ally. The Colts reached the New York 13 yard line with seven seconds on the clock.

This was just enough time for Steve Myhra (not Rechichar) to attempt a 20-yard field goal. The kick was good, the game was tied, and little time remained. Rechichar kicked off to the Giants, the ball reaching the end zone. It was fielded by Don Maynard and run back to the New York 18. The Giants ran one play—Conerly keeping the ball for a quarterback sneak of one yard—and the clock ran out with the score 17–17.

Championship games do not end in ties. Always a winner is declared. The only thing about this circumstance was that it had never happened in a title game in NFL history, dating back to the league's start in 1920.

At least a handful of players did not know the rules, did not know at the fourth quarter gun that they would continue playing. Imagine listening in on some of the talk.

"Sudden death? What the hell is he talking about?" Huff said when he heard the referee indicate that play would resume shortly. "What happens now?" Summerall asked Rote. "I think we play some more," Rote said. Conerly was sitting on the bench next to Gifford and indicated that he had given his all. "Wow, I can't go anymore," he said. "Boy, you're gonna have to go some more," Gifford responded. "I can't. I just can't," said the weary Conerly.[7] But of course he could—and did.

It seems odd to ponder so many years later, but many players on the field did not know what came next. The NFL had implemented a "sudden death" rule a few years earlier, but it had never been needed. This was the first overtime scenario in league history, and "sudden death" meant that the first team to score was the winner. At that time, regular-season games could conclude in a tie without any overtime. For this game, the teams met at mid-field after a three-minute break, and another coin-flip, the same as was performed at game's start, took place.

Kyle Rote and Bill Svoboda represented the Giants, and they won the toss and elected to receive. Rechichar kicked off once more. Maynard caught the ball at the 10 yard line, fumbled, then recovered, the ball blown dead at the 20.

New York had its chance to run the table. On first down, Gifford gained four yards rushing. On second down, Conerly threw incomplete to Schnelker. On third down, in somewhat of a surprise, Conerly kept the ball, ran, and was marked down after five yards gained, just short of the first down. Don Chandler punted for the Giants.

Baltimore took over on its own 20 and began its march to glory and into history. Halfback L.G. Dupre cut left and gained 11 yards on a run. Unitas attempted a deep one to Lenny Moore, but the throw was incomplete. Dupre ran again, gaining two yards. Unitas threw to Ameche, who cut over the middle and gained eight yards. Dupre broke free for another four yards, but when Unitas faded back on the next down, Modzelewski knocked him down for a sack and a loss of eight yards.

Berry grabbed a short pass, but Ameche, about to become the hero of the hour, ripped off a 22-yard gain on the ground, setting the Colts up on the Giants' 20-yard line. Dupre ran again but was stopped at the line of scrimmage. There was something inexorable about this possession. Unitas hit with a 12-yard completion to Berry, placing the ball on the eight.

The Colts were in rhythm. Unitas fired a strike to tight end Jim Mutcheller, who was downed a body's length from the end zone. When the next play unfolded, there was a gigantic hole in the Giants' defensive line, and Ameche, head down, ran to daylight, covering the two yards for the winning touchdown. No one bothered with an extra point. The Colts won, 23–17.

Almost immediately, the buzz about the game ricocheted around the country. The next morning, in offices, it was "Did you see that?" At NFL headquarters, there was a glow about what a great show fans had seen. The TV exposure was phenomenal and led to pro football having the door opened wider and wider on national TV in the coming years.

No one who was part of the Giants–Colts championship game and no one who watched it ever forgot it. It quickly took on cache as "the best game" or "the greatest game." Giants players, disappointed by the loss, did not always agree with the statements, because, after all, they felt they could have played better and could have won. Then maybe they might have felt they could view the game as the best ever.

Periodically, newspapers and sports magazines revisited the topic. Was this really the greatest football game ever? There was always parsing of what that might mean, but over time it was pretty well settled that Giants–Colts 1958 was likely the most important pro football game ever played. That game was pointed to when pro football began to take over the sporting landscape across the land.

Players who participated in the game, especially those who became enduring stars or Hall of Famers, were often enough asked if they believed it was the best game and if it really did have the meaning for NFL growth ascribed to it.

"I think that basically that it was going to happen anyway," Unitas said years later. "But I think because of the exciting way that the game was tied with the field goal and then the first overtime ever played, I think that added to the excitement. All the things added up."[8]

That comment was made 40 years later and was simultaneous to an announcement that the NFL was going to honor living Hall of Famers who participated in the game at the following Super Bowl and that the coin used in the game toss, featuring the Colts and Giants helmets, would be part of the next Super Bowl logo.

"The world of professional football was forever changed by that one game," Robustelli said. "But for me, it was a lousy way to make history."[9]

If you played for the New York Giants, it was hard not to share Robustelli's outlook.

It helped to be a member of the Colts to maintain the "greatest game" perspective. Giants players understood it was a special occasion, but they didn't revel in it quite so much because they lost.

CHAPTER 23

1959: Giants–Colts Again

A sadness permeated the New York Giants organization less than two months after the Giants fell to the Baltimore Colts. Team founder Tim Mara passed away on February 16, 1959, at age 71.

His small investment 34 years earlier had turned into the family business—which it remains today—and while he was no longer involved in daily operations, he was a figure connected to the team who was missed. Just a few years later, in 1963, when the new Professional Football Hall of Fame opened in Canton, Ohio, Mara was a member of the original class of inductees.

In a very different way, probably the weirdest thing that happened with the New York Giants and Charlie Conerly between the end of the sudden death championship game loss to the Baltimore Colts and the start of 1959 training camp was the declaration by Frank Gifford that he wanted to try out for quarterback.

This was bizarre on several fronts. Gifford and Conerly were close friends and roommates on the road. Gifford was already the starting halfback. Conerly was already the starting quarterback. They had been partners and teammates since 1952. They socialized evenings and in free time. Often, Gifford had been Conerly's staunchest defender standing against boobirds and critics.

And now Gifford wanted to take away Conerly's starting position? That sounded pretty selfish. Yes, Gifford had been called on to unleash the periodic halfback option pass, and he threw for occasional touchdowns. But how could this not be considered a personal affront?

Gifford approached coach Jim Lee Howell and asked for a chance to try out for quarterback. It would be an overstatement to suggest that Howell was enthused. He didn't say no outright, but he didn't embrace the suggestion with a broad smile and a slap on the back. He must have thought very hard about how to handle the situation in training camp without alienating two of his most important players. No doubt sportswriters would pick apart this circumstance and analyze it to death.

Then there was the Gifford-Conerly dynamic. Conerly was the elder statesman of the team, in place at the QB slot since 1948, one of the most prominent Giants on the roster. How was he going to take this? Would Gifford's power play leave him embittered? Would the two men develop serious friction? Would it upset the chemistry of the team? Those were all reasonable questions.

Gifford indicated that he had thought about the idea of being a quarterback for many years. "This was no passing fancy," Gifford said. "For openers, beginning in high school, a quarterback is always what I wanted to be. Yet, every time I got a shot at it something interfered and I ended up somewhere else. I also knew I could handle the job."[1]

Gifford had done his own math and figured he had thrown 12 touchdown passes off the halfback option in just 41 attempts. He believed the statistic showed he could become a quarterback. As an acknowledgment that this was an unusual situation, Gifford wrote a letter before training camp to Howell outlining his goal and desire. He pledged in writing that if things did not work out, "I will not moan and groan. I will not give you a problem."[2]

Given the sensitivity of his plan, Gifford did not telephone Conerly or write him a letter. Instead, he traveled to Clarksdale, Mississippi. They were out fishing together when Gifford broke the news. He said Conerly was very gracious and shrugged off the matter, saying, "Fine with me. I'll help you all I can."[3] Gifford attributed Conerly's nonchalance to his usual placid demeanor and also to his dislike of practice, believing some of the practice burden would be shifted from his shoulders. Perhaps.

In his long career as New York Giants quarterback between 1948 and 1961, Charlie Conerly tried to avoid scrambling, preferring to call a passing game, but sometimes he had to run (courtesy Pro Football Hall of Fame).

Chapter 23. 1959: Giants–Colts Again   181

Somewhere along the way, at least one newspaper got the situation slightly twisted and reported that the men were playing golf when Gifford informed Conerly he was going to go for the quarterback job. The supposed response from Conerly was something on the order of "Don't you know not to talk to me when I'm putting" and nothing else. Good story. It also would have demonstrated Conerly not being flustered. But Perian Conerly backed the other version, saying Gifford came to Mississippi and Conerly told him he would provide all the help he needed.

Some of Conerly's tightest teammates did not appreciate this so-called sneak attack by Gifford. They supported Conerly, who was playing football as well as he ever had and was a veteran friend, feeling that Gifford was needed in his own slot.

When training camp began, Howell gave Gifford some turns taking snaps. But the Giants had also acquired George Shaw from the Colts, the previous quarterback before Johnny Unitas wrested the job from him there. Plus, they drafted Lee Grosscup, an All-American who had played at Utah and the University of Washington. They also still had perennial back-up Don Heinrich around for his final season in New York. Jack Kemp had departed for the Calgary Stampeders in the Canadian Football League, but it was quite crowded at the position.

Conerly wrote a letter home to Perian assessing the situation.

> There are so many men trying out for quarterback this year I'm not getting much practice. I have to stand around so long waiting for my turn I've been running extra laps to keep in shape, and, as you know, I'm not all that fond of running. Even my own roommate is trying to take my job away from me![4]

Given the glut of quarterback candidates, this was not the best preseason for Gifford to inject himself into the picture. He got fewer turns behind center than he might have liked before Howell sent him back to halfback for good. The other survivors were Conerly, Shaw, and Heinrich. Grosscup was out but returned the next year.

While this scenario was on players' minds, when all was settled Conerly remained the starting quarterback. However, the big off-season change for the offense was the departure of Vince Lombardi. He left to become the Green Bay Packers' head coach and began his rise to glory in Wisconsin, where his voice was the only voice that counted in making decisions, and the payoff was rich as he formed the Packers into a powerhouse.

There would have been only one way to keep Lombardi in New York. The Maras would have had to fire Jim Lee Howell and turn over the head job to Lombardi. Howell had just led the Giants to the championship game, so that wasn't happening. Lombardi was on his way to greatness, but in 1959, before he had coached a game in the NFL, that would have been difficult to predict.

At the time, the Maras were not criticized for letting Lombardi go.

"That's the hardest decision you have to make in this business. Deciding whether the successful assistant can make the step up to be a successful head coach," John Mara, Wellington's son, said much later. "There's many more failures than there are successes. You tell me, looking at NFL history, how many highly thought-of assistants fail as NFL head coaches. He [Lombardi] ended up becoming the greatest NFL coach of all time."[5]

Allie Sherman, who had been Giants backfield coach in the early 1950s, replaced Lombardi as offensive coordinator. Sherman, who served a lengthy apprenticeship as an assistant in the sport, was only an average player and could even joke about it. "I was the league's best left-handed ball-holder for place kicks," he said.[6]

This was a period when the Giants were winners and had roster stability, especially with their biggest names. Two new key players were added in 1959, though, guard Darrell Dess and defensive back Dick Lynch. They missed the earliest days of this Giants era but were very good contributors once on board.

Dess was a six-foot, 245-pound offensive lineman out of North Carolina State who was an 11th-round draft pick of the Washington Redskins and played one season for the Pittsburgh Steelers before joining the Giants and sticking with them through several top-notch years until 1964. Twice he was selected for the Pro Bowl with New York.

Baltimore's Big Daddy Lipscomb, who pushed 300 pounds, once referred to Dess as a little guy who could block. Dess appreciated the compliment.

"I don't mind hitting people," Dess said. "I love the contact. It's getting hit in the head that bothers me. We're just taught to block with our heads. If you block with a shoulder, the defensive man can slide off. I break helmets. Sometimes everything goes black. I'm woozy a lot. And I have a headache after every game."[7] Apparently, Dess was one of the earliest athletes to recognize that pro football could be dangerous to a player's long-term health. Yet he was still living at 87 in 2022.

Lynch, who played collegiately at Notre Dame, started with the Redskins and after one season joined the Giants. He ended up intercepting 37 passes in his career, with a high of nine in 1961. Lynch had the daunting task of replacing Emlen Tunnell. The aging Tunnell was gone after a decade of affiliation with the Giants. He followed Lombardi to Green Bay and spent his last three seasons playing there. Lombardi, who had the dual role of coach and general manager, initiated the purchase of Tunnell's contract.

Chapter 23. 1959: Giants–Colts Again

When the 1959 season started on September 26 against the Rams at the Los Angeles Memorial Coliseum, Charlie Conerly was the main quarterback. It was time to learn whether the Giants would be crushed by their famous Colts defeat or the players would become more determined because of it.

The Coliseum was a huge stadium, opened in 1923 and famously the site of the opening ceremonies and other events at the 1932 Summer Olympic Games. For their opening game the Rams pulled in 71,297 fans who saw a good game though the Giants prevailed, 23–21. Pat Summerall's kicking was the essential element this day. He scored the first points of the season on a 23-yard field goal in the first quarter, and his field goal boots of 14 and 18 yards won the game as the New York defense shut out the Rams in the fourth quarter.

The biggest blow for the Giants was a 66-yard Conerly-to-Schnelker touchdown pass in the second period, and Gifford scored on a one-yard run in the same quarter. After the hullabaloo of training camp, Conerly went all the way at quarterback and turned in one of his finest games, completing 21 of 31 passes for 321 yards. He did not throw an interception and was not sacked.

It was a good start, but the Giants were manhandled by the improving Philadelphia Eagles the next week, falling 49–21. It was as bad as 42–7 at one point. Tommy McDonald, the sprite of a wide receiver and a shifty runner, tallied four touchdowns, one on an 81-yard punt return. Norm Van Brocklin threw two touchdown passes and ran for another. The only New York scoring through the air was a TD toss by Shaw to Rote.

Observers could argue that the Giants' season was already at a crossroads as they prepared to meet the Cleveland Browns. Hard to call a third-week game a must, but this one kind of was. The contest was not flashy, more hard-nosed, but the Giants won, 10–6. Conerly was nine for 17 for 106 yards through the air and scored on a one-yard run. Add a Summerall 31-yard field goal, and that accounted for New York's points. But it was enough with the Giants taking a 10–0 lead. Jim Brown was contained, with only 86 yards rushing.

After the Eagles debacle, the defense turned its helmets around facing forward again. New York held five teams to seven points or less and led the NFL by permitting only 170 points all season, or 14.2 per game. The offense likewise responded to Sherman's coaching and finished second in points at 23.7 per game.

Linebacker Sam Huff, who was gaining celebrityhood on the New York sports scene, said the players adjourned to Toots Shor's for drinks. The host welcomed them effusively, praising the D. "Toots would come up to us and say, 'I looooove the defense. I looooove the defense,' and he always gave us the best seat in the house," Huff said.[8]

There was a lot to like, and the Browns victory propelled the Giants to a five-game winning streak. They followed by reversing the results with the Eagles, dominating Philadelphia 24–7, a whole 'nother world of a game. Harland Svare delivered a crushing play on a 70-yard pass interception. Although Conerly played acceptably, Shaw came on and outplayed him, completing seven of nine passes for 156 yards, including a 13-yard touchdown toss to Schnelker.

After that, the Giants topped Pittsburgh, 21–16, Green Bay, 20–3, and the Chicago Cardinals, 9–3. This was the first meeting of the Giants and Packers with Lombardi coaching for the other side. Lombardi was at the beginning of his quick rebuild.

Versus Pittsburgh, Conerly twice found Gifford open for long touchdowns of 77 and 28 yards, was nine for 14 for 199 yards, did not throw an interception, and had a quarterback rating of 147.3. Although Lombardi was thoroughly familiar with the Giants' offensive personnel, his new guys could not stop New York. Summerall kicked two 49-yard field goals in this one, and Alex Webster scored touchdowns on rushes of three and seven yards. The Cardinals game was pretty ugly. New York fans could thank Summerall for his showing. His field goals of 37, 49, and 20 yards accounted for the Giants' points. The defense deserved the best seats at Toots Shor's after holding an opponent to only three points for the second week in a row. The Cardinals gained just 63 yards passing.

A banged-up Conerly was sidelined to restore his aching body. "Conerly had taken a pretty good beating all season," Huff said. "Hell, he was always taking a beating."[9]

The five-game winning streak ended with a 14–9 loss to the Steelers. Summerall kicked three field goals, but Bobby Layne threw two touchdown passes. Conerly missed this game, too, and Howell went with Don Heinrich, whose accuracy was limited. Heinrich was only seven for 24.

The loss left New York at 6–2. The Browns were also 6–2. It seemed entirely possible this season would continue with these regular rivals in a pitched fight for the division title again. That is not how things played out, however. The Giants had no more lapses. The offense began playing better than ever. All things were clicking on both sides of the ball. After the slip-up against the Steelers, the Giants went on a winning spree.

First, they took out the Cardinals, 30–20. Conerly was back and fired two touchdown passes, 33 yards to Gifford and 45 yards to Schnelker. Summerall kicked three field goals and three extra points. The game shouldn't even have been that close, but the Cardinals burned

New York with two long punt returns for touchdowns, marking special teams collapses.

Then the Giants—and Conerly—feasted on the Washington Redskins, pummeling them, 45–14. Conerly was superb, tossing touchdown passes of two, seven, and 34 yards by halftime. Gifford, in shades of what might have been, threw a TD pass, but more notably rushed for 159 yards as New York gained 351 yards on the ground.

That day, November 29, was declared "Charlie Conerly Day" at Yankee Stadium, the Giants honoring their long-time quarterback's service since 1948. The ceremonies took place on the field before the game versus Washington. Conerly entered from the locker room to a standing ovation from the 60,982 fans in attendance.

Perian was part of the line-up, as was the team chaplain, long-time Clarksdale buddy Tony Malvezzi, and darned if Charlie wasn't presented with a new Corvette. Perian got her car. But wait, the Giants also kicked in a 1960 Cadillac. The Conerlys received a trip to Europe, a movie camera, a vacuum cleaner, a knitting machine, a silver tea service, clothes for Charlie, luggage, a dinette set, an encyclopedia set, binoculars, cotton seed, fertilizer and a cotton trailer, a sterling silver football signed by Giants teammates, and a five-year supply of vitamins. They really did think he was old! Perian was singled out with a gold charm in the shape of Conerly's No. 42 with the inscription: "To our Perian on her Charlie's day." Don Heinrich and his wife, Barbara, were behind that gift.

Perian said that Giants president Jack Mara walked her off the field to her seat for the game, and she noticed a sign held up in the stands reading, "CONERLY FOR PRESIDENT." It wasn't clear if John F. Kennedy or Richard Nixon should step aside.

Later that evening, the Giants' Section Five Club threw a testimonial dinner and presented Conerly with a Sportsman Award which allegedly weighed 35 pounds. The message inscribed on the award read: "To Charles Conerly for his distinguished achievement as a football great who has contributed his outstanding ability and sportsmanship to the great game of football which has extended the appreciation of the sport to the world."[10]

Conerly did not rush to the spotlight at any time, and this time he pretty much moseyed into it. At the end of the festivities, though, as is common on such an occasion, the microphone was handed to Conerly. To anyone who knew the man, it was obvious his speech would be short, and sure enough, Conerly stayed true to form.

"Ah've had mah ups and downs heah with the Giants," Conerly said in his thick Southern accent. "An' I want to thank you all foh stickin' by me. Thank you."[11] End of show. That was a *Sports Illustrated* impression of his speech pattern, but he was not always quoted in that manner.

Someone remembered Conerly was originally a Washington Redskin, that day's opponent, if only as a draft pick years before, until that club traded him to New York and suffered consequences twice a season. Dick McCann, a public relations official for the Redskins, figured it was appropriate that this Conerly holiday took place against his team. "Hell, it's only fitting," McCann said. "We've been giving Conerly 'days' ever since he came into the league."[12]

Next up were the Browns, for the second time. While the Giants had fine-tuned their play, the Browns were in a freefall. They had lost two in a row leading up to the December 6 game at Yankee Stadium that drew 68,436 fans. The Giants were ascendant, the Browns sinking, and the Giants rubbed it in, overpowering Cleveland, 48–7. New York led 24–0 at halftime and added 24 more points in the third quarter. This was an uncharacteristically lopsided rout in the rivalry series.

For the second week in a row, Conerly threw for three touchdowns. He hit Schnelker on a three-yarder in the first quarter, Gifford on a 31-yarder, and then Rote for 19 yards. Conerly gained 271 yards through the air. Throw in Heinrich and Gifford, and New York torched the Browns for 401 yards passing. Meanwhile, Cleveland QB Milt Plum was harassed into a skimpy 36-yard passing day. Jim Brown gained only 50 yards on the ground.

Heading into the last weekend of the season, New York was 9–2 and Cleveland was 6–5. The Giants concluded the regular season by brushing aside Washington for a second time, this time 24–10. Conerly tossed two more touchdown passes, finding back Joe Morrison on a nine-yarder and Rote on a 26-yard strike. Chuckin' Charlie was 15 for 23 for 207 yards. He may have been 38 years old, but Conerly looked as crisp as ever.

New York finished 10–2, Cleveland, 7–5. The Eagles matched the Browns with the same record. For the second year in a row, the Baltimore Colts captured the Western Division. Their 9–3 record was one game better than the Chicago Bears' 8–4. Giants-Colts II. This was the rematch the country's football fans wanted to see.

Little separated Baltimore and New York in 1958 in the exciting, suspenseful, dramatic, historic sudden-death overtime game. Most fans wanted to see more of the same. Baltimore fans wanted a repeat. New York fans sought vengeance. The location was Memorial Stadium in Baltimore. There were 57,545 ticket buyers for the December 27 game.

The Colts struck first, Johnny Unitas completing a toss to Lenny Moore for a 60-yard touchdown in the first quarter. The Giants clawed back with a 23-yard field goal by Summerall, making it 7–3 after one quarter. The only scoring in the second quarter was another field goal,

Chapter 23. 1959: Giants–Colts Again

this one traveling 37 yards by Summerall. It was 7–6 at the half, low-scoring, defenses ruling.

Same deal in the third period. Summerall hit for a 22-yard field goal that gave the Giants a 9–7 lead. However, Summerall was pretty sure he received a gift from the officials when the kick was ruled good. "I wasn't sure it was good, but I turned around to the official and thrust both of my arms straight up in the air like I had not a doubt in the world that it was good as gold," Summerall said.[13]

Good break, but then the wheels came off for New York. The Colts scored 24 straight points in the fourth quarter before a Conerly-Schnelker 32-yard touchdown pass completed the scoring. No ties this time. No sudden death. Just another L in the title game, 31–16.

Conerly threw for 226 yards that day, but Unitas ate up the Giants' secondary by throwing for 264.

Speculation began soon enough about whether Conerly would retire. It almost seemed as if the Giants may have had inside information or they wouldn't have thrown him a special day. But no, Conerly would be returning for the 1960 season when he was 39.

There were going to be big changes, though. First, Tom Landry was departing as defensive coordinator to take over as head coach of the expansion Dallas Cowboys, a logical career step. But surprisingly, New York coach Jim Lee Howell was also leaving, despite his success in winning one NFL title and capturing three division titles. He cut a deal with the Maras to stay through the 1960 season and then move into the front office. Howell admitted that the constant pressure was getting to him and disrupting his life.

> It got so bad in 1959 that I was sacrificing everything, my life and my family, to football. I'd spend all day at practice, snapping at my players, then take my snarling disposition home with me. I couldn't sleep and I couldn't unwind. It just wasn't worth it anymore. It reached a point where I couldn't stand to lose and I didn't get any kick out of winning.[14]

Quarterback Charlie Conerly, the one guy affiliated with the Giants everyone always talked about retiring, wasn't retiring. For the third time, along with 1956 and 1957, in 1959 he had been named first-team All-Pro by *The Sporting News*. The old-timer had just been named Most Valuable Player of the NFL for the 1959 season. For the ninth time, Conerly had finished in the top six in the league in passing.

As it so happened, aside from his honors and statistics being so fine in 1959, Charlie Conerly had outlasted Tim Mara, Steve Owen, Vince Lombardi, Tom Landry, and Jim Lee Howell in New York.

Chapter 24

The 1960s

Maybe Jim Lee Howell should not have delayed retirement for a year. Maybe losing assistant coaches Vince Lombardi and Tom Landry was too much to handle. Maybe getting used to new assistant coaches Allie Sherman and Harland Svare was a lot to ask.

Or despite the look and feel of an experienced, big-name group of players on the roster, some aging eroded the New York Giants' effectiveness in 1960. This time the Eastern Division did not belong to New York but to the rising Philadelphia Eagles.

Also, coming off an MVP season, Charlie Conerly, 39 years old, was not as sharp, and while he played in all 12 games, he did more sharing of the quarterback job with George Shaw than he had with Don Heinrich. It may have been in closed-door coaching meetings when the leadership wondered if Conerly's time was up and if it might have been thought necessary to test-drive Shaw more to see if he could be the signal-caller of the future.

And then there was the medical reality. Conerly suffered from an infected tooth, which doesn't sound like much by way of injury in the context of the football wars, but to anyone who must deal with such an ailment, the nagging pain nearly prevents any clear thought. More significantly, Conerly came down with a lame arm. Much like a baseball pitcher, a football quarterback's bread and butter is earned by throwing, and an inability to maintain accuracy and make the clutch tosses when called for can wreck his performance. Conerly's arm strength was sapped. He could still throw short, but throwing long was a challenge and an adventure.

This season Shaw, no doubt quite pleased to get another chance to lead an NFL team after the way he was shoved aside in Baltimore, attempted more passes, completed more, and hit for more touchdowns than Conerly. Shaw, then 27, started five of the 12 games and completed 76 of 155 attempts for 1,263 yards and 11 TDs. Conerly, 12 years older, went 66 for 134 for 954 yards and eight touchdowns. Lee Grosscup did

Chapter 24. The 1960s

reappear on the scene as a third-stringer and played a little bit in four games.

Mel Triplett was the number one rusher with 563 yards, but Alex Webster played in just eight games and started one. Frank Gifford also played in only eight games. He was the victim of one of the most devastating defensive hits with severe consequences in NFL history, now simply known as "the Chuck Bednarik play."

Until that November 20 game against the Philadelphia Eagles, despite their changes and adjustments, the Giants had worked through the 1960 season acceptably with a 5–1–1 record. That 17–10 loss to the eventual Eastern Division champs truly sent New York into a tailspin. The stretch of 1–3–1 gave the Giants a season record of 6–4–2. The critical turning point also nearly ended Gifford's career.

Chuck Bednarik, a future Hall of Famer, was the last NFL player to go both ways, on offense and defense, at center and linebacker. At 35, Bednarik was late in his career, but the Eagles needed his two-way help because of injuries. Bednarik was an extraordinary competitor who in no way broke any rules when he clobbered Gifford with a clean hit that sprawled him out cold on the turf at Yankee Stadium. Gifford caught a fourth-quarter pass from George Shaw and was running toward the sideline when Bednarik tackled him. The contact knocked the ball loose for a fumble and knocked Gifford unconscious. Philadelphia gained possession in the close game, and Gifford was carried off the field on a stretcher. "I feel sorry for the guy," Bednarik said. "But at the same time, I feel justified. It was a good, perfect tackle."[1]

No penalty was called on Bednarik for the hit during the game, and the league office did not apply one afterward. He was correct in his description, even if the result was horrible for Gifford and the Giants.

The Eagles won that game and, in a rematch a week later, beat the Giants again, 31–23, coming back from down 23–17. Norm Van Brocklin threw three touchdown passes. The race for first was over. Philadelphia was 8–1, the Giants 5–3–1.

Gifford was out for the year, and his concussion was so severe, he did not play in 1961 either. It was believed that he was going to retire, but he came back to play for the Giants in 1962, though focusing on receiving rather than rushing the ball until he did retire after the 1964 season. To this day, Bednarik's hit and the consequences remain one of the most infamous plays in league history.

Before Gifford married television personality Kathie Lee Gifford, he informed her that despite all of his football accolades, the word she would hear most often connected to him was "Bednarik." She asked, "What's that—a pasta?" Gifford's explanation of the tackle went like this: "[Bednarik] caught me from the blind side and really nailed me. It was a great shot and down and out I went." He said he didn't truly remember the play, but his recollection was established by so many viewings of it on television.²

The Giants began the season by defeating the San Francisco 49ers, 21–19, the St. Louis Cardinals (who had moved from Chicago), 35–14, and the Pittsburgh Steelers, 19–17, and tying the Washington Redskins, 24–24, before losing their first game, 20–13, to the Cardinals the second time around.

Conerly and Shaw threw one touchdown pass each in the opener. Then Shaw made a splash with four TD throws versus St. Louis. Against Pittsburgh, they each tossed a touchdown pass. Shaw registered the only score through the air against Washington. Shaw did not play in a 17–13 win over Cleveland, and Conerly threw for 105 yards. Shaw also did not play in a 27–24 win over the Steelers when Conerly sparked a fourth-quarter rally.

Against Pittsburgh, Conerly threw for 233 yards and two touchdowns. It was a highlight showing, one that had others marveling, especially because Conerly was at less than 100 percent full-strength. His leadership reeked of athletic heroism and provoked Allie Sherman to race onto the field after the final gun; get into Conerly's face; and emotionally declare, "Oh, Charlie, Charlie, I'm so proud of you, so proud. I want to say so much...."³

Sherman was not alone in admiring Conerly's clutch play. Shaw was not playing but was observing. "You can play this game all your life, but watching Charlie Conerly, you realize you never stop learning."⁴

After the double losses to the Eagles, who did win the NFL crown that year, the Giants tied Landry's Dallas Cowboys, 31–31, bested the Redskins, 17–3, and lost to the Browns, 48–34.

Conerly didn't play against the Cowboys, who did not even win a game that season. He did throw a TD pass against Washington in an overall poor New York offensive game. The Browns game was a wild slugfest with the teams combining for 836 yards from scrimmage, Jim Brown contributing 110 of them on the ground and Conerly good for 282 through the air. His production included three touchdown passes.

Along the way, as he analyzed his aches and the Giants battled disappointment at falling behind the Eagles, Conerly was asked if he was going to return to play in 1961.

"I want to play because I figure I can play," Conerly said. "If I make this one, I'll be back, again, again and again." He almost made it sound like a true declaration when Perian joked that as age 40 approached, "I think he'll try for 50."⁵

Chapter 24. The 1960s

There was one fault with that thinking. By the time the 1961 season was about to begin, Conerly's right arm still wasn't back to its old form. New head coach Allie Sherman had inherited a great deal of talent, and as an offensive-minded coach he installed a new offense. He needed his guys—healthy ones—to execute it. The Giants were already without Frank Gifford, a setback right there. Now they were worried about Conerly. It was one thing to gut it out and play hurt, but no human being can overcome every injury at the highest level of professional sport. Giants management was worried.

During training camp, as the season loomed, the Giants made some aggressive changes. They acquired long-time quarterback Y.A. Tittle from the San Francisco 49ers and Los Angeles Rams wide receiver Del Shofner to catch his passes. These deals represented awesome returns for the Giants—Tittle for back-up lineman Lou Cordileone and Shofner for draft picks.

Tittle, like Conerly, had been playing pro football since 1948, though he started in the old All-America Football Conference. The 49ers made him available because they had a rising John Brodie and Bill Kilmer and plans to run a shotgun offense more suitable for them.

At his age, freshly recovered from his own groin injury and operator of an insurance agency in the Bay area, Tittle was hesitant to move to New York. "I was pretty sure I was going to retire," Tittle said of his life game plan instead of playing for the Giants. "No one, not even the trainer, knew how serious that injury was." Tittle said Frank Gifford, who was scouting while sidelined, telephoned him and talked him into joining the Giants, a move he was always glad he made.[6]

Tittle lobbied the Giants to grab Shofner, an explosive player who ended up making the Pro Bowl five times. Tittle-to-Shofner became a memorable tandem, and Tittle, who was 35 years old to Conerly's 40, gradually relegated the long-time leader to second-string. Other excellent additions were rookie offensive lineman Greg Larson, defensive back Erich Barnes, who came over from the Chicago Bears, and tight end Joe Walton, who succeeded Bob Schnelker.

In the face of the creation of the American Football League, the NFL embraced expansion and now had 14 teams. The New York defensive unit, still featuring so many of its legendary stars in Jim Katcavage and Andy Robustelli at the ends, Rosey Grier and Dick Modzelewski at the tackles, Jim Patton, Dick Lynch and Dick Nolan in the secondary, and Sam Huff and Cliff Livingston at linebacker, was the no. 1 ranked defense. Tom Scott was the new linebacker, in for Harland Svare, now defensive coordinator.

A boost to the offense came with the healthy return of Alex

Webster, who rushed for 928 yards and caught 26 passes. The Giants scored 368 points, averaging more than 26 points a game, and the offense was ranked no. 2 in the league. Oh, and Shofner grabbed 68 balls, gained 1,125 yards, and scored 11 touchdowns through the air.

Conerly ended up starting four games, completing 44 passes in 106 attempts for seven touchdowns. Tittle was 163 for 285 for 2,285 yards and 17 touchdowns. The numbers didn't lie. The Giants were better with Tittle behind center. NFL teams played 14 games that year for the first time, an increase from the old 12-game schedule.

Tittle, new to the team, did not play in the opening game loss to the St. Louis Cardinals. Conerly started the second game, but Tittle came in after a while, much as Conerly had done behind Don Heinrich. Conerly threw one touchdown pass and Tittle two the next week in a close win over the Washington Redskins.

The next game was a rematch win over the Cardinals, and Tittle started. After that the Giants won most weeks, first tromping on Tom Landry's Cowboys, 31–10. The feature there was a 102-yard interception return TD by Barnes.

There was an intriguing dynamic when the Giants bested the Rams, 24–14, at Yankee Stadium the following week. Svare had received his start in Los Angeles. So had Robustelli. So had Shofner. Tom Scott came over from L.A. This time Conerly flung two touchdown passes in the late going. Tittle threw one early.

The Cowboys took down the Giants, 17–16, but then New York won four in a row, including a 38–21 decision over the defending champion Eagles on November 12. Tittle threw three touchdown passes, and when the game ended both teams were 7–2. The Giants gained a satisfying victory over the Browns by a 37–21 margin. Pat Summerall kicked three field goals, and Barnes ran another interception back for a touchdown. Tittle scored on a short run but did not put points on the board through the air. Conerly did not play.

New York finished the regular season with a 20–17 loss to Green Bay, another win over Philadelphia, and a 7–7 tie against Cleveland for a record of 10–3–1, just ahead of the 10–4 Eagles and the 8–5–1 Browns.

Meanwhile, Vince Lombardi had swiftly worked his magic in Green Bay, winning the Western Division with an 11–3 record, far ahead of the 8–5–1 Detroit Lions. That set up a championship game on December 31 in Wisconsin. This was the moment the football world truly realized the Lombardi-led Packers were to be feared.

Green Bay crushed the Giants, 37–0. Bart Starr threw for three touchdowns, and Paul Hornung scored in most imaginable ways, with three field goals, three extra points, and a six-yard touchdown run.

Chapter 24. The 1960s

Neither Tittle (six for 20 for 65 yards and four interceptions) nor Conerly (four for eight for 54 yards), who had his chance, too, could move the New York offense. The Giants gained just 31 yards on the ground.

This was the fourth NFL title game for Conerly, the triumph of 1956, plus the losses to the Colts of 1958 and 1959 and now this one to the Packers. The Giants went on to win the Eastern Division title again in 1962 and 1963, though Conerly was no longer with them.

Much had been made for years about what a pounding Conerly took while fading back to pass and holding onto the ball as long as he could. He felt it was his job to give his team every chance to advance or to score. He never kept it a secret that it hurt to get hit, if anyone asked, but he didn't shirk that aspect of his role.

"Man, it hurts when those fellows smack into you," Conerly said. "You seldom feel it on impact. It's numbing. But the next day, and the day after that, you really hurt. And the older you get, the longer it takes to get over the bumps and bruises. It's all part of the game—all part of what they're paying you for."[7]

Conerly was not chased out of the game by large defensive lineman. More realistically, he understood that Y.A. Tittle was now the top-ranked field general, and he didn't want to sit on the bench. After the 1961 season, when Conerly returned to Mississippi, he stayed there, concluding a 13-year, 14-season New York Giants NFL career with a passel of team records.

Conerly walked away after appearing in 161 games in the National Football League, throwing 173 touchdown passes, completing 1,418 passes on 2,833 tries for 19,488 yards gained.

In a very different era of pro football, "Chuckin'" Charlie, "Chunkin' Charlie," or just plain Charlie Conerly made $25,000 in salary in his final season as a New York Giant.

Epilogue: Retirement

About seven weeks into 1962, less than two months after the New York Giants were thrashed, 37–0, by the Green Bay Packers in the NFL title game, Charlie Conerly announced his retirement.

This was not unanticipated, since Conerly would be 41 by the time the fall season began and because there had been speculation about the likelihood of his giving up the game every off-season for at least a half-decade.

Reality caught up to rumor when Conerly informed the world that he had taken his last quarterback snap in a Giants uniform. "Football got tougher every year," Conerly said at a retirement party–press conference at Toots Shor's. "And I mean mentally, as well as physically. The other players on the club took pretty good care of me the last few years so I wasn't bumped around much. But it was tough to get set mentally for so many games."[1]

Excepting times while coping with injuries and despite the Giants employing the bizarre strategy of Conerly entering games after his back-up felt out the defense, Conerly was the team's main quarterback from 1948 into the 1961 season, when Y.A. Tittle took over. Although it is not clear whether everyone believed his protestations, Conerly said the arrival of Tittle and his ascension was not the reason he was retiring. "That didn't figure in my decision at all," Conerly said.[2]

Given the manner in which he played, Tittle proved the Giants were well equipped to deal with a Conerly retirement, and Tittle did excel over the following couple of seasons, setting a single-year NFL mark of 36 touchdown passes in 1963 on his way to the Hall of Fame.

Tittle, who was in California, where he ran his off-season insurance business, was notified of Conerly's decision and said, "It was a privilege to be associated with Conerly."[3]

Conerly intended to remain associated with the Giants, if only as a scout. He said he was not particularly interested in coaching football and previously had deflected some feelers about college coaching opportunities at Mississippi State and at Tulane in Louisiana. He owned the 225-acre cotton farm in Mississippi and had shown he could happily spend his free time playing golf.

Due to his concussion, Frank Gifford did not play in 1961, and longtime teammate Kyle Rote became Conerly's road roommate. Rote said he was pretty sure from training camp on that 1961 would be Conerly's final year. He traced it to a night they went out for some liquid refreshment and suddenly realized the 11 p.m. training camp curfew was creeping up on them. They made a dash for their room to beat bed check by coaches.

"We made it just in time, popped into bed, and turned out the lights," Rote said. "It was quiet for a little and then Charlie spoke, 'Imagine, a 40-year-old man having to be in bed by 11 o'clock.'"[4]

The cover of the game program versus Alabama for October 3, 1970, featured (from left) then-senior quarterback Archie Manning, coach Johnny Vaught, and Charlie Conerly (courtesy University of Mississippi Athletics Department).

While Giants friends and teammates Gifford and Pat Summerall later became two of the most popular and best-known faces in sports television, Conerly also said he did not have the passion to go into broadcasting, especially not the play-by-play variety. This should not have been much of a surprise for any of the sportswriters who followed Conerly for years and could barely coax commentary out of him.

For years, Conerly had been casually teased in print about resembling Methuselah in football gear, for looking like an old athlete rather than a distinguished, aging man. That began to change near the end of his career when advertisers took a closer look at his craggy face, handsome appearance, and strong build. Suddenly, he was getting modeling work for magazines and other outlets.

Johnny Vaught (left) and Charlie Conerly meet up in the Ole Miss press box much later in life and pose for a picture together (courtesy University of Mississippi Athletics Department).

Rote used that development to push Conerly into his future. "He should retire," Rote said, who was also thinking back to a testimonial dinner they attended the previous year. "Anyone who looks that good in a tuxedo doesn't belong in pro football."[5]

The makers of Marlboro cigarettes also thought Conerly was a dashing dude in a variety of outfits. For a period of time, the company hooked its wagon to the solid-looking, strong, silent type of a guy as a product endorser, plastering his face on billboards and in magazine ads. "The Marlboro Man" became an iconic advertising figure for a period of time, and Conerly became one of the guys representing the company. He fit the image, even if he otherwise never wore a cowboy hat at work playing football. No claims were made about the man under the hat, about Conerly or the others selected for the role over time. Their job was to look a part, project an image.

The string of Marlboro men went on and on, adhering to a certain mystique. At one point, in 1975, Marlboro had 10 Marlboro men going, and most of their names were not even publicly known. They wore ten-gallon hats, and some of them roped cattle in ads. They were mature-looking males, many in their 40s, as was Conerly when he started, and thousands upon thousands, if not a reported million women, wrote to the company asking for their names. They would probably have been disappointed to learn that most of the men were married and many had children.

This approach to selling cigarettes turned into a startlingly successful campaign, perhaps one of the most successful in decades. Marlboro gradually overtook Winston as the leading brand in the United States and supplanted a Japanese brand worldwide.

"The Marlboro men have been doing their job for about 15 years," a 1975 newspaper report stated, "giving credence to industry research showing that virility sells cigarettes. And the Marlboro cowboys have proven to be the most virile image in the advertising world."[6]

The Marlboro guys earned about $300 a day for still photography shoots that could take up to three weeks and perhaps $10,000 for TV commercial residuals. The Marlboro man cowboy campaign began in 1954, and the original guy came to the role accidentally. The advertising company brought an actor to his property to film while renting his livestock, then chose owner Robert C. Norris over the professional for the commercial. Norris did not even smoke.

Charlie Conerly did smoke. Whether it was New York hype or not, he was sometimes referred to in print as the first Marlboro man, but he was not. The Marlboro man advertising program became more and more oriented to cowboys as it went on before ending in 1999.

Noted suspense writer Don Winslow once inserted Conerly-as-Marlboro-man into a 1996 novel, *Isle of Joy*. Two characters are drinking and making small talk. One abruptly toasts Giants defensive end Jim Katcavage. "To the entire Giants' defense." His friend says, "To Charlie Conerly. Did you know he's the Marlboro Man?" "No, I didn't," his companion says. "The truth," the first man says. "Charlie Conerly, quarterback of the sainted New York Football Giants, was the model for the original Marlboro Man."[7] Not 100 percent accurate, but the protagonists were drinking, so perhaps memories were blurred, and it was a novel.

When Conerly left the Giants, Perian stopped writing about pro football for newspapers, and they spent much of their free time back in Mississippi.

They still made visits to New York, and people knew where to find Conerly when they needed him for one honor or another. He was not forgotten. He had a Clarksdale business, a shoe store, shared with his longtime friend Tony Malvezzi, and it expanded from one store to a handful.

"We just had a blessed life," Perian Conerly said in 2019, thinking back to the immediate period following Charlie's football retirement. "He played golf and tennis and walked five miles each afternoon no

Epilogue: Retirement

Charlie Conerly (left) and Jake Gibbs, both members of the College Football Hall of Fame, participated in a book signing party in 1993 to announce the publication of *Ole Miss Football—A Century of Heroes*. Both were also first-team All-America picks, Conerly in 1947 and Gibbs in 1960. Gibbs turned down an opportunity to play in the NFL and opted for a baseball career, spending 10 years as a catcher for the New York Yankees (courtesy University of Mississippi Athletics Department).

matter what the weather. I played golf, tennis and bridge. We had a very active social life."[8]

The season after Conerly departed the playing field, the Giants retired Conerly's no. 42. There was good reason for that. Conerly's 173 touchdown passes were tops in franchise history, and he claimed many other marks. There had been so much Conerly retirement discussion for so long, there was the passing thought among some, not many, that he might yet change his mind and turn up in uniform. Owner Jack Mara made the crack that even after he presented Conerly with a retirement watch, he could still keep it if he came back to play. For decades after his retirement, Conerly held onto numerous other single-season records.

The Mississippi Sports Hall of Fame and Museum began selecting the top college football player in the state each autumn, and the recipient is awarded the C Spire Conerly Trophy. Later, Conerly was inducted into the U.S. Marine Corps Sports Hall of Fame.

In 1966, Conerly was inducted into the College Football Hall of Fame. At the festivities surrounding the event, one of the couple's favorite photographs was snapped. It posed the Conerlys with Bobby Kennedy and his wife, Ethel. A large mat was passed around for all the luminaries present to autograph, and Perian kept it as family keepsake. Of course, there was a party at Toots Shor's.

After spending so much time in New York, away from Mississippi during the football season, the Conerlys took up the habit of attending as many Ole Miss games as they could. Still, they were on the A list for Giants activities, so they sometimes took off for New York for special occasions. After the Super Bowl got started, they became regular attendees and rendezvoused with old friends from the football world at the game's site. Once, their goddaughter Lulu Maness recalls, the Super Bowl was scheduled for a Northern, open-air stadium, so instead of showing up for a possible snowy game, they traveled to Hawaii and watched on television.

There is one sore spot, one omission. Charlie Conerly is not a member of the Pro Football Hall of Fame. He has never been elected. To those who watched him play up close and to those who knew him well, this is a sad oversight. Seven times, Conerly has been a finalist for selection to the Canton, Ohio, shrine and missed out.

Many of Conerly's old teammates were firm supporters, and whenever a sportswriter contacted them to reminisce about Conerly's quarterback smarts and skills, they let loose with a series of compliments, especially Frank Gifford.

"He played one whole season, '52 or '53, with a shoulder separation," Gifford said, noting it as an example of physical courage displayed without complaint. Of 1956, the championship season, Gifford said, "I got most of the accolades that year, but we knew who got us there."[9]

Whenever historians reviewed Conerly's contributions with the University of Mississippi and the Giants, they reminded readers how much of a star he was. A few years ago, a writer ranked the GOATS, as the list was called, Greatest of All Time Rebels football figures, for Ole Miss. Long-time coach Johnny Vaught was first, followed by dad Archie and son Eli Manning, then Conerly. In 2015, the school publication *Rebel Nation* printed a story about Conerly headlined "Charlie Conerly: The Gold Standard."

Eddie Crawford, who played three sports for Ole Miss several years after Conerly graduated and was a teammate on the 1957 Giants, said, "I will say this about Charlie Conerly—he was very unselfish. He was one of those that just knew how to play the game. And he could always make the big play when he had to."[10]

Charlie Conerly is interviewed by Ole Miss alumna Mary Ann Mobley during the gala held in 1993 to honor its Team of the Century. Mobley was selected Miss America in 1959 and went on to enjoy a successful career as an actress and as a television personality (courtesy University of Mississippi Athletics Department).

Once in a while, Conerly returned to New York to watch the Giants play, though he always seemed to catch them during a down period when they lost. On one of those visits, Dave Anderson, the Pulitzer Prize–winning columnist for the *New York Times*, hung out with Conerly for one of those take-me-back stories.

The men kept company as the Giants played the Los Angeles Rams in 1981, when Conerly was 60. "Finally saw 'em win one," said Conerly, citing a few other games he watched his old club lose in New York in the years since retirement. "I still wear my championship ring. Not as big as the ones they get now. But that's all right. The ones now are a little too big."[11]

Life was pretty good for the Conerlys, with the exception of the periodic close-call Hall of Fame ballots that left the old quarterback on the outside of the hallowed shrine.

Then, on September 19, 1995, Conerly's 74th birthday, Charlie was hospitalized and underwent triple-bypass heart surgery. On the following February 13, Conerly died of heart failure in Memphis, Tennessee. He and Perian had been married nearly 47 years.

In one obituary, it was mentioned three times that Conerly was "a strong, silent Southerner" or "a man of few words."[12]

Long-time Mississippi sports columnist Rick Cleveland, who knew the Conerlys well, wrote a story about Charlie's funeral in Clarksdale at the First United Methodist Church, and it was reprinted by the Mississippi Sports Hall of Fame later. The headline was "Remembering the Great Charlie Conerly." There was prayer, and there was reading from the Bible, and there were eulogies that spoke of Conerly as "a kind, humble and very modest person."[13]

The surprise for most, altering the mood somewhat, was the organist playing the song "New York, New York." Perian Conerly said that was her suggestion, something emblematic of the link to the big city and to the Giants. "He loved that song, and we had so many great times in New York. I just thought it would send everyone out on a happy note. He would have liked that."[14]

Athletic stars from across Mississippi turned out, and Archie Manning said he inherited his hero worship of Conerly. "It was probably because he was my dad's hero," Archie Manning said. "We used to watch him playing for the New York Giants on Sunday afternoons. I didn't know much about football back then, but I knew he was from Ole Miss and Clarksdale and that was enough for me."[15]

Conerly was buried at Oakridge Cemetery, and there was a post-

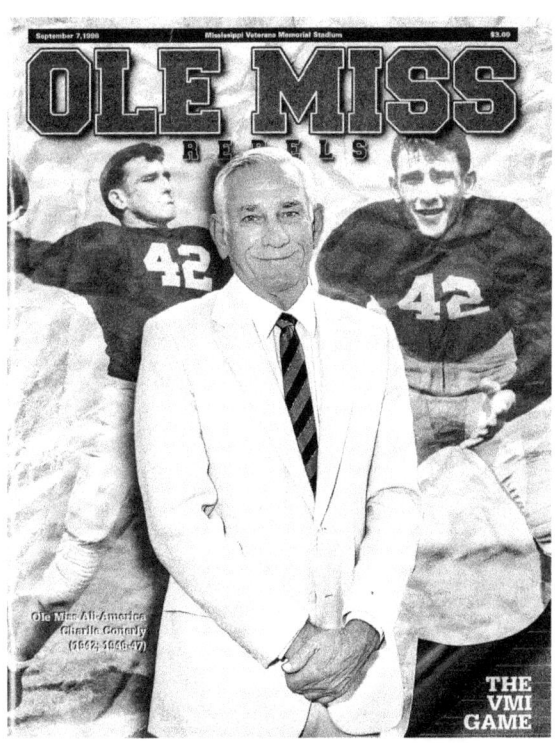

Dressed in a flashy sport coat, Charlie Conerly poses in front of images of himself as a younger man playing football (courtesy University of Mississippi Athletics Department).

ceremony gathering at The Ranchero, a local drinking establishment where Conerly regularly stopped in. "I've been lucky enough to know Gale Sayers, Joe Namath and Charlie Conerly," said Roscoe Word, who played for Jackson State in the state capital and for the New York Jets. "They are all special, not only because they were great players. They all had class. You know, there's no substitute for class."[16]

Perian Conerly stayed active in Mississippi and represented Charlie at awards events in the football world. Lulu Maness, her goddaughter, was a caretaker for her the last years of Perian's life, and they attended Ole Miss football games as long as Perian was able.

In April of 2019, Perian was asked what she thought about her husband not being a member of the Pro Football Hall of Fame. She sounded philosophical.

"I wish he could have been inducted but realize that the voters nowadays don't even know who he is," she said. Maness said that after Conerly retired and went into business with her father selling shoes, he was better known in Mississippi by the younger generations for that. More recently, Maness said, some people know Conerly more for the trophy named after him than for what he accomplished playing.

"There was a journalist in New York who hated him because he couldn't get a good interview," Perian said. "Charlie was not a great talker, and it was like pulling teeth to get him to say anything about himself." Perian wondered if that sportswriter blackballed him when it came to Hall of Fame voting.[17]

Periodically a manufacturer will issue football cards highlighting former players. This card appeared in 1994 (author's collection).

Epilogue: Retirement

On June 17, 2021, Perian Conerly passed away at the age of 94 in Oxford, Mississippi.

From Lulu Maness to University of Mississippi athletic department officials, to sportswriters with good memories or who know their history, however, the dream of Charlie Conerly one day being inducted into the Pro Football Hall of Fame by the Veterans Committee stays alive.

"The state of Mississippi obviously recognizes greatness on the gridiron," one writer said, referring to the trophy named after Conerly. "The Pro Football Hall of Fame, not so." Citing Conerly's record as a three-time Pro Bowl player, Rookie of the Year, league champion, and having his number retired by his only team, it was said, "Conerly deserves a longer look, a better look from Canton."[18]

Many times, Conerly has been called the best quarterback not in the Hall of Fame. It is not a title anyone wishes to wear.

At Ole Miss in Oxford, they haven't given up that someday Conerly will be recognized in Canton.

"Charlie was a quiet leader and played his entire 14-year NFL career for the Giants [1948–1961]," said Langston Rogers, special assistant to the athletic director at the University of Mississippi, noting how Conerly's successes uplifted football in a town that had been baseball-centric. "Charlie and his wife, Perian, were the toast of New York in the 1950s and much loved during their

Charlie Conerly, who fought for the United States in World War II, was posthumously inducted into the Marine Corps Sports Hall of Fame in 2010, and the trophy is on display in a glass case at the University of Mississippi (photograph by the author).

days in the Big Apple." Noting how much time has passed and how close Conerly came to election before, Rogers said:

> Unfortunately, there may not be any members of the selection committee left who actually saw Charlie play for the Giants. We remain hopeful that someone on the Veterans Committee will see fit to rekindle his name during the selection process and seek support to pave the way for Charlie Conerly to finally gain induction into the Pro Football Hall of Fame.[19]

It was quite something that when old friend and teammate Frank Gifford was elected to the Hall of Fame in 1977, he bluntly and forcefully said he was "embarrassed to be in it if Charlie's not in it."[20]

Most of Charlie Conerly's teammates and NFL contemporaries have passed away, but football-wise men populate the Veterans Committee for the Hall of Fame, and they may yet bring justice to Conerly's career.

Chapter Notes

Introduction

1. Rick Cleveland, "Remembering the Great Charlie Conerly," Mississippi Sports Hall of Fame and Museum, November 27, 2012.
2. Booton Herndon, *Football's Greatest Quarterbacks* (New York: Bartholomew House, 1961), 100.

Chapter 1

1. Tex Maule, "The Titans Were Tied," *Sports Illustrated*, December 3, 1956.
2. *The Big One! The 1956 NFL Championship Game*, an NFL and NBC production, announcers Earl Gillespie and Chris Schenkel.
3. https://www.ihavenet.com/nfl/index.html.1956-NFL-Championship-The-Game-That-Made-The-NFL.html.
4. Maule.
5. Richard Goldstein, "Ben Agajanian, Square-Toed Kicking Star, Dies at 98," *New York Times*, February 13, 2018.
6. Perian Conerly, *Backseat Quarterback* (Jackson: University of Mississippi Press, 2003), 219.
7. *Ibid.*
8. *Ibid.*

Chapter 2

1. Lulu Maness, personal interview, April 20, 2022.
2. Hugh Wyatt, "The Original Giants' Quarterback from Ole Miss," Old School Football, www.coachwyatt.com, 2008.
3. *Ibid.*
4. Richard Whittingham, *What Giants They Were* (Chicago: Triumph Books, 2000), 109.
5. Maness interview.
6. Charlie Tillis, "Eleven Lettermen Are Back This Fall with Clarksdale," *Delta Democrat-Times*, September 7, 1941.

Chapter 3

1. Todd Starnes, "Old Miss Dumps 'Dixie' from Football Games," Fox News, August 21, 2016.
2. *Ibid.*
3. Richard Whittingham, *What Giants They Were* (Chicago: Triumph Books, 2000), 66.
4. Steve Jacobson, "He Gave the NFL a Legacy of Class," *Newsday*, February 18, 1996.

Chapter 4

1. Lulu Maness, personal interview, April 20, 2022.
2. *Ibid.*
3. Jack Cavanaugh, *Giants Among Men* (New York: Random House, 2008), 38.
4. *Ibid.*
5. Langston Rogers, personal interview, April 15, 2019.
6. Paul Tiblier, "Ole Miss Comes of Age in Porker Win, Rebs Now Win," *Clarion-Ledger* (Jackson, MS), October 28, 1946.
7. "Vaught Sees Little Hope in Vandy Go," *Clarion-Ledger* (Jackson, MS), October 8, 1947.
8. Ed Thilenius, "Ole Miss-Vandy Game Takes Dixieland Grid Spotlight,"

Clarion-Ledger (Jackson, MS), October 9, 1947.
  9. Perian Conerly, *Backseat Quarterback* (Jackson: University of Mississippi Press, 2003), 9.
  10. *Ibid.*, 38–39.

Chapter 5

  1. Conerly, *Backseat Quarterback*, 6.
  2. *Ibid.*
  3. *Ibid.*, 7.
  4. Perian Conerly, personal interview, April 8, 2019.
  5. Conerly, *Backseat Quarterback*, 7.
  6. *Ibid.*, 8.
  7. *Ibid.*, 10.
  8. Richard Whittingham, *Giants in Their Own Words* (Chicago: Contemporary Books, 2000), 136.
  9. *Ibid.*, 135.
  10. *Ibid.*
  11. *Ibid.*
  12. Richard Whittingham, *What Giants They Were* (Chicago: Triumph Books, 2000), 74.
  13. Conerly, *Backseat Quarterback*, 11.
  14. *Ibid.*
  15. Whittingham, *What Giants*, 75.
  16. Conerly, *Backseat Quarterback*, 12.

Chapter 6

  1. Seph Anderson, "The Grove at Ole Miss," www.hottytoddy.com, April 18, 2012.
  2. Lulu Maness, personal interview, April 20, 2022.
  3. *Ibid.*
  4. Anderson, "The Grove at Ole Miss."
  5. *Ibid.*
  6. "Sports Illustrated Road Trip: University of Mississippi," *Sports Illustrated*, September 28, 2015.
  7. Jack Cavanaugh, *Giants Among Men* (New York: Random House, 2008), 39–40.
  8. *Ibid.*, 43.
  9. *Ibid.*
  10. Maness interview.
  11. *Ibid.*
  12. DeNeen Brown, "Lynchings in Mississippi Never Stopped," *Washington Post*, August 8, 2021.
  13. Parrish Alford, "John Vaught: Change Catches Up with the Rebels," *Northeast Mississippi Daily Journal*, June 8, 2003.
  14. Associated Press, September 7, 1966.
  15. Rick Cleveland, "Gentle Ben Williams, Who Broke Football Color Line at Ole Miss, Became 'Colonel Rebel,'" *Biloxi Sun-Herald*, May 19, 2020.

Chapter 7

  1. Richard Whittingham, *What Giants They Were* (Chicago: Triumph Books, 2000), 51.
  2. *Ibid.*, 66.
  3. *Ibid.*
  4. *Ibid.*, 109.
  5. Richard Whittingham, *Giants in Their Own Words* (Chicago: Contemporary Books, 2000), 138.
  6. Carlo DeVito, *Wellington: The Maras, The Giants, And the City of New York* (Chicago: Triumph Books, 2006), 113–114.
  7. Emlen Tunnell with William Gleason, *Footsteps of a Giant* (Garden City, NY: Doubleday, 1966), 113.
  8. Tunnell and Gleason, 113.
  9. *Ibid.*
  10. *Ibid.*, 114.
  11. *Ibid.*, 115.
  12. Perian Conerly, *Backseat Quarterback*, 16.

Chapter 8

  1. Michael Elson, "Giant of the Decade—1940s: Steve Owen," *NFL GameDay*, October 23, 1994.
  2. Hank Gola, "1956 Giants Player Profile: Charlie Conerly," *NFL GameDay*, September 15, 1996.
  3. *Ibid.*
  4. T.J. Troup, "The Pathway Back To Contention: Emlen Tunnell & Charlie Conerly," *Football Journal*, March 28, 2017.

Chapter 9

  1. Conerly, *Backseat Quarterback*, 9.
  2. *Ibid.*, 16.

3. *Ibid.*
4. *Ibid.*, 67.
5. *Ibid.*
6. *Ibid.*, 68.
7. David Halberstam, *Summer of '49* (New York: William Morrow, 1989), 124.

Chapter 10

1. Ernie Palladino, *Lombardi and Landry* (New York: Skyhorse Publishing, 2011), xxi.
2. *Ibid.*
3. Jack Cavanaugh, *Giants Among Men* (New York: Random House, 2008), 41.
4. *Ibid.*
5. *Ibid.*, 4.

Chapter 11

1. Frank Graham, "Steve Owen—The Man Behind the Giants," *Sport*, December 1947.
2. *Ibid.*
3. Steve Owen, "Pro Football Isn't for Sissies," *Sport*, November 1950.
4. *Ibid.*
5. *Ibid.*
6. Richard Whittingham, *What Giants They Were* (Chicago: Triumph Books), 93.
7. *Ibid.*, 95.
8. *Ibid.*, 118.
9. Gene Roswell, "Soft-Stepping Giant," *New York Post*, August 6, 1966.
10. Ernie Palladino, *Lombardi and Landry* (New York: Skyhorse Publishing, 2011).

Chapter 12

1. Perian Conerly, *Backseat Quarterback* (Jackson: University Press of Mississippi, 2003), 38.
2. *Ibid.*, 39.
3. *Ibid.*
4. *Ibid.*
5. Red Smith, "Learning by Rote," *New York Herald-Tribune*, October 29, 1961.
6. *Ibid.*
7. Frank Gifford with Harry Waters, *The Whole Ten Yards* (New York: Random House, 1993), 41.
8. *Ibid.*, 53.
9. *Ibid.*, 66.
10. *Ibid.*, 67.
11. *Ibid.*
12. *Ibid.*, 81.
13. *Ibid.*, 82.
14. *Ibid.*
15. Whittingham, *What Giants They Were*, 134.

Chapter 13

1. Conerly, *Backseat Quarterback*, 197.
2. *Ibid.*, 194–195.
3. Frank Gifford with Harry Waters, *The Whole Ten Yards* (New York: Random House, 1993), 87.
4. *Ibid.*
5. *Ibid.*
6. Carlo DeVito, *Wellington: The Maras, the Giants and the City of New York* (Chicago: Triumph Books, 2006).
7. Gifford and Waters, 88.
8. Jimmy Cannon, "Sports Today," *New York Journal-American*, May 18, 1964.
9. *Ibid.*
10. Richard Whittingham, *Giants in Their Own Words* (Chicago: Contemporary Books, 2000), 143.
11. Conerly, *Backseat Quarterback*, 28.
12. *Ibid.*
13. Lulu Maness, personal interview, April 8, 2019.
14. *Ibid.*
15. Conerly, *Backseat Quarterback*, 36.
16. *Ibid.*

Chapter 14

1. Dave Klein, *The New York Giants: Yesterday, Today, Tomorrow* (Chicago: Henry Regnery, 1973), 166–167.
2. *Ibid.*, 167.
3. Ernie Palladino, *Lombardi and Landry* (New York: Skyhorse Publishing, 2011), 63.
4. *Ibid.*, 47.
5. Carlo DeVito, *Wellington: The Maras, the Giants and the City of New York* (Chicago: Triumph Books, 2006), 128.

6. David Maraniss, *When Pride Still Mattered: A Life of Vince Lombardi* (New York: Simon & Schuster, 1999), 160.
7. Richard Whittingham, *Giants in Their Own Words* (Chicago: Contemporary Books, 1992), 139.
8. *Ibid.*

Chapter 15

1. Ernie Palladino, *Lombardi and Landry* (New York: Skyhorse Publishing, 2011), 76.
2. H.R. Horning, "Schnelker," *Pro Magazine*, November 3, 1974.
3. *Ibid.*
4. Dave Eisenberg, "Wietecha Tops on Attack," *New York Journal-American*, October 21, 1961.
5. *Ibid.*
6. Arthur Daley, "The Iron Man," *New York Times*, November 4, 1962.
7. *Ibid.*
8. Jack Cavanaugh, *Giants Among Men* (New York: Random House, 2008), 138.
9. Murray Olderman, "Offensive Guards Who Think They Would Be Missed If They Weren't There," *Newspaper Enterprise Association*, December 23, 1961.
10. *Ibid.*
11. Don Williams, "How Great Is Jack Stroud? Just Ask Colts' Marchetti," *Long Island Press*, September 16, 1963.
12. Paul Zimmerman, "Rosey: From 27th to No. 1," *New York Post*, August 24, 1966.
13. *Ibid.*
14. Bill Wallace, "Rosey's Lament: Couldn't Move Without Us," *New York Herald-Tribune*, October 19, 1962.
15. Ernie Palladino, *Lombardi and Landry* (New York: Skyhorse Publishing, 2011), 77.
16. Frank Gifford with Harry Waters, *The Whole Ten Yards* (New York: Random House, 1993), 97.

Chapter 16

1. Conerly, *Backseat Quarterback*, 76.
2. *Ibid.*, 136.
3. *Ibid.*, 139.
4. Booton Herndon, *Football's Greatest Quarterbacks* (New York: Bartholomew House, 1961), 100.
5. Don Smith, editor, *The Quarterbacks* (New York: J. Lowell Pratt, 1963), 65.
6. Herndon, 100–101.
7. *Ibid.*, 101–102.
8. Jimmy Cannon, "He's a Winner When It Counts," *Los Angeles Herald & Express*, December 13, 1961.
9. Jimmy Cannon, "Charlie," *New York Journal-American*, September 23, 1963.
10. Conerly, *Backseat Quarterback*, 143.
11. Perian Conerly, personal interview, April 8, 2019.
12. Conerly, *Backseat Quarterback*, Table of Contents.
13. *Ibid.*, 190–191.
14. *Ibid.*, 194.
15. *Ibid.*, 201.
16. Rick Cleveland, "Perian Conerly, Who Dazzled with Her Warmth, Looks and Words, Dies at 94," *Mississippi Today*, June 19, 2021.

Chapter 17

1. Frank Gifford with Harry Waters, *The Whole Ten Yards* (New York: Random House, 1993), 140.
2. *Ibid.*, 141.
3. Richard Whittingham, *Giants in Their Own Words* (Chicago: Contemporary Books, 2000), 177.
4. *Ibid.*, 178.
5. Charlie Conerly, "Webster Solid Man of Giants," *New York Mirror*, December 15, 1961.
6. *Ibid.*
7. Dave Klein, *The New York Giants: Yesterday, Today, Tomorrow* (Chicago: Henry Regnery, 1973), 169.
8. Jonni Falk, "They Were Giants: Dick Nolan," *The Giant Insider*, November 9, 1998.
9. Berry Stainback, "The Specialist in Pro Football: Jim Patton, Safety," *Sport*, February, 1966.
10. *Ibid.*
11. *Ibid.*
12. Jonni Falk, "LB Harland Svare," *The Giant Insider*, October 3, 1999.

13. Milton Gross, "SPORTS," *New York Post*, December 19, 1962.
14. Roosevelt Grier with Dennis Baker, *Rosey: An Autobiography, The Gentle Giant* (Tulsa: Harrison House, 1986), 71.
15. *Ibid.*
16. *Ibid.*, 75.
17. Klein, 168.

Chapter 18

1. Ernie Palladino, *Lombardi and Landry* (New York: Skyhorse Publishing, 2011), 64.
2. Frank Blauschild, "Don on Toes When It Counted," *New York Mirror*, November 19, 1962.
3. Andy Robustelli with Jack Clary, *Once a Giant, Always ... My Two Lives with the New York Giants* (Boston: Quinlan Press, 1987), 13.
4. *Ibid.*, 22.
5. "Katcavage Beats Rivals to Punch," *New York World-Telegram*, November 23, 1961.
6. Dick Kaplan, "Katcavage, the Commuter," *Sport*, January 1965.
7. Palladino, 67.
8. *Ibid.*
9. *Ibid.*
10. Hank Gola, "1956 Player Profile, Charlie Conerly," *NFL Game Day*, September 15, 1996.
11. Jonni Falk, "Looking Back: Jim Katcavage," *NFL Game Day*, August 26, 1989.
12. Emlen Tunnell with William Gleason, *Footsteps of a Giant* (Garden City, NY: Doubleday, 1966), 155.
13. Frank Gifford with Harry Waters, *The Whole Ten Yards* (New York: Random House, 1993), 102.

Chapter 19

1. Andy Robustelli with Jack Clary, *Once a Giant, Always ... My Two Lives with the New York Giants* (Boston: Quinlan Press, 1987), 40.
2. Richard Whittingham, *Giants in Their Own Words* (Chicago: Contemporary Books, 1992), 178.
3. Joe King, "Conerly's Passing Helps Turn Game Into Romp; 56,836 See Stadium Contest in 20-Degree Cold," *New York World-Telegram*, December 31, 1956.
4. *Ibid.*
5. Hank Gola, "Game of the Decade—The 1950s, the 1956 Championship," *NFL Game Day*, October 30, 1994.
6. *Ibid.*
7. Robustelli with Clary, 41.
8. Frank Gifford with Harry Waters, *The Whole Ten Yards* (New York: Random House, 1993), 128–129.
9. *Ibid.*, 138.
10. *Ibid.*
11. *Ibid.*
12. *Ibid.*

Chapter 20

1. Conerly, *Backseat Quarterback*, 36.
2. *Ibid.*, 238.
3. Emlen Tunnell with William Gleason, *Footsteps of a Giant* (Garden City, NY: Doubleday, 1966), 159.
4. Sam Huff with Leonard Shapiro, *Tough Stuff* (New York: St. Martin's, 1988), 69.
5. Tunnell and Gleason, 119.
6. *Ibid.*

Chapter 21

1. Sam Huff with Leonard Shapiro, *Tough Stuff* (New York: St. Martin's, 1988), 72.
2. Frank Gifford with Harry Waters, *The Whole Ten Yards* (New York: Random House, 1993), 103.
3. *Ibid.*
4. *Ibid.*
5. *Ibid.*, 105.
6. Pat Summerall, *Summerall: On and Off the Air* (Nashville: Nelson Books, 2006), 5.
7. *Ibid.*, 55.
8. *Ibid.*, 56.
9. Huff and Shapiro, 73.
10. *Ibid.*, 63.
11. *Ibid.*, 65.
12. *Ibid.*
13. *Ibid.*, 66.
14. Richard Whittingham, *Giants in Their Own Words* (Chicago: Contemporary Books, 1992), 139.

Chapter 22

1. Pat Summerall, *Summerall: On and Off the Air* (Nashville: Nelson Books, 2006), 67.
2. Andy Robustelli with Jack Clary, *Once A Giant, Always ... My Two Lives with the New York Giants* (Boston: Quinlan Press, 1987), 68.
3. Sam Huff with Leonard Shapiro, *Tough Stuff* (New York: St. Martin's, 1988), 82.
4. Frank Gifford with Harry Waters, *The Whole Ten Yards* (New York: Random House, 1993), 173.
5. John Steadman, "December 28, 1958," *Inside Sports*, January 1989.
6. Perian Conerly, personal interview, April 8, 2019.
7. Mark Bowden, *The Best Game Ever* (New York: Atlantic Monthly Press, 2008), 192.
8. Pro Football Hall of Fame transcript, multi-player Colts–Giants conference call, December 15, 1988.
9. Robustelli with Clary, 70.

Chapter 23

1. Frank Gifford with Harry Waters, *The Whole Ten Yards* (New York: Random House, 1993), 176.
2. *Ibid.*, 177.
3. *Ibid.*
4. Conerly, *Backseat Quarterback*, 85.
5. Ernie Palladino, *Lombardi and Landry* (New York: Skyhorse Publishing, 2011), 253.
6. Myron Cope, "Allie Sherman: The Most Unlikely Coach," *Sport*, January 1964.
7. William N. Wallace, "Dess of Giants: A Man Who Uses His Head," *New York Times*, November 13, 1963.
8. Sam Huff with Leonard Shapiro, 94.
9. *Ibid.*, 99.
10. Conerly, 232–233.
11. Tex Maule, "The Old Quarterback and the Youngster," *Sports Illustrated*, December 7, 1959.
12. Don Smith, editor, *The Quarterbacks* (New York: J. Lowell Pratt, 1963), 76.
13. Summerall, 76.
14. Huff and Shapiro, 98.

Chapter 24

1. Sam Robinson, "When Frank Gifford Was Knocked Out by One of the Most Vicious Tackles in NFL History," www.history.com, September 20, 2021.
2. Frank Gifford with Harry Waters, *The Whole Ten Yards* (New York: Random House, 1993), 181–182.
3. Booton Herndon, *Football's Greatest Quarterbacks* (New York: Bartholomew House, 1961), 108.
4. *Ibid.*
5. *Ibid.*, 109.
6. Jonni Falk, "They Were Giants: Tittle—The San Francisco Treat," *The Giant Insider*, October 6–12, 1997.
7. Don Smith, editor, *The Quarterbacks* (New York: J. Lowell Pratt, 1963), 71.

Epilogue

1. "Conerly Ends Football Life at 40," United Press International/ *Washington Post*, February 22, 1962.
2. *Ibid.*
3. George Girsch, "Conerly Calls Quits, to Scout for Giants," *New York Daily Mirror*, February 22, 1962.
4. Harold Rosenthal, "Conerly Retires, 'Played Enough,'" *New York Herald-Tribune*, February 22, 1962.
5. *Ibid.*
6. Nicholas C. Chriss, "Puffaroos ... Marlboro Men Lean 'n Mean," *Los Angeles Times*, April 30, 1975.
7. Don Winslow, *Isle of Joy* (London: Arrow Books, 1996), 153.
8. Perian Conerly, personal interview, April 8, 2019.
9. Mark Weinstein, "Charley Conerly, December 3, 1956," *BLUENATIC*, July 7, 2008.
10. John Davis, "Charlie Conerly: The Gold Standard," *Rebel Nation*, September/October 2015.
11. Dave Anderson, "Old Giant Can Cheer," *New York Times*, December 7, 1981.
12. Bob Oates, "Charlie Conerly Dead at 74," *Los Angeles Times*, February 14, 1996.
13. Rick Cleveland, "Remembering the Great Charlie Conerly," *Mississippi*

Sports Hall of Fame and Museum, November 27, 2012.
 14. *Ibid.*
 15. *Ibid.*
 16. *Ibid.*
 17. Perian Conerly and Lulu Maness personal interviews, April 8, 2019.
 18. Rick Gosselin, "State Your Case: Charlie Conerly," *Sports Illustrated Talk of Fame Network*, August 16, 2016.
 19. Personal interview with Langston Rogers, June 20, 2022.
 20. Dave Anderson, "Old Giant Can Cheer," *New York Times*, December 7, 1981.

Bibliography

Books

Bowden, Mark. *The Best Game Ever.* New York: Atlantic Monthly Press, 2008.

Cavanaugh, Jack. *Giants Among Men.* New York: Random House, 2008.

Conerly, Perian. *Backseat Quarterback.* Jackson: University of Mississippi Press, 2003.

DeVito, Carlo. *Wellington: The Maras, the Giants, and the City of New York.* Chicago: Triumph Books, 2006.

Gifford, Frank, with Harry Waters. *The Whole Ten Yards.* New York: Random House, 1993.

Grier, Roosevelt, with Dennis Baker. *Rosey, An Autobiography: The Gentle Giant.* Tulsa: Harrison House, 1986.

Halberstam, David. *Summer of '49.* New York: William Morrow, 1989.

Herndon, Booton. *Football's Greatest Quarterbacks.* New York: Bartholomew House, 1961.

Huff, Sam, with Leonard Shapiro. *Tough Stuff.* New York: St. Martin's Press, 1988.

Klein, Dave. *The New York Giants: Yesterday, Today, Tomorrow.* Chicago: Henry Regnery, 1973.

Maraniss, David. *When Pride Still Mattered: A Life of Vince Lombardi.* New York: Simon & Schuster, 1999.

Palladino, Ernie. *Lombardi and Landry.* New York: Skyhorse Publishing, 2011.

Robustelli, Andy, with Jack Clary. *Once A Giant, Always ... My Two Lives with the New York Giants.* Boston: Quinlan Press, 1987.

Smith, Don, editor. *The Quarterbacks.* New York: J. Lowell Pratt, 1963.

Summerall, Pat. *Summerall: On and Off the Air.* Nashville: Nelson Books, 2006.

Tunnell, Emlen, with William Gleason. *Footsteps of a Giant.* Garden City, NY: Doubleday, 1966.

Whittingham, Richard. *Giants in Their Own Words.* Chicago: Contemporary Books, 2000.

———. *What Giants They Were.* Chicago: Triumph Books, 2000.

Winslow, Don. *Isle of Joy.* London, Arrow Books, 1996.

Newspapers

Biloxi Sun-Herald (Mississippi)
Clarion-Ledger (Mississippi)
Delta Democrat-Times (Mississippi)
Long Island Press
Los Angeles Herald & Express
Los Angeles Times
Mississippi Today
New York Herald-Tribune
New York Journal-American
New York Mirror
New York Post
New York Times
New York World-Telegram
Newsday
Northeast Mississippi Daily Journal
Washington Post

Magazines

Football Journal
Inside Sports
NFL Game Day programs
Sport
Sports Illustrated

Personal Interviews

Perian Conerly
Lulu Maness
Langston Rogers

Institutions

Mississippi Sports Hall of Fame and Museum
NFL (1956 championship game film)
Pro Football Hall of Fame

News Services

Associated Press
Fox News
Newspaper Enterprise Association
United Press International

Team Publications

The Giant Insider
Rebel Nation

Websites

www.coachwyatt.com.
www.history.com
www.hottytoddy.com
https://www.ihavenet.com/nfl/index.html

Index

Aaron, Hank 49
Abdul-Jabbar, Kareem (Lew Alcinder) 132
Afghanistan 11
Agajanian, Ben (Toeless Wonder) 10, 11, 73, 114, 115, 120, 129, 135, 144, 146, 150, 157, 158, 160, 161
All-America Football Conference 11, 42, 46, 58, 62, 65, 75, 76, 78, 79, 81, 191
All-American 36, 53, 77, 85, 86
Ameche, Alan 171, 172, 177
American Football League (1925) 62
American Football League (1960) 11, 75, 96, 171, 191
American League (baseball) 42, 62, 151
Anderson, Dave 200
Antebellum 14
Aristotle Greek Lyceum 24
Arizona Cardinals 80
Arkansas 107, 110, 135, 158
Arkansas National Guard 157
Arnold College 139, 140
As I Lay Dying 21
Associated Press football poll 47
Auburn University 32
Austin, Bill 73, 156

Backseat Quarterback 123
Badgro, Red 16, 64
Bakersfield, California 93, 94
Baltimore Colts 75, 80, 81, 96, 115, 118, 136, 166, 169, 170, 171, 172, 173, 174, 175, 177, 178, 179, 181, 182, 183, 186, 187, 193
Barnes, Erich 191, 192
Barnett, Ross 23, 24
Barry, Al 161
Bates College 33
Battles, Cliff 131
Baugh, Sammy 25, 41, 43, 49, 65, 85, 91, 97

Beck, Ray 135, 156
Bednarik, Chuck 189, 190
Bell, Bert 173
Benners, Fred 95, 96, 97
Berle, Milton 113
Berra, Yogi 27, 32, 62, 174
Berry, Raymond 170, 173, 174, 175, 177
Birmingham-Southern 33
Blaik, Earl "Red" 110
Blanda, George 9, 10, 145
The Blues 13, 21
Bobo Cemetery 17
Bobo Senior High School (Clarksdale, Mississippi) 17, 48
Boston Celtics 156
Boston College 78
Boston Patriots 97
Bowen, John (Bud) 18, 39
Bowling Green University 114
Branca, Ralph 58
Brewer, Billy 47
Brickhouse, Jack 9
Briggs Stadium 167
Britt, R.C. 18
Broadway 4, 46, 71, 124, 144, 164
Brodie, John 191
Bronx County Courthouse 71
Brooklyn (New York) 109
Brooklyn Dodgers (baseball) 42, 43, 62, 122, 151
Brooklyn Dodgers (football) 42, 44, 57, 58, 62, 65, 75
Brooklyn Eagles (football) 110
Brown, Ed 145
Brown, Jim 158, 159, 160, 165, 166, 167, 168, 183, 186
Brown, Paul 50, 75, 120, 169
Brown, Roosevelt 50, 108, 116, 118, 119, 152, 156, 171
Brown vs. Board of Education 51
Bryn Mawr, Pennsylvania 59

216 Index

Buffalo Bills 52
Bureau of Prisons 24

C Spire Conerly Trophy 198
Calgary Stampeders 64, 141, 142, 181
California 94, 134, 140, 194
Campanella, Roy 49
Canada 130, 131, 173
Canadian Football League 64, 102, 130, 141, 181
Cannon, Jimmy 103, 125
Canton, Ohio 4, 62, 199
Canton Bulldogs 62, 64
Card-Pitt (NFL team) 27
Carlisle Indian Industrial School 63
Carmody, Jim 52
Caroline, J.C. 150
Carpenter, Ken 79
Casares, Rick 10, 150
Catholic University of America 22
Chandler, Don 139, 143, 144, 157, 176
Charlottesville, Virginia 119
Chicago 14, 15, 44, 51, 135
Chicago Bears 4, 7, 8, 9, 10, 11, 25, 49, 65, 66, 81, 84, 85, 97, 145, 146, 148, 150, 151, 153, 156, 165, 170, 186
Chicago Cardinals 25, 27, 44, 45, 66, 79, 87, 89, 100, 113, 114, 115, 117, 124, 130, 132, 135, 136, 141, 144, 145, 147, 159, 160, 161, 164, 165, 184, 190
Chicago Tribune 42, 84
Chicago White Sox 113
Chicasaws (Native Americans) 13
China 30
Choctaws (Native Americans) 13
Civil Rights Act 51
Civil Rights movement 21, 23, 24, 50, 51, 157
Civil War 13, 14, 21, 24, 51
Clarion-Ledger (Jackson, Mississippi) 33
Clark, Ed 148
Clark, John 13
Clarksdale, Mississippi 3, 5, 13, 14, 16, 18, 20, 22, 23, 25, 29, 30, 32, 38, 41, 46, 52, 60, 68, 70, 71, 103, 104, 123, 180, 185, 197, 201
Clarksdale High School (Mississippi) 17, 19, 71
Clarksdale Press Register (Mississippi) 123, 124
Clatterbuck, Bobby 7, 115, 120, 150
Clay, Randy 77, 81, 82
Cleveland, Rick 127, 201
Cleveland Browns 42, 50, 75, 76, 79, 81, 82, 87, 88, 89, 95, 96, 98, 100, 102, 114, 119, 125, 136, 137, 141, 142, 144, 145, 147, 158, 160, 165, 166, 167, 168, 170, 172, 183, 184, 186, 190, 192
Cleveland Bulldogs 63
Cleveland Rams 49
Cleveland Municipal Stadium 79, 81, 87, 101, 144, 165
Coahoma County, Mississippi 13
Cobb, James C. 14
College Football All-Star game 44, 45, 55, 84
College Football Hall of Fame 4, 24, 36, 64, 92, 199
Columbia University 55
Comiskey Park 113, 130
Concourse Plaza Hotel 70, 104, 123, 147
Conerly, Charles (father) 15
Conerly, Charlie 1, 3, 4, 5, 7, 8, 9, 10, 12, 13, 14, 16, 17, 18, 19, 20, 21, 22, 24, 25, 26, 28, 29, 30, 31, 32, 33, 34, 35, 36, 37, 38, 39, 40, 41, 42, 43, 44, 45, 46, 47, 48, 49, 50, 52, 53, 54, 55, 56, 57, 58, 59, 60, 61, 63, 65, 66, 67, 68, 69, 70, 71, 72, 73, 74, 75, 76, 77, 78, 79, 80, 81, 82, 83, 84, 85, 86, 88, 89, 90, 91, 93, 94, 95, 96, 97, 98, 99, 100, 101, 102, 103, 104, 105, 107, 108, 109, 111, 112, 113, 114, 115, 117, 118, 120, 122, 124, 125, 126, 127, 129, 130, 131, 133, 135, 136, 137, 138, 142, 143, 144, 146, 147, 149, 150, 152, 153, 154, 155, 156, 157, 158, 159, 160, 162, 163, 164, 165, 166, 167, 168, 169, 171, 172, 173, 174, 176, 179, 180, 181, 183, 184, 185, 186, 187, 188, 190, 191, 192, 193, 194, 195, 196, 197, 198, 199, 200, 201, 202, 203, 204
Conerly, Perian 1, 4, 11, 13, 18, 24, 29, 30, 35, 37, 38, 39, 40, 41, 44, 45, 46, 52, 53, 59, 60, 61, 68, 69, 70, 71, 72, 73, 90, 91, 94, 103, 104, 105, 122, 123, 124, 126, 127, 153, 155, 175, 181, 185, 190, 197, 199, 201, 202, 203
Conerly, Ray (sister) 16
Conerly, Ruth (sister) 16
Conerly, Winford (mother) 15, 16, 30, 31, 41
Confederate flag 22
Congressional Medal of Honor 27, 30
Connecticut 140, 148
Connie Mack Stadium 100, 129
Considine, Bob 73
Cooke, Sam 14
Cooperstown, New York 42, 64
Cordileone, Lou 191
Cotton Belt 13
Cotton Bowl 47
Crawford, Eddie 199

Cronkite, Walter 143
Crosby, Bing 73
Crossroad Blues 15
Crow, Linden 161, 172
Crowley, Jim 109
Crump Stadium (Memphis) 36
Cuff, Ward 131
Czarobski, Zig 45

Daley, Arthur 102
Dallas Cowboys 77, 88, 96, 132, 134, 187, 190, 192
Dallas Texans 96
Davis, Glenn 88
Dayton Triangles 62
Dayton University 139
Dean, Dizzy 42, 43
Dean, Paul 42
Delta Bowl 35, 36, 39, 41
Delta Times-Democrat 19
Dempsey, Jack 73
DeRogatis, Al 73, 79, 130
Dess, Darrell 182
Detroit Lions 66, 92, 95, 102, 120, 137, 142, 147, 164, 167, 192
Detroit Tigers 155
DiMaggio, Joe 27, 62, 72, 125, 154
Disney, Walt 113
Dixie (song) 22
Dixie (the South) 50
Donovan, Art 170
Doolittle, Jimmy 30
Downey's 72
Drew, Red 33
Drew, Mississippi 4
Driscoll, Paddy 10, 149, 151
Dublinski, Tom 162
Dupre, L.G. 176, 177
Dyer Brook, Maine 33

East Chicago, Indiana 116
Eddie Condon's 72
Edmonton Oilers 156
Eisenhower, Dwight D. (president) 157
Empire State Building 46
Europe 27, 30, 185
Evers, Medgar 51
Ewbank, Weeb 166, 170

Faubus, Orval 157
Faulkner, William 21
Feathers, Beattie 130
Feller, Bob 27
Fennema, Carl 70
Fennema, Joanne 70, 71
Filipski, Gene 8, 149, 150

First Methodist Church (Clarksdale, Mississippi) 60, 201
Flaherty, Ray 64, 148
Florida-Georgia football 47
Forbes Field 56, 78, 120
Ford, Len 76
Ford, Whitey 62
Fordham University (Rams) 109, 110
Fox News 23
Friedman, Benny 64
Frisch, Frankie 42

Galiffa, Arnie 100
Gashouse Gang 42
Gedeon, Elmer 27
Georgetown 28
Georgia 135
Germany 27, 30
Gibbs, Jake 198
Gifford, Frank 1, 10, 11, 70, 86, 92, 94, 95, 96, 100, 101, 102, 105, 107, 111, 112, 115, 120, 121, 125, 127, 129, 130, 135, 136, 143, 144, 146, 147, 149, 150, 152, 153, 156, 159, 160, 162, 163, 165, 166, 167, 169, 171, 172, 174, 175, 176, 179, 180, 181, 185, 186, 189, 191, 195, 199
Gifford, Kathie Lee 93, 189
Gillespie, Earl 9
Gillman, Sid 140
Gilmer, Harry 34, 65
Gloster, Mississippi 35, 56
Governali, Paul 55, 57
Graham, Otto 75, 79, 87, 88, 98, 120, 137, 147
Grandelius, Sonny 99
Grange, Red 9, 62, 84, 155
Great Britain 19
Great Depression 18
Great Migration 15
Great Mississippi Flood 22, 30
Great Plains 13
Greatest Game 170, 177
Greatest of All-Time Rebels 199
Green Bay Packers 11, 25, 57, 64, 65, 66, 84, 85, 97, 106, 109, 115, 116, 139, 156, 159, 181, 182, 184, 192, 193, 194
Greenberg, Hank 155
Greenville, Mississippi 104
Greenwich, Connecticut 9
Greenwood, Mississippi 15
Grey Cup 130
Grier, Mike 134
Grier, Rosey 50, 128, 134, 135, 136, 139, 142, 157, 161, 171, 191
Griffith, Forest 79
Griffith Stadium 146

Index

Grisham, John 21
Grosscup, Lee 181, 188
The Grove 47, 48
Groza, Lou 75, 82, 87, 88, 96, 120, 158, 167
Guam 29, 30, 163
Guglielmi, Ralph 139
Gustavus Adolphus College 119
Guyon, Joe 16, 63

Halas, George 10, 84
Hammond Pros 62
Harlem, New York 13, 50, 157, 158
Hawaii 19, 29, 199
Hazelhurst, Mississippi 14
Hein, Mel 16
Heinrich, Barbara 185
Heinrich, Don 7, 9, 115, 124, 129, 130, 135, 143, 144, 146, 150, 162, 165, 167, 172, 184, 185, 186, 188, 192
Heisman Trophy 146
Hemingway, Ernest 72, 124
Hemingway, William 33
Hemingway Stadium 33, 47
Henry, Wilbur "Pete" 16, 64
Herber, Arnie 85
Hill, Harlon 146
Hiroshima 30
Hollywood, California 93, 94, 95, 140, 158
Hooker, John Lee 14
Hornung, Paul 192
Houston Oilers 146
Howell, Dixie 36
Howell, Jim Lee 8, 9, 106, 107, 108, 109, 110, 112, 117, 118, 119, 121, 128, 131, 133, 135, 137, 138, 148, 149, 150, 151, 152, 167, 175, 180, 181, 184, 187, 188
Hubbard, Cal 16, 64
Hubbell, Carl 125
Huff, Sam 1, 26, 139, 142, 143, 152, 156, 158, 159, 162, 165, 171, 174, 176, 183, 184, 191
Hughes, Ed 8, 149, 157
Huntington, Indiana 28
Hutson, Don 25, 85, 86

Indiana 60
Isbell, Cecil 85
Isle of Joy 197
Iwo Jima 163

Jackson, Mississippi 123
Jackson Clarion-Ledger News 124
Jackson State 202
Japan 19, 27, 29, 307

Jenkins, Eulas 39
Jim Crow laws 51
Johnson, Herb 120
Johnson, Joe 36
Johnson, Lyndon Baines (president) 51
Johnson, Paul, Jr. 23, 24
Johnson, Robert 14
Jones, Dub 88

Kansas City Chiefs 65, 96
Kansas City Cowboys 65
Kansas City Star 72
Karilivacz, Carl 165
Katcavage, Jim 139, 140, 141, 142, 145, 157, 191, 197
Kemp, Jack 171, 181
Kenna, Doug 18
Kennedy, Ethel 134, 199
Kennedy, John F. (president) 23, 24, 185
Kennedy, Robert F. 23, 24, 134, 199
Kentucky Derby 48
Kezar Stadium 144
Kilmer, Bill 191
King, Martin Luther, Jr. 51
Kosciusko, Mississippi 23
Ku Klux Klan 51
Kuharich, Joe 141

Lake City, Florida 164
Lambeau, Curly 84, 85
Landis, Kenesaw Mountain 27
Landry, Tom 77, 78, 79, 87, 88, 89, 95, 96, 97, 106, 108, 109, 110, 111, 121, 128, 132, 133, 134, 135, 139, 142, 143, 152, 158, 161, 171, 187, 188, 190, 192
Laramie, Wyoming 38
Larsen, Don 10
Larson, Greg 191
Las Vegas 118
Lavelli, Dante 75
Layne, Bobby 166, 184
Leahy, Frank 45, 109
LeBaron, Eddie 97
Leemans, Tuffy 64, 131
Lewis, Jerry 94
Light in August 21
Lipscomb, Gene "Big Daddy" 104, 171, 182
Little Rock, Arkansas 157
Little Rock Central High School (Arkansas) 157
Live! (TV show) 93
Livingston, Cliff 41, 115, 129, 139, 156, 173, 191
Livingston, Howie 41, 55, 115
Lombardi, Vince 106, 109, 110, 111, 112,

Index   219

114, 115, 116, 121, 128, 129, 135, 143, 152, 161, 164, 168, 169, 171, 181, 182, 184, 187, 188, 192
Lone Okie, Arkansas 110
Long, Buford 116, 130
Long Island 61
Lopat, Ed 62
Los Angeles 72, 93
Los Angeles Memorial Coliseum 49, 183
Los Angeles Rams 49, 81, 88, 89, 95, 100, 120, 128, 133, 134, 139, 140, 142, 170, 183, 191, 192, 200
Louisiana State University 28, 35
Louisville, Kentucky 48, 52
Luckman, Sid 49, 85
Lummus, Jack 27
Lyceum 24
Lynch, Dick 182, 191

MacAfee, Ken 120, 136, 144, 147, 156, 159, 165
Madison Square Garden 80
Major League Baseball 27, 32, 42, 46, 49, 61, 64, 70, 154, 156, 173
Major League Baseball All-Star game 42
Mallouf, Ray 66
Malvezzi, Angelo 29
Malvezzi, Tony 29, 104, 185, 197
Maness, Lulu (goddaughter) 15, 18, 29, 30, 47, 50, 104, 105, 199, 202, 203
Manhattan College 148
Manning, Archie 4, 5, 48, 199, 201
Manning, Buddy 4
Manning, Eli 4, 48, 199
Manning, Peyton 4
Mantle, Mickey 62, 70, 141
Mara family (Jack, Tim, Wellington) 43, 55, 57, 58, 64, 65, 66, 78, 82, 83, 84, 88, 102, 103, 105, 108, 109, 110, 111, 113, 118, 140, 151, 154, 155, 162, 171, 179, 181, 182, 185, 187
Marchetti, Gino 118, 131, 132, 170, 175
Marchibroda, Ted 160
Maris, Roger 70
Marlboro cigarettes 3, 196, 197
Marlboro Man 3, 196, 197
Marshall, George Preston 41
Martin, Dean 94, 140
Martin, Pepper 42
Matson, Ollie 96, 160
Mayer, Louis B. 72, 73
Maynard, Don 161, 171, 176
Mays, Willie 49
McBride, Jack 63
McCann, Dick 186

McCaskey, Ed 10
McChesney, Bob 81, 87, 96
McColl, Bill 145
McDonald, Tommy 165, 183
McGraw, John 62
McHan, Lamar 160
Medwick, Joe 42, 43
Mehre, Harry 26, 28, 32
Memorial Stadium (Baltimore) 186
Memphis 28, 33, 35, 36, 39, 201
Memphis State University 28
Meredith, James 23, 24, 48, 51, 52
Michener, James 71
Michigan State University 116
Mike Manouche's 72
Minisi, Skippy 59
Minneapolis Marines 28
Minnelli, Liza 61
Minnesota Vikings 114, 132
Minoso, Minnie 49
Mission, Texas 78
Mississippi 1, 16, 25, 30, 32, 42, 46, 51, 52, 55, 56, 57, 59, 60, 61, 65, 68, 70, 73, 94, 103, 104, 105, 127, 135, 153, 154, 162, 181, 193, 197, 199, 201, 202
Mississippi Blues Trail 14
Mississippi Delta 4, 13, 14, 21, 46, 51, 103
Mississippi Flood (athletic teams) 22
Mississippi River 13
Mississippi Sports Hall of Fame and Museum 104, 198, 201
Mississippi State College for Women 38, 68, 123
Mississippi State Teachers College 17
Mississippi State University 28, 32, 35, 195
Mize, Johnny 42, 43
Mobile, Alabama 155
Mobley, Mary Ann 200
Modzelewski, Dick 109, 139, 141, 142, 157, 174
Modzelewski, Ed 109, 139, 141, 142
Money, Mississippi 51
Montgomery, Alabama 51
Montreal Alouettes 130
Montreal Canadiens 156
Montreal Royals 42
Moore, Lenny 170, 175, 176, 186
Morris, Willie 21, 48
The Most Southern Place On Earth 14
Mote, Kelley 89
Motley, Marion 50, 75
Muncie Flyers 62
Musial, Stan 27
Mutcheller, Jim 177

My Fair Lady 10
Myhra, Steve 172, 175

NAACP 51
Nagasaki 30
Namath, Joe 202
National Baseball Hall of Fame 27, 42, 64, 155
National Basketball Association 27, 46, 61, 132, 156, 173
National Football League 4, 7, 9, 11, 12, 16, 25, 27, 28, 31, 32, 36, 41, 42, 44, 45, 49, 50, 55, 56, 57, 59, 62, 64, 65, 70, 73, 75, 76, 78, 81, 84, 85, 86, 90, 91, 94, 95, 97, 104, 108, 112, 113, 114, 116, 117, 118, 128, 130, 139, 140, 141, 142, 147, 148, 152, 153, 154, 155, 156, 164, 166, 169, 170, 172, 173, 174, 176, 177, 182, 183, 187, 188, 189, 190, 191, 193, 194, 204
National Guard 24
National Hockey League 27, 46, 61, 134, 156
National League 42, 62, 140, 151
Naziism 27
NBC-TV 9
NCAA 25, 57, 59, 65, 146
Neale, Greasy 74, 81
Needlepoint for Men 134
Negro All-American team 118
Nelson, Andy 171
New England Patriots 156
New Guinea 11
New Jersey 110, 130
New Orleans (The Big Easy) 21
New Orleans Saints 132
New York Bulldogs 66
New York City (Big Apple) 1, 3, 5, 7, 11, 16, 19, 37, 44, 46, 50, 52, 53, 57, 60, 61, 68, 70, 71, 72, 93, 94, 100, 103, 105, 110, 115, 122, 123, 132, 140, 152, 171, 183, 197, 199, 200, 202
New York Daily News 61
New York Giants (baseball) 16, 26, 62, 122, 140, 151
New York Giants (football) 1, 4, 7, 8, 9, 10, 11, 12, 16, 19, 27, 31, 37, 41, 43, 44, 45, 46, 50, 54, 55, 58, 60, 62, 63, 64, 65, 66, 67, 69, 70, 73, 75, 76, 77, 78, 79, 80, 81, 82, 83, 84, 86, 87, 88, 89, 92, 93, 95, 98, 99, 100, 102, 103, 104, 105, 106, 108, 111, 112, 114, 116, 117, 118, 119, 120, 121, 122, 124, 126, 128, 129, 130, 131, 133, 134, 135, 136, 137, 138, 139, 140, 141, 142, 143, 145, 146, 147, 148, 150, 151, 152, 153, 155, 156, 157, 159, 160, 161, 164, 165, 166, 167, 168, 170, 171, 172, 173, 174, 175, 176, 177, 178, 179, 180, 182, 183, 184, 185, 186, 187, 188, 189, 192, 193, 194, 197, 198, 199, 200, 204
New York Giants Section Five Club (football) 185
New York Islanders 156
New York Jets 202
New York Knickerbockers 61, 122
New York, New York (song) 61, 201
New York Post 61
New York Rangers 61, 80, 122
New York Times 48, 61, 102, 123, 200
New York Yankees (baseball) 10, 61, 72, 122, 151, 153, 156
New York Yankees I (football) 62
New York Yanks (football) 56, 81, 89
Newcombe, Don 49
Newsday (newspaper) 61
Nixon, Richard (president) 185
Nolan, Dick 128, 132, 139, 157, 191
Noll, Chuck 109
Norris, Robert C. 197
North American Newspaper Alliance 124
North Carolina State University 130, 182
Northington, Nate 52
Northwestern University 116
Norton, Jerry 129
Notre Dame 28, 45, 84, 109, 182

Oakridge Cemetery (Mississippi) 201
O'Brien, Davey 35
Ohio 132, 158
Oklahoma 64, 83, 94
Oklahoma A&M 36
The Old Man and the Sea 162
Old South 23
Olney, Texas 34
O'Neill, Harry 27
Orange Bowl 22, 35
Oregon State University 73
Ott, Mel 16
Outer Mongolia 11
Outland Trophy 139
Owen, Steve 16, 26, 55, 64, 65, 66, 67, 73, 74, 75, 77, 78, 81, 83, 84, 85, 94, 95, 97, 101, 103, 107, 108, 109, 110, 112, 118, 119, 125, 131, 148, 152, 187
Oxford, England 20
Oxford, Mississippi (The Little Easy) 3, 19, 20, 21, 23, 25, 26, 28, 32, 33, 37, 47, 52, 53, 57, 203

Panama City, Florida 105
Parilli, Babe 97

Index

Parks, Rosa 51
Patton, Jimmy 104, 128, 132, 133, 135, 139, 157, 159, 160, 166, 171, 191
Pearl Harbor 19, 27, 29, 30
Pelfrey, Ray 100, 102
Penn State University 134, 135
Philadelphia, Mississippi 51
Philadelphia Eagles 27, 64, 66, 76, 79, 80, 81, 87, 89, 95, 96, 100, 102, 114, 120, 129, 130, 137, 145, 147, 159, 165, 167, 183, 184, 188, 189, 192
Philbin, Regis 93
Pihos, Pete 100
Pittsburgh 54
Pittsburgh Courier 118
Pittsburgh Pirates (baseball) 62, 155
Pittsburgh Steelers (Pittsburgh Pirates football) 27, 55, 62, 66, 78, 79, 87, 89, 97, 100, 101, 109, 114, 120, 130, 135, 139, 142, 144, 159, 160, 165, 166, 182, 184, 190
P.J. Clarke's 72
Plasman, Dick 25
Plum, Milt 160, 186
Polo Grounds 8, 16, 57, 63, 70, 81, 88, 98, 102, 107, 135, 136, 137, 144, 148
Poole, Barney 34, 35, 56, 57
Poole, Jim 35, 56
Poole, Ray 34, 35, 56, 57, 59, 79, 80, 96, 97
Pottsville Maroons 64
Price, Eddie 77, 79, 80, 89, 96, 99, 116, 120
Pro Football Hall of Fame 1, 4, 9, 49, 50, 63, 64, 76, 77, 92, 97, 102, 118, 131, 138, 142, 146, 160, 161, 166, 170, 171, 177, 179, 180, 189, 194, 199, 200, 202, 203, 204
Pro Football Writers Association of America 123, 126
Pyle, C.C. (Cash and Carry) 62

Radnor Township, Pennsylvania 59
The Ranchero (Mississippi) 202
Raschi, Vic 62
Rebel Nation 199
Rechichar, Bert 174, 175, 176
Reconstruction 13
Reed, James 52
Reese, Pee Wee 125
Reynolds, Allie 62
Rickey, Branch 42, 43, 44, 57, 62, 75, 155
Rickles, Don 140
Ring of Honor (New York Giants) 130
Riverside Hotel (Mississippi) 14
Roaring Twenties 84

Roberts, Gene (Choo-Choo) 57, 66, 79, 86
Robinson, Jackie 42, 49
Robustelli, Andy 1, 9, 49, 139, 140, 141, 142, 143, 146, 148, 151, 152, 157, 171, 173, 174, 178, 191, 192
Rock Island Independents 62
Rocky Mountains 13
Rogers, Langston 32, 203, 204
Roosevelt, Franklin D. (president) 19, 27, 29, 32
Rote, Kyle 4, 10, 31, 86, 91, 98, 99, 100, 101, 115, 116, 120, 121, 124, 127, 130, 135, 136, 137, 143, 144, 150, 152, 156, 159, 165, 166, 173, 176, 183, 186, 195, 196
Rote, Kyle, Jr. 86
Rote, Betty 92
Rowan Oaks 21
Rowe, Harrison 77
Ruth, Babe 70, 73, 153

St. Louis 35
St. Louis Cardinals (baseball) 42, 43
St. Louis Cardinals (football) 79, 190, 192
St. Peter, Minnesota 119
Salem, Oregon 164
San Antonio, Texas 86, 92
San Diego Chargers 133, 142
San Francisco 49ers 42, 75, 95, 97, 132, 144, 160, 191
San Francisco Giants (baseball) 63
San Jose Sharks 134
Santa Ana, California 10
Santa Monica, California 93
Saranac Lake, New York 87
Saskatchewan 95
Saskatchewan Roughriders 64
Sayers, Gale 202
Schenk, William "Bud" 35
Schenkel, Chris 9
Schnelker, Bob 114, 115, 116, 120, 129, 130, 143, 146, 156, 159, 165, 166, 167, 174, 176, 183, 184, 186, 187, 191
Schnellbacher, Otto 77, 88, 89
Scott, Joe 79, 88, 98
Scott, Tom 191, 192
Screen Actors Guild 94
Seattle 70
Senior Bowl 155
Seven Blocks of Granite 109
Shaughnessy, Clark 25
Shaw, George 136, 166, 181, 183, 184, 188, 189, 190
Sheboygan Redskins 62

222 Index

Sherman, Allie 117, 182, 188, 190, 191
Sherrod, Bud 96
Shibe Park 81
Shofner, Del 86, 191, 192
Shor, Bernard "Toots" 72, 73, 152
Sinatra, Frank 61, 73, 140
Sirhan Sirhan 134
Smith, Bessie 14
Sneakers Game 8, 148
Sneakers Game II 8, 148
Soldier Field 44
The Sound and the Fury 21
South Pacific (geographic region) 3, 27, 29, 30, 31, 37, 86, 91
South Pacific (play) 71
Southeastern Conference 3, 22, 32, 35, 50, 52, 117
Southern Methodist University 86, 91, 95
Spahn, Warren 27, 32
Spanish-American War 29
The Spectator (college newspaper Mississippi State College for Women) 40
Speedie, Mac 75
Spinney, Art 171
Sport magazine 133
The Sporting News 47, 187
Sports Illustrated 7, 8, 47, 185
Springfield College (Massachusetts) 33
Square Bookshop (Oxford, Mississippi) 21
Stamford, Connecticut 140
Stanford University 25
Stanton, Harry 35, 57
Starr, Bart 192
Staten Island, New York 107
Statue of Liberty 46
Stautner, Ernie 78
Steagles 27
Stengel, Casey 62
Stouffer, N.P. 22
A Streetcar Named Desire 14
Stribling, Bill 96, 97, 98
Strode, Woody 49
Strong, Ken 16, 64
Stroud, Jack 108, 116, 117, 118, 156, 161
Subway Series 62
Sugar Bowl 47, 51
Summer Olympics 183
Summerall, Pat 114, 117, 124, 127, 161, 164, 165, 166, 167, 168, 171, 172, 174, 176, 183, 184, 186, 187, 192, 195
Sunflower River 13, 17
Super Bowl 7, 109, 116, 178, 199
Sutherland, Jock 74
Svare, Harland "Swede" 128, 133, 134, 139, 156, 166, 184, 188, 191

Svoboda, Bill 160, 176
Swiacki, Bill 57, 80, 86
Syracuse University 158, 173

Tales of the South Pacific 71
Tarawa 163
Tennessee 28
Texas 135
Texas Christian University 34, 35, 36, 41
That's My Boy 94
Thomason, Bobby 100
Thompson, Tommy 81
Thorpe, Jim 63, 64
Tiblier, Jerry 39
Tidwell, Travis 79, 80, 81, 87
Till, Emmett 51
Times Square 46, 164
Titanic 99
Title IX 52
Tittle, Y.A. 97, 118, 160, 191, 192, 193, 194
Today Show 93
Tony Award 144
Toots Shor's (nightclub) 72, 73, 74, 81, 122, 140, 152, 160, 183, 184, 194, 199
Topp, Bob 120
Toronto Argonauts 64
Toronto Star 72
Triplett, Mel 128, 132, 135, 144, 145, 150, 156, 165, 173, 189
Trippi, Charlie 44, 96
Truman, Harry (president) 49, 113
Tulane University 34, 77, 195
Tunnell, Emlen 1, 50, 57, 58, 59, 66, 67, 73, 77, 87, 88, 89, 119, 137, 139, 146, 150, 152, 156, 157, 158, 159, 160, 171, 182
Turnage, Allen H. 30
Turner, Ike 14
Tuscaloosa, Alabama 33
21 (nightclub) 72

Unitas, Johnny 170, 173, 174, 175, 176, 177, 181, 186, 187
United Nations 61
United States 3, 19, 27, 29, 30, 42, 61, 64, 78, 84, 173, 196
United States Air Force (Army Air Corps) 27, 54, 78
United States Army 27, 54, 104
United States Coast Guard 59
United States Court of Appeals Fifth Circuit 24
U.S. Marine Corps Sports Hall of Fame 198, 203
United States Marines 27, 28, 29, 31, 37, 41, 46, 54, 86, 91, 163

Index

United States Naval Academy 32
United States Navy 27, 33, 54
United States Supreme Court 23, 51
University, Mississippi 20
University of Alabama 32, 33, 34, 65
University of Arizona 35, 57
University of Arkansas 28, 33, 35, 107, 164
University of Bridgeport 139
University of California–Los Angeles (UCLA) 49, 115
University of Florida 32, 33, 34, 139
University of Georgia 27, 28
University of Illinois 84, 155
University of Iowa 59
University of Kansas 77
University of Kentucky 32, 34, 52
University of Maryland 132, 139
University of Mississippi (Ole Miss Rebels) 3, 4, 5, 19, 20, 22, 23, 24, 25, 26, 28, 29, 31, 32, 33, 34, 35, 36, 37, 38, 40, 43, 45, 47, 48, 51, 52, 54, 55, 56, 60, 68, 69, 75, 85, 90, 91, 105, 133, 196, 198, 199, 200, 201, 203
University of New Mexico 10, 73
University of North Carolina 34, 56
University of Oregon 136
University of South Carolina 34
University of Southern California 92
University of Southern Mississippi 17
University of Tennessee 28, 32, 35, 117
University of Tennessee at Chattanooga 35, 57
University of Texas 77, 78
University of Texas at El Paso 161
University of the South 95
University of Toledo 59, 132
University of Utah 162, 181
University of Washington 9, 70, 115, 181
University of Wyoming 38
U.S. Rubber 148

Van Brocklin, Norm 165, 183, 189
Vance, Rupert 14
Vanderbilt University 28, 32, 34, 92
Vaught, Johnny 3, 34, 36, 47, 50, 51, 52, 56, 196, 199
Vaught-Hemingway Stadium 33
The Violent World of Sam Huff 143

Walk of Champions 47, 48
Walker, Doak 92

Walker, Ed 22
Walking Blues 15
Walston, Bobby 100
Walton, Joe 191
Ward, Arch 42, 44, 84
Warner, Glenn "Pop" 26, 63
Washington, Kenny 49
Washington & Jefferson College 64
Washington, D.C. 115, 146
Washington Post 51
Washington Redskins 25, 31, 32, 41, 43, 49, 54, 55, 65, 79, 80, 81, 87, 91, 97, 100, 101, 105, 115, 130, 131, 135, 137, 139, 141, 142, 146, 159, 165, 166, 182, 185, 186, 190, 192
Washington University in St. Louis 35
Waters, Muddy (McKinley Morganfield) 14
Webster, Alex 86, 105, 128, 130, 131, 132, 135, 136, 143, 144, 146, 149, 150, 152, 156, 159, 160, 164, 166, 167, 169, 171, 172, 173, 184, 189, 191
Weinmeister, Arnie 77, 95
Welty, Eudora 21
West Point (Army football) 32, 110
West Virginia University 139, 142
Western Kentucky University 28
White House 23
Wietecha, Ray 108, 116, 117, 156, 168, 171
Wilkie, Curtis 21
Wilkinson, Bob 96, 98
William & Mary 36
Williams, Ben 52
Williams, Ted 27
Williams, Tennessee 14, 21, 162
Willis, Bill 50, 75
Winslow, Don 197
Winston cigarettes 196
Wisconsin 181, 192
Woodward, Ray 18
Word, Roscoe 202
World Series 62, 122, 145, 151
World War II 3, 19, 25, 27, 29, 30, 33, 42, 49, 56, 61, 64, 78, 83, 86, 90, 91, 107, 163
Wright, Richard 21

Yankee Stadium 7, 10, 70, 107, 136, 144, 145, 146, 148, 149, 151, 160, 165, 166, 167, 168, 171, 185, 186, 189, 192
Yazoo City, Mississippi 52
Youso, Frank 161

www.ingramcontent.com/pod-product-compliance
Ingram Content Group UK Ltd.
Pitfield, Milton Keynes, MK11 3LW, UK
UKHW041950140426
5217IPUK00014B/738